Praises for Eritrea's Hard-won Independence and Unmet Expectations

Semere Solomon's book, "Eritrea's Hard-won Independence and Unmet Expectations", transcends mere historical documentation; it serves as a catalyst for constructive dialogue and critical analysis of Eritrea's past, present, and future. By presenting a multifaceted perspective and confronting uncomfortable truths, it lays the groundwork for a more informed and introspective approach to nation-building. Personally, the book exceeded my expectations and challenged long-held beliefs regarding Eritrean history.

By providing personal anecdotes and historical accounts, Solomon exposes the mechanisms through which dictatorship takes root, casting a critical eye on the current Eritrean government. His unbiased assessment invites readers to draw their own conclusions while serving as a cautionary tale for future generations, urging vigilance against authoritarian tendencies.

—Dr. Shiden Solomon
Post-doctoral Research Fellow,
Molecular and Cellular Neuroscientist, King's College, UK

Semere Solomon's book offers an in-depth exploration of Eritrea's colonial history, the prolonged struggle for independence, and the subsequent challenges faced by the nation post-independence. Merging historically significant events with his own firsthand experiences, Solomon, a seasoned freedom fighter turned scholar, provides a unique blend of narrative and analysis, enriching the book with insights only an educated and experienced individual like him could offer. His transition to an international development expert adds further depth to his observations, making the book a rich resource for understanding the complexities of the region's socio-political environment.

What distinguishes Solomon's work is his systematic approach to unraveling the complex challenges Eritrea and Eritreans faced in the post-independence period. By integrating historical facts with theoretical concepts and eyewitness testimonies, he conducts a thorough investigation into the fundamental issues plaguing the nation. This book transcends a simple chronological recounting of events to serve as a profound critique of the socio-political forces at play, providing insightful commentary on possible solutions. Solomon's book is not only a must-read for those keen on comprehending the dynamics of liberation movements and nation-building but also an invaluable resource for scholars, activists, and policymakers interested in the broader implications of personalist authoritarian regimes.

—Dr. Tomas Solomon

I am honored to have had an opportunity to review this important work. It comes at a time when the whole world is concerned about what happens after conflict and nations have an opportunity to be formed or to rise up over the ashes of conflict to create a haven for its citizens, one that is nurturing and on the path to thrive. This book, from the perspective of a once hopeful freedom fighter, tells the story of what happened in clear terms. It is informed by a wealth of firsthand and deeply researched knowledge of the situation of someone who has spent his life and career to being a development practitioner. Anybody who seeks insight into the phenomena of why and how "things fall apart" must read this book. I highly recommend it.

—Sharon T. Freeman, Ph.D.
President, Gems of Wisdom Consulting, Inc., USA

This book is a gem and thank you for writing it! I hope my generation fully appreciates and takes in all the lessons to be learned. It is very rare to have a multi-dimensional history for one of the most isolated nation-states be documented, much less complemented by personal accounts. I am a proud Eritrean American whose family contributed to the fight for Eritrea's independence. The fascinating aspect of this book is that it is our history, our story, and one that we are NOT done writing. It is my dream that in my lifetime, I will get the opportunity to travel freely to Eritrea with my children *and share our rich and proud culture with them. I am hopeful because to not be is simply painful!*

—*Miriam Yohannes, Consumer Affairs and Outreach Division Chief, USA*

Semere Solomon's book is truly a reflection of the man whom I have known, trusted, and admired for almost 11 years. Meticulous in his research and unwavering in his commitment to facts about Eritrea's decades-long struggles for independence and a new national identity, Semere also intertwines his personal accounts as an idealist and a soldier on the frontlines. Frequently, those who are part of a major political, military or social event write a book to settle scores with old adversaries or rewrite history to serve their own personal needs. Fortunately, "Eritra's Hard-Won Independence and Unmet Expectations" is not that kind of book. It is a unique, insider's view of aspiration, war, sacrifice, hope, and disillusionment. The book does not end with Semere's exile. Semere intertwines his life after Eritrea to which he dedicated nearly three decades as an outstanding development practitioner in Iraq, Zambia, Pakistan, Central Asia, Ethiopia, and Nigeria— always with an eye to what his homeland could have been like. The hopes and desires of a true idealist never fade.

—*Michael Zamba, Senior Director, Communications, Creative Associates International, USA*

This book stands as a significant literary contribution, not only for its eloquent portrayal of the author's personal and professional journey but also for its profound impact on the discourse of Eritrea and its future. It has the potential to ignite a cascade of thought-provoking discussions and inspire positive actions. The commitment of Semere Solomon to the Eritrean cause, coupled with his optimistic vision for the future of Eritrea as a nation, serves as an inspiring narrative. In essence, the book is not just a personal memoir but a catalyst for a broader literary exploration of challenges and solutions. I am confident that the impact of this work will extend beyond its pages, encouraging other Eritreans to share their narratives and contribute to the ongoing dialogue on the pressing issues of our time.

—Yussuf Hassen,
Stockholm, Sweden

I wanted to take a moment to let you know that I have finished reading your book, and I must say, it was an absolute delight. I couldn't be prouder of your accomplishment. Your talent as a writer shines through on every page, and I have no doubt that this is just the beginning of a remarkable literary journey for you. I eagerly await the release of your future books, as I know they will be just as incredible as this one.

—Negasi S. Abraha, USA

Semere Solomon dedicated twenty-four years of his life to the birth and development of Eritrea, a small nation in the Horn of Africa, located just north of Ethiopia. He credits the courage and perseverance of, both, the ELF and the EPLF for Eritrea's independence from Ethiopia's control. In doing so, he even acknowledges the mistakes the fronts made along the way and offers an alternative approach rooted in first principles. His ability to publicly, yet thoroughly, reflect on past history (the good and the bad) is commendable, respectable, and inspiring.

He doesn't blame any one party or individual for the current state of Eritrea —which is important when discussing sensitive and complex topics involving human beings with a myriad of perspectives. Instead, Solomon takes the reader back in time, from the 1940s to the 1990s, and then propels them forward into the future (or present) and meticulously dissects the constellation of variables that contributed to the current state of Eritrea. Answering the "how did we get here" question. This is a wonderful read for anyone interested in a nuanced and sober analysis of Eritrea within a historical, political, social, and cultural context.

Thank you, Mr. Solomon, for eloquently and honestly articulating your very unique, precious, and valuable perspective. The world is better for it.

—*Seble S. Solomon, USA*

Cover page: The background color symbolizes the sacrifice of the Eritrean people, while the photograph showcasing Massawa, the Pearl of the Red Sea, embodies the promise of Eritrea's radiant future.

—Design by Seble S. Solomon

Eritrea's Hard-won Independence and Unmet Expectations

Eritrea's Hard-won Independence and Unmet Expectations

From the Perspective of a Veteran Freedom Fighter

Semere Solomon

ISBN: 979-8-218-39332-8

Second edition published in March 2024.

This book stands as a tribute to my beloved late parents, Madalena Yosief and Solomon Abbai. Through their boundless love, unwavering care, and enduring affection, they bestowed upon my siblings and me an upbringing that continues to shape our lives.

In addition, I dedicate this book to my youngest brother, Mehari Solomon, currently enduring unjust imprisonment under the oppressive regime in Asmara. His plight represents the thousands of prisoners of conscience unjustly detained. I also honor the memory of my two martyred brothers— Rufael Solomon and Bihon Solomon—symbols of the tens of thousands of Eritreans who sacrificed their lives for the cause of an independent Eritrea.

TABLE OF CONTENTS

FOREWORD
BY JERROLD KEILSON

T HE SECOND EDITION of the book you hold in your hands, "Eritrea's Hard-Won Independence", is in reality three separate stories. First and foremost, it is a case study of a country's economic and political development, targeting the political, economic, social, and foreign policy initiatives that should be in place for a country to achieve economic growth and development. In the case of Eritrea, it's more of a cautionary tale, what happens to a country that gains independence militarily but does not have the governance systems, policies or leadership in place to achieve development.

Second, the volume is a brief and intimate history of the Eritrean revolution and struggle for independence that played out over more than thirty years, culminating in Eritrea's independence from Ethiopia in 1991. It's also a glimpse at the betrayal of the ideals of that revolution and the current situation of Eritrea today, thirty years after independence.

Finally, the arc of the story is seen and told through the eyes and voice of the author, who lived through and was an active participant in the events he describes. With this revised text, the author, Semere Solomon, acknowledges the lost opportunities, and lost people, in the independence struggle. But he has not lost hope and remains optimistic that Eritrea retains the potential to achieve what its people set out to accomplish in the 1970s, to create a free, well-governed, and prosperous Eritrea.

I've known Semere Solomon not as a freedom fighter or Eritrean exile, but as a fellow practitioner in the field of international development, and I want to share my perspective on him. I first met Semere in 2003, when we both worked at Creative Associates, a well-known international development organization. Semere was based in Iraq, supporting a USAID-funded project to rebuild the basic education system in that country in the aftermath of Saddam Hussein and the US invasion of that country. Circumstances were challenging, but Semere seemed to take whatever happened in stride. After that project ended, and for more than a decade, Semere devoted himself to managing basic education projects in Nigeria, including an especially challenging project in northeastern Nigeria, in the region where Boko Haram, the terrorist organization, operates. Semere led these projects to accomplish a great deal, more than what was called for in the contracts. As impressive to me was his ability to work in highly complex, conflicted development environments, to effect change and make a difference in the lives of children and communities. I also was struck by the profound level of respect that the project team had for him. They referred to him as the General, which I thought was a sign of respect until I read this book and realized that he had, in fact, been a military commander.

Over the years Semere and I would talk, over coffee, about the field of development, what it accomplished and why it often failed. He is a voracious reader, and we would from time to time read the same book on development (me for classes I taught and he out of intellectual curiosity). Semere has developed an integrated set of principles on what contributes to successful development. Early in this book he highlights governance as perhaps the critical element of successful development. Good governance calls for the rule of law, transparency in decision making, low or no corruption, a free press, honest and forthright discussions, the ability to disagree, and a mechanism to resolve differences amicably. Underpinnings of good governance include an educated and engaged population, which means all the people-men, women, and youth. It includes ethnic and religious minorities, and both urban and rural populations. Semere has, in his career, worked in different countries around the world. He has seen firsthand how progress can be made when there is an open and transparent governance system. And he has seen the converse, where nations with potential for wealth fail when systems of governance either are not in place or are undermined by one-party rule or a charismatic strongman/dictator. His noteworthy contribution to the development field is the recognition that the desire and willingness for economic, political, and social change cannot be imposed from outside, by donors. Rather, it must come from within the nation, from government and the people together. Donor funding has a role to play as a catalyst for change but cannot lead the change. Semere makes that point powerfully when describing the history and present situation in Eritrea.

"Eritrea's Hard-Won Independence" is an easy and interesting read. I started it on a Sunday night, and finished mid-day Monday. Semere is telling a story, several stories actually, and he interweaves them and tells them well. The text flows, and his ability to write about complex political situations and juxtapose them with personal anecdotes results in a compelling book.

This volume is an updated second edition of the book. This is a more personal story than the first edition, with new material on the author's early years and upbringing, and with further discussion on important issues that deserved a fuller discussion. Of note is that the additional information was inserted in response to requests from early readers who wanted to know more. In my mind, this speaks volumes about Semere's personality, that he would take such comments seriously and make an effort to respond.

It's important to note that the recent history of Eritrea is relatively unknown in the US and the West. Semere's writings, in this book and previously, provide a corrective to the lack of attention that is generally paid to that strategic country. At some point in the near future, as Semere writes, there will be changes in Eritrea's leadership and system of governance. Knowing how the country got to where it is, knowing its history, will be crucial to US policymakers as they determine how to respond to changes in Eritrea, and its neighbors. This knowledge also will be important to the next generation of Eritrean citizens as they navigate their new reality.

"Eritrea's Hard-Won Independence" is an important contribution to the literature of development, along the same lines as Dambisa Moyo's "Dead Aid." The focus on one country, and the attention Semere Solomon pays to the interplay of development, politics, and governance, is what gives the book its importance. And it is the personal experience and reflections of the author that make the book compelling and gives the story power.

Jerrold Keilson
Co-founder, Center for Development History
Professorial Lecturer, American University
Senior Consultant, International Development
February 20, 2024

PREFACE

AFTER THE INITIAL launch of the first edition a few months ago, I have been fortunate to receive substantial feedback from readers. The insights provided by these inputs have proven invaluable in steering me toward a more in-depth exploration and improvement of the subjects discussed in the book.

Some readers pointed out the need for increased rigor, analysis, and insight in certain chapters. There was a strong desire that I should include additional chapters that expand on the areas that they felt were overlooked or insufficiently explored within the existing content. A segment of readers emphasized the importance of incorporating more anecdotes to substantiate specific arguments. Additionally, there were suggestions to incorporate insights into my childhood or upbringing.

I have diligently worked to incorporate this constructive feedback, and I am thrilled to present the second edition of my book. This updated edition endeavors to fill gaps by offering a more comprehensive and enriched reading experience for my audience.

I hope the second edition meets the expectations of my esteemed readers.

In this book, I delve into and examine various historical phases and epochs central to Eritrea's struggle for independence transcending the mere pursuit of national sovereignty and territorial integrity of Eritrea. The independence movement was driven by a broader vision centered on achieving social justice as its primary goal. At its core, the movement sought to safeguard basic human rights, encompassing the right to a better life, the right to freely express oneself without fear of persecution, the right to organize and participate in political parties, the right to access equitable social services, the right to pursue economic gains, the right to religious freedom, the right to develop and preserve one's culture, the right to live and lead one's life as desired and rooted in freedom and choice, the commitment to upholding the rule of law, and the belief in negotiating differences and finding ways to live together. Additionally, it aimed to foster peaceful and harmonious coexistence with neighboring communities. Whether the above-mentioned goals have been met or not is the question the book is trying to answer.

I also try to answer whether the emergence of an authoritarian regime was an inevitable consequence of the independence movement or if preventive measures could have been taken to mitigate the phenomenon observed in present-day Eritrea. The goal is to extract valuable lessons from the past and use them to avoid similar mistakes in the future.

I attempt to maintain a focus on objectivity, offering interpretations of significant events rather than delving into intricate historical minutiae. The primary aim is to address a series of pressing questions that have cast a shadow over the nation's journey to independence and its subsequent aftermath.

I will dive into the "whys" of the sequence of events that transpired, further extrapolating on the various factors that may have contributed to the nation's historical trajectory. I examine the influence of the socioeconomic formation of the Eritrean society (as it evolved), the nature of the power dynamic within the society, and the impact of the international world order i.e., geopolitics. The role of foreign-bred influences on the country and the region in shaping events will also be explored. In other words, I will try to answer questions of relevance to the "whys" regarding certain historical events/ revelations.

Furthermore, the book will explain the significance of individual figures like President Isaias Afwerki—PIA—in shaping this historical phenomenon as well as evaluate if the responsibility lies on the collective or with specific individuals. The book will also try to address the issue of timing—why it took so long to detect certain developments. In cases where deterrence is possible, I offer strategies to achieve those goals as well as highlight which lessons can be gleaned from past experiences.

In addition to referencing various sources of information, I will also incorporate my personal experiences and the knowledge I gained during my tenure as a former member of the Eritrean People's Liberation Front (EPLF).

I lived the life of a freedom fighter. I breathed the air of Sahel, Gash, Barka, Semhar, Senhit, Hamasien, Akeleguzai, Seraye, and Dankalia. I was tested under different circumstances. I experienced political isolation, social seclusion, and character assassination during my tenure with the EPLF. My firsthand experience allows me to minimize potential subjectivity in the analysis.

I dedicated twenty-four years of my life to the cause (seventeen years in the field and seven years post-independence) in the endeavor to establish and nurture the nation of Eritrea. In post-independent Eritrea, I took pride in serving in the capacity of Director General for the Department of Planning and Development at the Ministry of Education until I left the country in 1998. My hands-on experience and extensive network within the country ensure that my views and perspectives are firmly rooted in reality. Continual interactions with former colleagues keep me apprised of ongoing developments.

After obtaining a diploma in Education Planning and Administration and an advanced degree in Sustainable Development and International Diplomacy, I had the opportunity to serve in various capacities for different international organizations, including the United Nations (UN) and the United States Agency for International Development (USAID), for over twenty-five years after leaving my home country, Eritrea. My involvement in international development work took me to various parts of the world, such as Africa, the Middle East, South East Asia, and Central Asia, among others. This experience significantly broadened my international perspective on various political and developmental issues. Therefore, when I write, I do so from a position of knowledge and experience coupled with years of honestly reflecting on the events (and choices) that led to the present moment.

It is important to acknowledge, however, that history is inevitably influenced by one's interpretation of events. Regardless of the abundance of factual information at one's disposal, how these facts are interpreted, the interlinkages established among them, and the contextualization applied, will almost always contain an element of personal bias. In essence, history is a matter of perspective because individuals approach the past from their subjective value systems and worldviews. As such, I am not exempt from such biases. However, I want the reader to be rest assured that I will openly share my inner perspective regarding my beliefs and experiences without hesitation. Unlike the majority of former EPLF members, I won't shy away from using the pronoun *I* to refer to myself. This is my personal history, and I aim to embrace it authentically.

This book endeavors to present a thorough and thought-provoking analysis of Eritrea's quest for independence. It aims to illuminate the intricate web of factors that shaped its historical trajectory, with the goal of offering insights that can contribute to a more promising future. It will also raise a series of assumptions that some people may have hesitated to explore or deliberately dismissed (often due to personal biases or due to some conventional thinking). I am open to correction and welcome more persuasive or alternative viewpoints. I believe in engagement conducted in the spirit of civility and honesty.

At times, I may choose not to divulge my sources to safeguard the security of my informants. This discretion is understandable, particularly in situations where the safety of some individuals could be easily jeopardized.

I will occasionally provide anecdotal pieces of evidence to bolster my arguments or analyses when it is deemed necessary. These anecdotal accounts are specifically intended to support certain assumptions and may not have been previously disclosed to anyone.

The book combines a chronological narrative with thematic explorations derived from these events. I hope that readers will find these themes interesting. It should be noted that the stand-alone chapters are interrelated – I will try to highlight how these connections influence one another throughout the book.

This book is not exclusively intended for an academic audience, it is tailored for the general public. It is written in a clear and accessible manner, designed to assist any interested reader in comprehending the complex events that unfolded in a small country once hailed as the "beacon of hope" in Africa.

The book will have a chapter for conclusions. This is where I will make final contextual remarks about what has been said in the book. This chapter will highlight some lessons learned and make some recommendations the young generation may wish to consider in shaping the future of Eritrea.

Primarily, this book serves as an expression or a statement of my beliefs, akin to a position paper. Every statement I make is rooted in political convictions and principles I have cultivated over the years.

This book also serves as a sincere plea for forgiveness from the betrayed Eritrean people extended on behalf of all justice-loving compatriots, including myself, who deeply regret the wrongs committed against you. You rightfully deserved acknowledgment and rewards for the significant sacrifices you made. Regrettably, we brought a monster into your lives. For that, we take full responsibility. May this book stand as a tribute, honoring all your sacrifices. Be assured, we will emerge from this predicament stronger.

Finally, I would like to make a confession and reveal one of my secrets. I have been writing under various pen names, such as Zeineb Ali, Tedros Tesfai, and Dehab Mussie, since 2000. Those who were following political developments in Eritrea in the 2000s will for sure have a recollection of these articles. They are also featured in the first edition of this book.

ACKNOWLEDGMENTS

THE CREATION OF this book has been a profound journey, enriched by the invaluable support, guidance, and encouragement of numerous exceptional individuals. I extend my deepest gratitude to all those who played a part in shaping this work. My heartfelt appreciation goes to Hebret Berhe, former Ambassador of Eritrea to Sweden, whose generosity in reviewing the entire manuscript was critical. Her meticulous fact-checking, insightful feedback, and thoughtful inquiries have profoundly enriched the content of this book. Her contributions have been pivotal in shaping the book's direction and enhancing its depth.

I also extend my deepest gratitude to my friend, Jerrold Keilson a former coworker at Creative Associates, who, without a moment's hesitation, graciously wrote the foreword for my book upon my request.

I express my sincere gratitude to Dr. Sharon Freeman, my esteemed colleague and former coworker at Creative Associates International, for her dedicated review of the manuscript. Her perceptive feedback and constructive criticism undeniably elevated the quality of this book to new heights. I also extend my heartfelt appreciation to Dr. Shiden Solomon, Dawit Mesfin, Miriam Yohannes, Dr. Tomas Solomon, and Semere T. Habtemariam for generously investing their time in extensively reviewing the book and engaging with me soon after its release. Their valuable insights played a pivotal role in addressing certain gaps within the book and expanding on certain topics.

To my family—my beloved wife, Faiza Adem, and my cherished children, Seble, Aida (Dorina), and Semir—who have been the driving force behind the life I have led. I owe them an immeasurable debt of gratitude for their unwavering support, patience, and understanding during the countless hours of writing and revision. Their enduring encouragement propelled me through the most challenging moments of this journey. I hope this will serve as an invitation for them to gain insight into my journey; first and foremost as a human being and later on as an activist and international development practitioner.

I express my profound gratitude to my daughter, Seble. S. Solomon, who graciously devoted her valuable time to meticulously reviewing the entire manuscript of this edition, for which I am deeply indebted. Her thorough examination ensured the absence of any spelling, punctuation, or grammatical errors. Her editorial suggestions were very helpful too. I cannot help but admire her attention to detail. This contributed to enhancing the overall excellence of the manuscript. I want to thank her for being a partner in this endeavor.

My heartfelt appreciation extends to the individuals who not only encouraged but also insisted that I document my experiences and thoughts in this book for the benefit of others. Many graciously shared their own experiences and knowledge, significantly enriching the depth and breadth of this work. Above all, I am profoundly grateful to those who dedicated their time to peruse the initial edition of the book and provided valuable feedback, enhancing its depth and quality.

Finally, I extend my deepest gratitude to the readers whose unending curiosity and thirst for knowledge led to the pursuit of learning. Your interest in this book is genuinely cherished and profoundly appreciated.

To each one of you who have contributed to this incredible journey, thank you for being an integral part of this endeavor.

1

MY LIFE'S JOURNEY: NAVIGATING TOUGH CHOICES AND EMBRACING UNIQUE EXPERIENCES

I WAS BORN IN Asmara, Eritrea, and grew up in an environment marked by rapid political transformation as the nation sought to define its identity. I willingly abandoned my higher education studies and dedicated my prime years to the cause of this nation, Eritrea.

In the warm embrace of a loving family, I was nurtured with an abundance of affection. My mother, a loving and caring woman with deep religious convictions, was not just a parent, but a friend. Her communication style mirrored that of a conversation with a confidant, freely sharing everything as if chatting with a trusted companion. She extended her friendship to all her children, fostering an atmosphere of understanding, honesty, and candidness.

My father was a no-nonsense man. You may have to carefully consider the consequences of your actions before making any misstep or foolish blunder. While he never resorted to physical discipline, his penetrating gaze and expressive countenance sufficed to convey the gravity of any wrongdoing. In the presence of my father, the house is enveloped in absolute silence. However, the moment the car leaves the driveway and the gates close, petty quarrels among the siblings promptly ensue. My school report card had to be signed by him every six weeks when I was attending Comboni College. He would look at the grades and sign. While I was walking out of the dining room, he would make one comment, "I think you could do better." And that's it. My father consistently advocated for originality. On a particular day, he observed my new hairstyle and inquired about my choice. I mentioned that several boys in the neighborhood were sporting a similar look. In turn, he told me to stand out from the crowd and nurture something distinctive and authentic. His words lingered with me long after that conversation.

My father was a member of Al Rabita Al Islamia - a political movement that aspired for the independence of Eritrea during the 1940s.

The life lessons instilled by my parents, a set of dos and don'ts, continue to serve as guiding principles of my life.

On Sundays, everyone had to be at the early morning church service, except my father. He had the right to attend the late-hour mass at Cattedrale. After the mass, he would drive us to Arberobu'e or Beleza.

My childhood, though ordinary, was a joyous tapestry woven with the threads of sibling rivalry and the cocoon of a caring community. Nicknames, initially a source of quarrels amongst siblings, eventually became endearing quirks. Despite occasional quarrels and fights, the bonds among siblings strengthened over time.

Playfulness and mischief were integral to my early years too, yet within tolerable bounds.

Against the backdrop of my upbringing, two exceptional souls emerged as my role models. Firstly, my late uncle, Medhanie Yosief, adorned with degrees from the American University of Beirut and the London School of Economics, was a distinguished civil servant, a university lecturer, and the secretary-general of the Eritrean

Chamber of Commerce. Secondly, my godfather, Beyene Debessai, boasting an advanced degree from Canada, excelled as an accomplished executive in the private sector. Both individuals were highly esteemed within their communities.

The YMCA played a pivotal role in shaping my youth, offering not only sports and entertainment but also invaluable leadership lessons. From basketball to chess, the YMCA was a melting pot of diverse activities. It also served as a hub where seniors from Hailesellassie I University assisted high school graduates in preparing for their university entrance exams.

Medhanie Yosief generously sponsored our basketball team and entrusted the team with the capable guidance of an American coach from Kagnew Station.

Movies and the camaraderie of trusted friends provided additional avenues for enjoyment and self-expression. I was privileged to own a bicycle from an early age (along with my siblings) and ventured into formal driving lessons at the age of 15. The way my father approached it was amusing. One bright Saturday morning, he asked me to accompany him without revealing our destination. As we drove, I remained in the dark about where we were heading. Eventually, we arrived at a driving school (Autoscuola Africa) near Mercato Coperto. Before I stepped out of the car, my father told me that the person awaiting us would tell me what I was supposed to do and he left. Fitsum was the name of the instructor who was assigned to give me driving lessons.

All members of the family attended the prestigious Comboni College of Asmara run by the Jesuits at various points, beginning with my eldest sister, Illen Solomon.

Completing my education up to grade 12 in Asmara, I subsequently joined Hailesellassie I University.

Academic diligence was a hallmark of my school years, with exceptional achievements in secondary school, culminating in securing the top position in the "Special Class" at Hailesellassie I Secondary School in Grade 12's French Section.

Early exposure to reading, fueled by a voracious appetite for knowledge, saw me finish almost all African Writers' Series in the school library by the age of 14-15 while I was attending grades 9 and 10.

In the literary realm, I borrowed books from the extensive libraries of my late uncle, Medhanie Yosief, and my godfather, Beyene Debessai as well as his younger brother, the late Yonas Debessai.

Kagnew station (an American military base in Asmara) introduced my siblings and me to comic books which were exchanged at a small kiosk near Albergo Italia, Asmara. My mother never liked them. She would always say, "Stay away from these "figurini" (sketches) and concentrate on your schoolbooks." My siblings and I had various secret locations where we stashed our comic books to ensure my mother couldn't find them.

Within my family, a culture of reading thrived. My father immersed himself in Italian magazines until the late hours. His favorite was the weekly "Domenca Del Corriere" (a weekly magazine published in Milan, Italy) and he played crossword puzzle ("Cruciverba") over lunch and dinner, while my late elder sister, Asmeret Solomon, enjoyed delving into books for days on end. I have never encountered a more voracious reader than Asmeret in my entire life. The elder sisters, Alganesh and the late Assefash, immersed themselves in both Italian and English magazines such as "Romanzo", "True Love", and "True Story."

I harbored a fervent passion for learning languages. I dedicated five years to studying Italian at Principé (also known as Dante Alighieri) Evening School, learned French in high school and Alliance Française, and took Arabic lessons at Jalia (Arab Community School) School after school or during winter breaks.

My mother's prayer books, cherished repositories of spirituality, were all in Italian.

Twenty-four years of my life were devoted to the birth, development, and nurturing of this young nation. My responsibilities during this period were closely tied to the establishment of a free Eritrea imbued with a sustainable socioeconomic framework that promotes social justice.

For reasons that require little explanation, most of my work, both within the EPLF and later within the Eritrean government, was carried out without any financial compensation. It was only in the mid-1990s that the government could afford to provide a token salary. Suffice it to say, I consider my involvement in the birth of Eritrea and the experiences of those tumultuous years to be a reward in itself.

I served the EPLF in various capacities, both in active combat and other roles. I was considerably young when I was chosen by the rank and file to represent the EPLF during its efforts to reconcile with the Eritrean Liberation Front (ELF) after five years of relentless civil war between the two organizations. Our platoon, known as Berhe Tsada's Platoon (ሓይሊ በርሀ ጸዓዳ) gathered in Fishe Mrara to choose a representative for a meeting to discuss the matter of unity with the ELF. I received an overwhelming mandate with 144 out of 145 votes from the platoon members. I was serving in the capacity of unit leader then.

Subsequently, I joined fellow freedom fighters from different platoons, all assigned the same mission. After deliberation on what our approach should be toward unity, the group convening in Solomuna, selected a five-member committee. I was one of the committee members.

It was an incredible experience to engage in dialogue and exchange of ideas with the rank and file and senior members of the ELF on matters pertaining to collaboration for the common cause (independence) and unity. The committee drawn from the EPLF conducted visits to all ELF platoons situated in the highlands of Eritrea, La'elai Barka, and the Sahel regions. During this expedition for reconciliation, the committee also had the privilege of meeting Osman Saleh Sabbe (Head of the Foreign Mission of EPLF) when he visited BleQat, which served as EPLF's base area in the Sahel region. He was accompanied by his delegation. In addition, the five-member Committee also met with Paulos Ba'atai and Menghisteab Isak – both representing the Eritreans for Liberation of North America (ELNA). They had traveled all the way from the United States to engage the leadership. The purpose of our meeting with them was to update them on the current status of the ongoing efforts to bring the two organizations (EPLF and ELF) closer.

The reception our team received from ELF members was warm, and our discussions took place in a friendly and cordial atmosphere. The enthusiasm was boundless, and both parties couldn't wait for the day when they could work together under a united platform. Members of the committee also met with EPLF platoons scattered all over EPLF operations areas. Despite a few differences harbored by each front, it was evident that there was no fundamental distinction between the two fronts on the question of independence and unity.

Prior to the dissolution of the committee, I was initially assigned to co-command a newly formed platoon drawn from the newly recruited members of the EPLF along with Amanuel Ainalem (Amanuel Qeshi) before being designated (by the EPLF leadership) as the Head of Information, Culture, and Education, alongside Ahmed Al Qeisi. However, I was temporarily frozen out from active duty and held in detention by the leadership before I was reassigned to the Department of Mass Administration, Asmara (Team 06 - ባይ ኣይኣት) in the outskirts of Asmara for a specific mission, which aimed to raise awareness and organize the urban population through various mass organizations.

The person overseeing the unit was Ermias Debessai, also known as Papayo. Key members of the Unit included Woldemichael Abraha (Herr Schmidt), Fessahaye Haile (Afro), the late Rezene Embaye (a pharmacist by profession), the late Tekle Bahlbi (Wedi Lbi) who was in charge of Operations in Ethiopia, the late Weini Menghesha, and me. All were senior-level cadres capable of operating independently without any supervision.

Our team would have been incomplete without the dynamic and highly dedicated leadership team operating from within Asmara disguised as civilians. Chief among these individuals were Kidane Solomon (my elder brother, nom de guerre Kebede), Afeworki Tewoldemedhin (nom de guerre Bureaucracy), Russom Teklemariam (nom de guerre Tarzan), Beyene Debessai, Kibrom Ghebremedhin (Wedi Bula), Kaleb Solomon (my younger brother), Iyob (ኣእዳወይ ይስበሩ), Ghebru, Alem Mekebeb, Kibreab Kidane (ጠቢቕ) and Tiquabo. Many served as branch (ጨንፈር) leaders, coordinating major operations in their respective branches and domains. These colleagues fearlessly faced the enemy and adversity, constantly walking on the edge of death at every second, minute, and hour of every day.

Mobilized members of EPLF (of the city of Asmara and the surrounding area) were organized in "cells" and "branches" (ዋህዮታትን ጨናፍራትን) under the Workers' and Students' Associations.

Operating within a radius of 3 – 7 kilometers from Asmara, our main base was Dirfo. We coordinated our operations from Karneshim, Minabé Zerai, and Seharti districts. Our primary responsibilities included rallying city and village dwellers in Asmara and its vicinity in support of the liberation movement led by the EPLF.

We were also entrusted with leading and coordinating military, intelligence, and other operations in Asmara. These involved recruiting new EPLF members, collecting intelligence from the enemy, infiltrating enemy ranks and recruiting them to serve on the side of the liberation movement, sabotaging enemy operations, pillaging enemy property and moving it to liberated areas, as well as combatting enemy agents. We were the night visitors of Asmara whenever the need arose, including pillaging goods from the enemy vital to the sustenance of the liberation movement. These included but were not limited to medicine, plastic sandals, fabric, sugar, oil, lentils, spare parts, and more. We would sometimes guide battalions into Asmara to undertake certain operations at night.

We published a monthly magazine called "Dimtsi Hizbi" ("The Voice of the People") aimed at raising political awareness of the population. The magazine's editors were Fessahaye Haile (Afro) and me, with Kidane Solomon (Kebede) making significant contributions to the magazine. Kidane Solomon was a brilliant idealogue and an excellent addition to the team. "Dimtsi Hizbi" was widely distributed in Asmara and nearby villages and played a major role in rallying the population behind the movement for independence.

Tekle Bahlbi (Wedi Lbi) was in charge of operations in Ethiopia, frequently traveling to Mekele, Dessie, Addis Ababa, and other cities as necessary, sometimes accompanied by Kidane Solomon (Kebede).

Our team maintained effective coordination with the Suicide Squad that was led by the late Brigadier General Mebrahtu Tekleab (Vinac).

I later became in charge of the unit that was responsible for operations in Asmara, from Adi Hawsha (a village located south of Asmara).

Two years later, at the request of Mr. Beraki Ghebresellasie, the Head of the Education Department, I was assigned to lead the Education Branch in the Semien Region. In 1978, following EPLF's famous strategic withdrawal, I was designated to join the combat units in the North Eastern Sahel region, where I served as a Battalion Commissar for almost six years. During this time, I had the opportunity to test myself in combat and had the privilege of participating in several military offensives (ወራራት), including the 2nd, 3rd, 4th, 5th, 6th, offensive launched by the Ethiopian Occupation Army and "The Initiative" (ተበግሶ)—a military offensive launched by the EPLF in 1979. I was wounded in combat and still have bomb fragments in the lower part of my body.

Regrettably, I also engaged in the capacity of a Battalion Commissar in numerous and extended military skirmishes against the ELF in Sahel and Gash Barka regions until the latter was eventually forced out of Eritrea into Sudan thereby restricting its operations in Eritrea.

In late 1983, I returned to the Department of Mass Organizations. Between late 1983 and 1987, I frequently ventured back and forth to the frontlines (Nakfa, Barka, and Noth Eastern Sahel), providing support to the combat units whenever it was deemed necessary, always serving as a Battalion Commander. One of my several assignments was in Brigade 4 serving in the capacity of a Battalion Commissar under the command of the late Major General Ghebrezghabiher Andemariam (Wuchu).

Then, in 1986, Simon Ghebredinghil (then in charge of Signals Unit) and I assumed the role of commanding the reserve/auxiliary forces in the base area, North Eastern Sahel. My pivotal role in organizing and training these forces led to their transformation into a full-fledged combat unit organized in a brigade which later was integrated into Division 85. In this capacity, I was appointed Brigade Commissar, working alongside Ahmed Dali, who served as Brigade Commander, and Berhane Tsehaye, who held the position of Deputy Brigade Commander. At a later stage, I handed over my responsibilities to Iyob Fessahaye (Halibay).

Years 1987–91 marked a significant period in my life. During this time, I had the privilege of working on the editorial board of an internal magazine called *Harbegna* (which translates to "Patriot"). This six-person team, as detailed in Chapter 9, included Ahmed Al Qeisi, Alemseghed Tesfai, Zemhret Yohannes, Kidane Solomon, Mahmoud Chirum, and me.

Harbegna was established as a laboratory for experimenting with new ideas, with the primary goal of enhancing the political consciousness of EPLF members through robust discussions and debates within its platform. The editorial board members were responsible for defining their scope of work, selecting relevant topics, and devising effective approaches to addressing and disseminating them. In addition to managing the magazine, the team was also entrusted with the important task of documenting the history of Eritrea. I also wrote a book on the pre-colonial history of Eritrea which served as a political education manual for the members of the front.

The pertinent issues raised by the magazine ignited controversies that the leadership found increasingly difficult to endure. Consequently, the leadership made the controversial decision to permanently shutter the magazine. Its life span was rather short-lived, lasting less than two years. The team responsible for overseeing the internal magazine *Harbegna* was disbanded, and its members were reassigned to various units within the organization. Ahmed Al Qeisi was incarcerated, a consequence of his association with the magazine's provocative topics, though not solely due to it. Meanwhile, I, after an eleven-year absence from the department, was reassigned to head the Curriculum Division of the Department of Education.

I was not a member of the clandestine political party, known as the Eritrean People's Revolutionary Party (EPRP), which was later rebranded as the Socialist Party. However, I was aware of the party's existence during its early years in 1979. I was summoned by a high-ranking party official— Teklai Habtesellassie, commander, Brigade 31—when it was discovered that I had come across party documents and had come to know about the party's presence within the front. I was threatened with death if I disclosed, insinuated, or hinted at anything about it. Every party member became aware of my knowledge regarding the existence of this clandestine party. In a dedicated chapter, I will delve into what it was like to participate in an organization while being aware of the presence of another hidden organization within it, and the feeling of being an outsider in an organization that one is supposed to be a part of.

Five brothers from my own family joined the EPLF. Two— Rufael Solomon and Bihon Solomon—were martyred in combat in the battles of Massawa and Barentu respectively. The youngest—Mehari Solomon— a former freedom fighter, was taken from a coffee shop one bright morning in 2014—and is languishing in the dungeons of the regime.

Mehari served as the Director of Finance at the Ministry of Local Governments. Having been a committed member of clandestine operations in Asmara when Asmara was the epicenter of all Dergue's activities in Eritrea, he transitioned to the field in 1981. Following military training, Mehari held various roles at the Department of Mass Administration.

His departure from Asmara became imperative when Dergue operatives discovered an AN/PRC 77 Radio Set buried in our family residence, Gejeret, Asmara. This radio set was used by Mehari to communicate secret messages to freedom fighters from the heart of Asmara. Unfortunately, a colleague who was captured and subjected to torture later tipped off the Dergue operatives, leading to Mehari's decision to flee. It was ironic how the Dergue operatives reacted when they saw my mother witnessing the situation with horror. One of them said, "The lady looks like a saint." And they left her alone.

I take pride in serving as the director general for the Department of Planning and Development, Ministry of Education from 1991 to 1998 until I was frozen out and sidelined. The Asmara regime routinely enforces this practice on numerous prominent civil servants, ostensibly for undisclosed reasons, though, in most cases, it is driven by political motives. Interestingly, I happened to be one of them. The affected civil servants are typically instructed to transfer their responsibilities to another official and are subsequently left in a state of uncertainty. The duration of this situation remains unknown, leaving the individuals in limbo regarding their potential reinstatement, a decision solely determined by circumstances beyond their control. Immediately after I was frozen out, I submitted a letter of resignation and stopped taking a salary from the government in defiance of the norms. The resignation letter read as follows,

After seven years of dedicated service to the Ministry of Education, I am formally tendering my resignation from the civil service. I want to underscore my conviction that continuing to draw my salary from taxpayer funds would raise ethical concerns, and as such, I have decided to cease accepting my salary.

The letter was addressed to Mr. Osman Saleh, the Minister of Education, and copied to the Minister of Local Governments (Mahmoud Sheriffo), and the Office of the President.

I will delve into this topic extensively in Chapter 15.

Subsequently, I embarked on an international assignment with UNESCO and the United Nations Office of the Humanitarian Coordinator in Iraq (UNOHCI) in Iraq and served there for five years as a senior planning officer.

After earning an advanced degree in Sustainable Development and International Diplomacy, I gained valuable experience through diverse roles in programs funded by USAID. Over the course of twenty-five years, I immersed myself in international contexts, embarking on assignments across the globe, including Africa, the Middle East, South East Asia, and Central Asia, among other regions. These experiences profoundly enriched my international outlook, deepening my understanding of a wide range of political and developmental challenges.

I am lucky to be a native speaker of Tigrigna, fluent in oral and written English, with working knowledge of French, Italian, and Amharic, and basic Arabic.

Tendering my resignation from civil service and subsequent departure from Eritrea evoked mixed feelings among my colleagues. This was unheard of before and came as a shock to many. Some did not agree with the decision I made, expressing that I could have exercised more patience, and they viewed it as a hasty choice and an action of defiance against the government. Some sympathized with my predicament but were reluctant to openly endorse my actions, saying, "He should not have put his safety and that of his family in danger." A few, however, believed that I had made the right decision.

The decision was critical for me as I knew that I would be under close surveillance from that day forward. Hence, I had to find a way to flee the country; which I did.

Interestingly, one individual—Filipos Woldeyohannes—supported my decision. After I left, during a casual conversation over drinks with other military commanders, Brigadier General Teklehaimanot Libsu criticized my actions as wrong, arguing that I should not have left the country while Eritrea was at war with the Tigray People's Liberation Front (TPLF). General Filipos, however, intervened and firmly stated that he supported my decision, adding that he would have done the same had he been in my position. He was referring to the decision to marginalize me from the civil service despite having much to offer. This discussion took place during a dinner held to celebrate the return of several military officers from China after completing a six-month-long military training. The narrator of this story was the late Colonel Mekonen Haile who happened to be one of the military officers who received training in China.

I met Beraki Ghebresellassie—former minister of Information—after I tendered my resignation. Beraki did not react. He was numb. Abdalla Jaber—former Executive Committee member, PFDJ, in charge of organizational affairs—visited my place to inquire about my decision and to explore the possibility of revisiting my decision. He left after I unequivocally told him that I was not going to change my mind.

2

ERITREA IN 1991

THE STRUGGLE FOR independence in Eritrea went beyond the mere quest for independence and self-determination. It was driven by a broader vision focused on achieving social justice as its primary objective. At its essence, the movement aimed to protect fundamental human rights, including the right to a better life imbued with dignity, the freedom to express oneself without fear of persecution, the right to organize and engage in political activities, access to fair social services, the pursuit of economic opportunities, religious freedom, the preservation and development of one's culture, the liberty to live life according to personal preferences, and a commitment to upholding the rule of law. Furthermore, it sought to promote peaceful and harmonious coexistence with neighboring communities.

It is an undeniable fact that Eritrea's victory over the Socialist Regime in Ethiopia in 1991 was mainly attributed to a long and sustained sacrifice paid by the Eritrean people. This being the case, the victory cannot be seen in isolation from other variables such as the shift in international power dynamic which culminated in the implosion of the USSR, the growth of opposition forces in Ethiopia, and the new development in the internal power dynamic within the Dergue. These latter factors are not to be underestimated.

A new nation, whether it is a product of decolonization or any other circumstance, typically has a range of opportunities to build itself. The extent of these opportunities can vary greatly depending on factors like historical context, resources, political stability, and international factors. Nascent states usually find themselves at a crossroads. Eritrea was not an exception.

In 1991, Eritrea found itself at an intersection, facing a myriad of challenges and opportunities as it emerged from the ashes of a thirty-year war of independence.

The birth of this new state came at a heavy price, with scars of conflict and uncertainty still fresh. Scores of freedom fighters gave their lives to a cause they believed was dear and sacrosanct.

Hundreds of thousands of residents were displaced, seeking refuge in neighboring countries and beyond. The country experienced a halt in social and economic development, with conditions either stagnant or deteriorating."

The political organization—the EPLF—that co-led the armed struggle and liberated the country from Ethiopian colonial occupation, had yet to be tested in post-independence Eritrea against a totally different set of criteria.

The war necessitated tenacity, resilience, courage, commitment, and high level of military configuration on the part of the liberation movements. It called for strict hierarchical structures and a disciplined chain of command. It demanded clear lines of authority and responsibility for maintaining order and effectiveness. It required the ability to adapt to rapidly changing circumstances and evolving threats; a tradition of continuous learning and adjustment to remain effective in dynamic environments. It dictated the prevalence of effective leadership, both at the tactical and strategic levels for guiding operations and making critical decisions under pressure. It also required value systems—codes of ethics and values—that emphasize adherence to the rules of engagement.

The question loomed: Could the EPLF successfully transition from a wartime movement possessing all the above variables to a movement or a political party that could address developmental issues? Could it prove itself to be understanding of the new circumstances and cope with them? Could the new norms be responsive to the demands of the day? Could the rule of law reign supreme? Could it successfully hand over power to its legitimate owners, the people of Eritrea? How would the organization evolve into a democratic institution, shedding its culture of secrecy and militarization while preserving its resilience and tenacity that evolved over the years? How could it slowly morph into an apparatus that embraces inclusivity, accountability, the rule of law, and individual freedom?

Building a sense of national unity and social cohesion was crucial to stability too. Promoting dialogue and a culture of tolerance would help prevent internal conflicts. Equally pressing was the task of preparing its former members to adapt to this new reality, working seamlessly while blending in with the civilian population. Another significant concern was addressing the needs of war-disabled veterans in a time of peace, a question that demanded answers.

The economic landscape posed yet another formidable challenge. Where would the resources come from to rebuild a war-ravaged nascent nation? How could the weak institutions inherited from the socialist state of Ethiopia be strengthened or recalibrated to respond to the new normal? How could the human resource asset be aligned with the demands of national reconstruction? And how could the country's infrastructure which was in a state of disrepair be revitalized? All the aforementioned questions called for the charting of a comprehensive roadmap for national reconstruction.

SEMERE SOLOMON

The issue of mass exodus, with Eritreans who sought refuge in neighboring countries, the Middle East, Europe, and North America, added complexity to the situation. Eritrean refugees in Sudan (in particular) deserved particular attention. According to UNHCR, when Eritrea won its independence in May 1991, some five hundred thousand Eritrean refugees were living in Sudan[i] (UNHCR, 1998). Amid these challenges, the imperative of gaining legitimacy in the eyes of the international community was paramount. Diplomatic efforts were needed to garner international recognition and support for rebuilding a nation coming out from the ruins of war.

The education system had to be revitalized to meet the demands of national reconstruction, and the deep trauma suffered by the population during thirty years of conflict needed healing, both physical and psychological.

Moreover, it was imminent that there could be political threats from the South (i.e., Ethiopia) from those who would not accept the status quo of a new independent Eritrea. A deeply ingrained myth deliberately cultivated and nurtured by the Amhara Royalty for centuries maintained that imperial Ethiopia's three-thousand-long history has a legitimate claim over territories bordering the Red Sea and current Eritrea. Generations of Ethiopians were indoctrinated by this myth.

This was despite the warmth in the relationship between the Eritrean People's Liberation Front (EPLF) and the Ethiopian People's Revolutionary Democratic Front (EPRDF) during that period.

Of major concern was the persistent specter of Islamic extremism in the world in general and the region in particular. In other words, the Horn of Africa and the neighboring Middle East were no strangers to this troubling phenomenon, and Eritrea was not immune.

How to navigate these challenges while grappling with the security and development of the new nation was a pressing question.

Despite these formidable obstacles, Eritrea also possessed significant opportunities.

Independence became a rallying factor for all patriotic Eritreans from all walks of life and all schools of thought. People had paid a steep price for its achievement and therefore felt that its independence was truly well-deserved. The path toward it was arduous and long. Speculations as to whether the Eritrean armed struggle was bound to fail were rampant at one time or the other. Everyone thus rejoiced. Everyone demonstrated their readiness to forget wounds inflicted upon each other during the armed struggle. The vast majority agreed to close the chapter once and for all and to start a new phase of history with an open mind and heart. To say bygones are bygones. This culminated in the most historically notable referendum where 99.98 percent of Eritreans voted for Eritrea's independence.[ii]

Society's respect and support for, and trust in the liberation front presented an opportunity to unite the entire nation for a common goal; a goal to create a sovereign, democratic, and prosperous Eritrea.

Eritrea's location along the Red Sea coastlines was a major asset if properly nurtured and taken advantage of too. More than 10 percent of the world's global trade transits through the Red Sea annually, spanning from the Bab al-Mandab at the sea's southern gateway to Egypt's Suez Canal in the north. The Red Sea serves as an indispensable economic maritime route and is poised to retain its significance in the forthcoming decades. The region encompassing the Red Sea littoral nations along the northeastern coast of Africa and the Arabian Peninsula holds immense growth potential. Projections indicate that the population in this area will surge by 100 percent, soaring from approximately 620 million to nearly 1.3 billion by the early 2050s. Concurrently, the gross domestic product (GDP) is anticipated to climb from $1.8 trillion to $6.1 trillion over the same timeframe[iii] (Due, 2021).

Eritrea's strategic location in this pivotal zone was likely to draw the attention of global powers, given the strategic importance of this vital corridor. Developments within this region would vigilantly be monitored, and the world's major economic, political, and military powers would exhibit little tolerance for any instability in this area. It was expected that interventions, whether military or diplomatic, may be considered should circumstances lean toward chaos or disruption.

Considering the aforementioned factors, it was imperative for Eritrean leadership to exercise prudence in light of the then-prevailing circumstances. This situation demanded utmost caution for the international community to perceive Eritrea's role as a stabilizing force, rather than a disruptive one, within the region. Whether the leadership perceived it well or not, the responsibility of ensuring regional security often extended beyond their immediate control. This necessitated a keen awareness of the power dynamics at play in the region and a clear understanding of their own role within that intricate equation. Neglecting to grasp the context of their existence and engaging in questionable actions could potentially lead to severe consequences.

The international community viewed the nascent nation favorably, offering a supportive environment for its development and ensuring its legitimate role within the international community. Several multilateral and bilateral funding organizations started engaging their Eritrea counterparts for consultations and to assess their strategic needs and priorities. Diplomatic missions started establishing protocols and rules of engagement to consider future collaboration. The implementation of an internationally sponsored and monitored referendum was the first milestone in the history of post-independence Eritrea. The international community recognized the will of the Eritrean people; the independence of Eritrea. Eritrea's legal entity—with its territorial boundaries—within the international community paved the way for formal interaction with individual sovereign nations, as well as regional (IGAD, AU, and others) and international organizations such as the United Nations and its official branches.

The lessons learned from various global experiences, including African liberation movements, provided valuable guidance on what to embrace and what to avoid. These movements were established to do away with European colonial domination and with setting up free and democratic states. These included the Front for National Liberation (FNL) of Algeria, the Popular Movement for the Liberation of Angola (MPLA), the South West African People's Organization (SWAPO) of Namibia, the Front for the Liberation of Mozambique (FRELIMO), the Zimbabwe African National Union (ZANU), the African National Congress (ANC) of South Africa, and the African Party for the Independence of Guinea and Cape Verde (PAIGC)[iv] (Mesfin, 2008).

These liberation movements have indeed echoed the political aspirations of their respective people and were instrumental in uprooting the colonial vestiges. Like the ELF and EPLF, they made huge sacrifices and displayed a great sense of commitment to their respective causes. These movements predominantly embraced Marxism as their path to salvation and social transformation. Most of them did not end up well as it increasingly became clear that they were led by tiny elites who were interested more in their narrow interests (power) at the expense of the common goal. Secrecy and ruthlessness cut across the behavior of most of these elite groups. Most of them displayed undemocratic tendencies and claimed a monopoly of the truth as compared to exercising democratic practices toward matters of national concern. They ended up staying in power for an unlimited period under the pretext of safeguarding national security or political stability.

Indeed, these narrow elites had been holding office for decades by establishing a system of secrecy and a culture of impunity, characteristics reminiscent of the struggle years[v] (Mesfin, 2008). These movements usually did not tolerate voices of dissension. They did not provide a platform for a diversity of opinions or world outlooks. Nor did they possess the mechanism to resolve differences or conflicts through consensual means, to say the least, and often resorted to violence or coercion.

Immediately after securing independence, these movements were not clear as to what they were going to do with it. Also, they did not have a clear sense of direction to translate their ideas into reality. They did not have a firm grip on societies' socioeconomic formation nor were they aware of their needs and aspirations. The phenomena we have witnessed were shattered dreams and frustrated aspirations of the common people and a total grip of power by a small elite and their minions, all rallying around deceptive slogans. Eritrea had a lot to learn from these lessons.

The positive working relationship between the EPLF and EPRDF (formerly the TPLF) offered avenues for cooperation and coordination on many fronts—economic, security, diplomatic, and so forth. Regardless of the ups and downs that unfolded since they started working together in 1975, the two organizations came a long way to mitigate suspicion, distrust, and to a certain extent their political differences. In 1991, this partnership culminated in framing a joint strategy and well-orchestrated multifaceted military, political, and diplomatic initiatives aimed at toppling the authoritarian regime in Addis Ababa. This did, however, call for (the two organizations) more effort to skillfully respond to and address the dynamic political situation that was unfolding between the two countries and in the wider region as two sovereign states and in a manner compatible with international law and norms.

Eritrea also had the opportunity to shape an all-encompassing development agenda that was inclusive, forward-looking, and anchored in the community's needs. This fresh start would allow the creation of a new constitution, the establishment of vital institutions, and the pursuit of economic growth. Cultural identity, infrastructure development, education, and human capital were to be prioritized to empower the nation's citizens.

Furthermore, there was an opportunity to craft a well-thought-out foreign policy to secure international support and benefit from a globalized world, promote social cohesion, uphold the rule of law, and embrace good governance vital for stability and legitimacy.

Eritrea's journey in 1991 was thus marked by both daunting challenges and promising opportunities. Navigating this delicate balance would be the key to building a stable, prosperous, and united nation from the ruins of war.

3

STATE OF THE NATION TODAY

O NCE HAILED AS a beacon of hope of Africa, a country of low crime, ethnic harmony, and can-do spirit located along the Red Sea, it has been a while since a bleak and somber tale started unfolding. The State of Eritrea, as assessed through various social, economic, and political criteria, reveals a landscape marred by economic downturn and turmoil, political disorientation, institutional malaise and dysfunction, and a social fabric fraying at the edges.

The situation in Eritrea, as it stands now, is characterized by wanton misuse/abuse of one full generation's potential, deliberate move toward dismantling the social fabric, carefully designed destruction of rich and diversified culture, undue harassment and control of religions and religious institutions, forceful/violent suppression of any dissenting voice/s, rounding up and confinement of the youth to military barracks, the alarming exodus of tens of thousands countrymen and women for fear of persecution, gross infringement of basic human rights, total marginalization of veterans of the war of independence, the forceful regimentation of society's way of thinking, and international isolation. The political situation has deteriorated to an alarming degree. It has been years since the nation witnessed any semblance of political stability. Political dissension resulting from lack of transparency has become the norm. Citizens are increasingly disillusioned by the inability of their leaders to steer the ship of state. According to the Fund for Peace (FFP),[vi] Eritrea (with a score of 94.5 from a maximum deterioration scale i.e., 120) is considered to be one of the twenty most fragile countries (chief among which are Somalia, Yemen, South Sudan, DRC, Sudan, Central African Republic, Chad, Ethiopia, etc.). Compare the score with that of Botswana (55.3), Namibia (60.3), Ghana (62.3), Morocco (68.20), South Africa (72.0), Gambia (76.1), and Tanzania (76.6). Criteria used to measure progress comprise cohesion, economic, political, social, and crosscutting indicators. Cohesion indicators measure security apparatus, factionalized elites, and group grievance. The economic indicators assess economic decline, uneven economic development, and human flight and brain drain. Politics is seen against state legitimacy, public services, human rights, and the rule of law. Social indicators address demographic pressures and refugees and internally displaced persons (IDPs). The cross-cutting factor deals with external intervention (Peace, 2023).

The rate of decline is specifically visible in areas such as security apparatus[vii] (Peace, 2023), group grievance[viii] (Peace, 2023), and economic decline[ix] (Peace, 2023) (this indicator considers factors related to economic patterns of progressive economic decline of the society as a whole as measured by per capita income, Gross National Product, unemployment rates, inflation, productivity, debt, poverty levels, or business failures, etc.), human flight and brain drain[x] (Peace, 2023), state legitimacy[xi] (Peace, 2023), and human rights and rule of law[xii] (Peace, 2023).

According to Human Rights Watch 2023 World Report,[xiii] the Eritrean government persisted in its severe suppression of its citizens. These include imposing limitations on the freedom of expression, opinion, and religious belief, as well as hindering independent over-sight by international observers. The government continues its practice of conscripting Eritrean citizens, predominantly males and unmarried females, into military or civil service without fixed terms, meager com-pensation, and no input into their choice of profession or work location (Watch, 2023).

Furthermore, widespread mass arrests and prolonged arbitrary detentions persisted without access to legal representation, judicial review, or family visits, with some individuals enduring such condi-tions for decades. These actions primarily target individuals perceived as opponents of the government, including those evading military conscription. For more than two decades, the government has denied religious freedom to those who do not adhere to the officially recog-nized religious denominations, which include Sunni Islam, Eritrean Orthodox, Roman Catholic, and Evangelical (Lutheran) churches. Those affiliated with "unrecognized" faiths continued to face impris-onment, with instances of torture used to coerce them into renounc-ing their religious beliefs.

It is worth noting that Eritrea has not ratified the 1951 UN Refugee Convention or the 1969 African Refugee Convention. As of the end of 2021, there were more than 580,000 Eritrean refugees and asylum seekers living abroad, and a significant majority cited the ongoing indefinite national service as the primary reason for their decision to flee the country, as documented in the May 2022 report by the UN special rapporteur on the human rights situation in Eritreaxiv (Human Rights Watch, 2023).

In its 2022/23 report, Amnesty International[xv] documented ongoing persecution by Eritrean authorities against political dissi-dents, leaders and members of religious congregations, leading to their arbitrary detention. The whereabouts of these persecuted indi-viduals remained unknown, and national service conscripts were often subjected to what seemed like an indefinite period of service. Disturbingly, there were widespread allegations of sexual violence committed by military commanders against conscripts in the Sawa Military Training Camp (International A., 2023).

The fate and location of eleven members of the G-15, a group of fifteen seasoned politicians who expressed their dissent regarding President Afwerki's misgovernance, remained undisclosed since their arrest by security forces in September 2001. These eleven members were apprehended following the publication of an Open Letter to the president, urging the implementation of the ratified constitution and the holding of open elections. Similarly, the whereabouts and destiny of Dawit Isaak, a Swedish journalist, and sixteen others assumed to have collaborated with the G-15, remained shrouded in mystery.

A prominent group of dissidents, consisting of high-ranking government, military, and party officials, initiated an endeavor known as the Forto Rebellion in January 2013, with the aim of overthrowing the Isaias-led government and installing a constitutional government. The key figures behind this movement, along with their supporters, have been apprehended, and their current whereabouts remain undisclosed. These comprise Abdalla Jaber (former chief, Organizational Affairs, PFDJ, Mustafa Nur Hussein (former governor, Southern Zone), Ahmed Haji Ali (former minister, Energy and Mines), Major General Omar Tewil (former commander, Southern Zone), and Ibrahim Totil (former Central Committee member, PFDJ). Said Ali (Wedi Ali) – a high-ranking army officer – who took part in the rebellion died in action. The attempt to overthrow the government failed, with government troops suppressing the would-be rebellion and no one rising up in the streets[xvi] (Gettleman, 2013). According to my confidential sources, even prominent figures such as Ramadan Mohammed Nur were not only aware of the rebellion but sympathized with it.

The aforementioned purges are comparable to no other but those committed by Saddam Hussein, Joseph Stalin, and Mao Tse-Tung—all vestiges of the leftist movements.

The two major incidents underscore a fundamental truth; the government's stability has always been shaky or under a question mark. It is evident that the government is deeply concerned about its security, given the prevalence of such grievances among both its members and the general public. These situations insinuate that change is not just a possibility but an eventuality. Furthermore, these incidents highlight that change could and is likely to originate from within, driven solely by insiders. This perspective aligns with the idea that regime change, as observed in many other countries, is primarily determined by internal power dynamics rather than external influences. I also believe that there may have been other, albeit minor, attempts to overthrow the government over the past three decades, which remain undisclosed. In a tightly controlled society like Eritrea, accessing information of this nature can be an arduous task. What we know for sure is that acts of dissent of this nature were and are prevalent and will persist.

The patriarch of the Eritrean Orthodox Church, Abune Antonios, passed away on February 9, 2022, at the age of ninety-four. He had been subjected to unlawful house arrest since 2006, a punitive measure taken by authorities after he openly criticized government policies, despite never being formally charged with or convicted of any recognizable criminal offense. On October 15, 2022, Abune Fikremariam Hagos (bishop of the Catholic Church), from Segheneiti, was arrested at Asmara International Airport upon his return from Europe. Multiple sources confirmed that he was detained without any charges in Adi Abieto prison. However, Bishop Fikremariam and Abba Mehretab (another Catholic priest) were eventually released from detention on December 28, 2022.

Additionally, government forces conducted numerous raids, known as "giffa" in Tigrinya, during which they apprehended young individuals from the streets for compulsory military service. Government officials allegedly coerced parents into bringing children who had avoided conscription to register for national service[xvii] (International A., 2023).

The annual report[xviii] from the United Nations High Commissioner for Human Rights (along with reports from the Office of the High Commissioner and the Secretary-General), provides an overview of the human rights situation in Eritrea. This assessment primarily focuses on the indefinite national/military service and its adverse effects on the economic, social, and cultural rights of the Eritrean population. It also delves into the status of the rule of law, the administration of justice, and instances of violations of civil and political rights, including prolonged and arbitrary detentions as well as enforced disappearances. The report draws attention to the plight of the Eritrean Afar indigenous communities who continue to endure discrimination, persecution, and interference with their traditional ways of life. Additionally, the report highlights the ongoing challenges in safeguarding the rights of Eritrean refugees and asylum seekers, both in the region and beyond. Despite recommendations put forth by various human rights organizations, there has been no discernible progress in reforming the national service system in Eritrea (Babiker, 2023).

The same report by the Special Rapporteur citing the conflict that broke out in November 2020 raised the alarm over the grave human rights violations committed by Eritrean troops in the context of the Tigray conflict, including the participation of the Eritrean Defense Forces in large-scale massacres, sexual and gender-based violence, looting, obstruction of humanitarian assistance, destruction of civilian infrastructure and refugee camps, and kidnapping and targeted attacks against Eritrean refugees (Babiker, 2023).

According to the Heritage Foundation,[xix] Eritrea's economic freedom score is 39.5, making its economy one of the least free in the 2023 index. Its score is 0.2 points lower than last year. Eritrea is ranked 45th out of 46 countries in the sub-Saharan Africa region, and its overall score is well below the regional and world averages.

Eritrea's long-standing problems include poor governance, a lack of commitment to structural reform, poor management of public finance, and underdeveloped legal and regulatory frameworks. Weak enforcement of property rights and the fragile rule of law have driven many people into the informal sector. Eritrea ranks no. 171 out of 176 countries in this regard (with the last on the list being North Korea (Kim, 2023). The overall rule of law is weak in Eritrea. The country's scores on property rights, judicial effectiveness, and government integrity are all below the world average. Eritrea is ranked 45 out of 46 countries in the sub-Saharan Africa region, and its overall score is well below the regional and world averages[xx] (Kim, 2023).

The World Bank Human Capital Project[xxi] updated its report in October 2022. The report provides country-level disaggregated data in perspective with Human Capital Complementary Indicators (HCCIs). The data covers 172 countries except Eritrea (Bank T. W., 2020).

The World Bank's lending program in Eritrea is inactive due to repayment arrears, and its role is limited to technical assistance, analytical work, and preparation for broader re-engagement[xxii] (Bank T. W., The World Bank IBRD IDA, 2021).

According to a report released by Mo Ibrahim Foundation, twenty-three out of fifty-four African countries are currently host to at least one non-African military presence. Fourteen non-African states have established a military presence on the African continent. Djibouti, with its strategically important location, now hosts seven non-African military bases. The UAE opened its first African military base in Eritrea in 2015, with airfield and deepwater port facilities that have been used to support the UAE's role in the Yemen conflict. However, in February 2021, under pressure from the United States, it dismantled parts of the Assab military base[xxiii] (VOA, VOA News, 2021). A report by the United States Institute for Peace (USIP)[xxiv] (USIP, 2020) citing the Washington Institute for Near East Policy revealed that as of early 2019, the Emirati base in Assab, Eritrea, reportedly hosted a battalion of ground forces in addition to eight hundred to twelve hundred naval, air, and support forces. This presence has reportedly decreased by up to 75 percent, although the UAE has, according to UN investigators, continued to use the air base to covertly ferry arms to the LNA in Libya[xxv] (USIP, 2020).

The AU's African Charter on Democracy, Elections and Governance (ACDEG), adopted in 2007 and entered into force in 2012, has been signed by forty-six countries and ratified by thirty-eight. Countries that have neither signed nor ratified include Botswana, Egypt, Eritrea, Libya, Morocco, and Tanzania[xxvi] (Foundation, 2023).

According to a report released by the International Monetary Fund (IMF), Eritrea's GDP growth[xxvii] stands at 2.9 percent in 2023. GDP per capita stands at USD 2.19 thousand as of 2023 (IMF, 2023).

Table A4. Emerging Market and Developing Economies: Real GDP *(continued)*
(Annual percent change)

	Average 2005–14	2015	2016	2017	2018	2019	2020	2021	2022	Projections 2023	2024	2028
Sub-Saharan Africa	**5.5**	**3.2**	**1.5**	**2.9**	**3.2**	**3.3**	**-1.7**	**4.6**	**3.9**	**3.6**	**4.2**	**4.4**
Angola	7.8	0.9	-2.6	-0.2	-1.3	-0.7	-5.6	1.1	2.8	3.5	3.7	4.2
Benin	4.2	1.8	3.3	5.7	6.7	6.9	3.8	7.2	6.0	6.0	5.9	5.9
Botswana	3.7	-4.9	7.2	4.1	4.2	3.0	-8.7	11.8	6.4	3.7	4.3	4.0
Burkina Faso	5.9	3.9	6.0	6.2	6.6	5.7	1.9	6.9	2.5	4.9	5.9	5.2
Burundi	4.5	-3.9	-0.6	0.5	1.6	1.8	0.3	3.1	1.8	3.3	6.0	5.5
Cabo Verde	3.7	1.0	4.7	3.7	14.6	5.7	-14.8	7.0	10.5	4.4	5.4	4.5
Cameroon	3.6	5.6	4.5	3.5	4.0	3.4	0.5	3.6	3.4	4.3	4.4	4.7
Central African Republic	-1.5	4.3	4.7	4.5	3.8	3.0	1.0	1.0	0.4	2.5	3.8	3.3
Chad	5.4	1.8	-5.6	-2.4	2.4	3.4	-2.1	-1.1	2.5	3.5	3.7	3.7
Comoros	2.9	1.1	3.3	3.8	3.6	1.8	-0.2	2.1	2.4	3.0	3.6	4.2
Democratic Republic of the Congo	7.2	6.4	0.4	3.7	4.8	4.5	1.7	6.2	6.6	6.3	6.5	6.5
Republic of Congo	5.5	-3.6	-10.8	-4.4	-4.8	1.0	-6.2	1.5	2.8	4.1	4.6	4.0
Côte d'Ivoire	3.6	8.8	7.2	6.1	3.8	8.3	1.7	7.0	6.7	6.2	6.6	6.0
Equatorial Guinea	4.6	-9.1	-8.8	-5.7	-6.2	-5.5	-4.2	-3.2	1.6	-1.8	-8.2	-0.3
Eritrea	4.5	-20.6	7.4	-10.0	13.0	3.8	-0.5	2.9	2.6	2.9	2.9	2.9

The population, once a source of strength, has become a cause for concern. The mass exodus of skilled and educated youth has left the country grappling with a brain drain of monumental proportions. The effects of this exodus are felt not only in the domestic job market but also in the eroding state of education, as schools struggle to find qualified teachers.

The bitterness, anger, and frustrations of the youth have given rise to movements like Brigade NHamedu or the Blue Wave, demanding change and accountability from the government. These voices represent the simmering discontent that threatens to boil over. It is a movement that began in 2021 and is predominantly spearheaded by the youth, many of whom are former members of the National Service. Their profound discontent stems from their perception of the regime as having played with their future and the future of the country. The movement is one of a kind that shattered the fear factor the government employed to intimidate the Eritrean diaspora. It operates through local chapters or branches and has a global presence. From an external perspective, there appears to be a degree of coordination among its various branches. Recent political events organized by Eritrean youth in several parts of the world, including Germany, Israel, the Netherlands, Sweden, Denmark, the USA, Canada, and Switzerland, among others, are concrete manifestations of this movement.

I contend that the Government of Eritrea bears responsibility for provoking this movement. The enduring policy of perpetual "National Service," the harassment of the youth, the dire circumstances faced by the Eritrean populace, ongoing military conflicts with neighboring countries, a deteriorating economy, and the suppression of religious institutions have all contributed to the deepseated bitterness, anger, and fury displayed by the youth in expressing their frustrations.

Does this movement need to enhance its strategy to counter the Eritrean regime's malicious attempts to weaken it? Should it prioritize greater organization to challenge the regime's deceptive campaign aimed at rallying Eritreans in the diaspora with its pseudo-nationalistic schemes (using the fear factor)? Should it outmaneuver the regime's old tactics and develop a more sophisticated strategy to engage the youth effectively? Could it further step up its efforts to disrupt the regime's primary source of revenue, the 2 percent tax? Should it stop the regime from milking the diaspora for its own political ends in perpetuity? Should it shed light on the regime's brutality to the outside world? Absolutely. Whether one agrees with it or not, this is a movement to reckon with and thus demands serious attention.

One can certainly critique the violent nature of this movement—an issue open to deliberation by all Eritreans. However, asserting that the movement is solely instigated and funded by foreign entities (as some government operatives maintain) does not do justice to its essence. It is essential to recognize that political movements of this kind, spearheaded by the youth, naturally emerge in response to repressive regimes' malpractices like the one currently in power in Eritrea.

Consider the Arab Spring that swept across the Middle East in the early 2010s —was it primarily driven by external forces? Was it not led by disgruntled youth who had suffered under their respective authoritarian regimes? Similarly, is the Palestinian Intifada solely the result of foreign instigation? I argue that these at their core are genuinely nationalist youth movements driven from within, despite their imperfections.

Another interesting characteristic of the Eritrean society is the once-vibrant social fabric that bound communities together has been weakened. Trust in institutions has eroded, giving way to a sense of alienation among citizens. Social divisions have deepened, and the country's diversity is no longer celebrated but exploited for political gains.

Amid this backdrop, the government's stance on the war in Ukraine has raised eyebrows. Its controversial position has isolated the country further on the global stage, deepening the divide between the nation and its international partners.

The nation's relationship with its neighbors has become increasingly strained, with tensions bubbling just beneath the surface. Rhetoric, against the West and international institutions, has become commonplace, further isolating the nation.

Eritrea is often called the North Korea of Africa because it is so isolated and authoritarian, with few friends and thousands of defectors in recent years as President Isaias tightens his grip and the economy teeters on the brink of ruin.

The opposition, though existent, remains divided and disorderly, unable to mount a coherent challenge to the ruling regime. In the absence of a credible alternative, the government continues to hold sway, unchecked and unchallenged.

As the nation descends further into turmoil, the road to recovery seems long and arduous. The challenges are daunting, and the future remains uncertain. In this narrative of decline, hope flickers dimly, awaiting a spark to ignite change and steer the nation toward a brighter tomorrow.

4

WHAT SHOULD HAVE BEEN THE
NASCENT NATION'S PRIORITIES

E RITREA'S POVERTY, ITS small economy, and modest population,
defined its reality in the aftermath of its independence.
Nonetheless, amid these challenges, Eritrea boasted a unique
and invaluable asset that holds the potential to shape its future—its
resilient people. Against formidable odds, the Eritrean populace
not only endured a three-decade-long war but also emerged victorious in securing its independence. This monumental achievement
set the stage for a promising journey toward development. And
hence was branded as the "beacon of hope" by many observers.

Nestled in a strategically vital location, it was obvious that geopolitics would cast a long shadow on Eritrea's destiny. Eritrea is a
small, coastal country strategically located along the Red Sea in the
Horn of Africa, bordered by Sudan, Ethiopia, and Djibouti.

In this intricate geopolitical puzzle, there was a constant threat
looming from the south. Ethiopia, Eritrea's vast neighbor, had
long maintained mainstream political aspirations that included the
Eritrean ports of Massawa and Assab. Ethiopia's 120 million land-
locked citizens added urgency to Eritrea's need for careful navigation.

A deeply ingrained myth cultivated and nurtured by the Amhara royalty for centuries maintains that the Ethiopian Empire was the legitimate owner of the coastlines of Eritrea— and Massawa and Assab in particular. While it is undeniable that the historical and cultural bonds between the populations of Eritrea and Ethiopia stemmed from the Axumite Era and subsequent periods, one must also recognize one notable historical reality. This has to do with the fifty years of Italian colonization of Eritrea and the subsequent occupation by the British for another ten years that resulted in forging a national identity.

Another persistent specter in the region was religious extremism. The Horn of Africa and the neighboring Middle East were no strangers to this troubling phenomenon, and Eritrea was not immune.

The war of independence also caused a monumental exodus that in turn drained its productive population.

Given the above, what could/should have been Eritrea's priorities?

Ensuring stability by paving the way to setting up a government of national reconciliation: Eritrea's path to independence was shaped by a complex interplay of internal dynamics and external influences. Various political organizations, each characterized by diverse ideologies and leadership styles, emerged and vanished at different junctures in time. This phenomenon can be attributed to several factors, including the socioeconomic formation of Eritrean society, the political climate of the 1940s and 1950s, and the global movement for democracy and justice. Additionally, the schisms within the Socialist Camp, particularly the tensions between the Soviet Union and China, as well as the influence of the Arab Renaissance Movement that swept through the Middle East in the 1960s and 1970s, played significant roles in shaping Eritrea's political landscape. Despite these disparities, the achievement of Eritrean independence can principally be credited to the prolonged and unwavering sacrifices made by the entire population, a fact that cannot be overstated.

Regrettably, the political disagreements among different Eritrean political organizations were not resolved through peaceful and democratic dialogue. The liquidation of the Eritrean Liberation Movement (ELM), also known as Haraka, in the harsh Sahel region, the brutal civil war between the EPLF and the ELF that persisted for nearly a decade (until the eviction of ELF from Eritrea), and sporadic military clashes between the EPLF and various splinter groups of the ELF from 1981 to 1991 are notable examples. These divisions among the fronts also had a divisive impact on the Eritrean population (both inside and outside Eritrea), leading to tensions between supporters of different factions.

In light of the aforementioned circumstances, the primary focus of the EPLF regime, which assumed power through its political and military dominance, should have been the establishment of an inclusive platform with the overarching goal of uniting the entire Eritrean populace, irrespective of their political, ideological, religious, or ethnic affiliations, in pursuit of national reconciliation and reconstruction. This endeavor could have culminated in the formation of a government dedicated to national reconciliation, exemplifying the behavior expected of dominant political entities—a sign of political maturity and wisdom. By undertaking this initiative, the EPLF would have stood to gain significantly.

The specifics of this political transition could have been delineated through a national conference that brings together representatives from diverse segments of Eritrean society, including opposition members, traditional and religious leaders, women, civic society representatives, and the diaspora, among others. The objective of such a gathering would have been to chart a comprehensive roadmap for the transition period and the nation's future. It could have also served as the beginning of the healing process. This roadmap could have remained a work in progress, subject to periodic review and refinement.

Initiating the Healing Process: The political schism between the EPLF and ELF has exacted a substantial toll on Eritrea. The domestic resources, particularly the sacrifices made on both sides during the civil war, the opportunity cost incurred, the ensuing political discord among their respective followers, and the lingering bitterness against each other demanded a set of guiding principles and approaches to swiftly de-escalate tensions and commence the healing process.

As the saying goes, "Resilience should be your critical attribute when you are a minority, magnanimity when you are a majority." This maxim should have been applied to post-independence Eritrea. Ideally, the EPLF could have demonstrated wisdom, prudence, far-sightedness, tolerance, and pragmatism to initiate the healing process. A crucial first step could have been the recognition of all those who sacrificed their lives for independence, followed by the issuance of a Certificate of Martyrdom for all Eritrean martyrs, irrespective of their political affiliation.

Moreover, the compensation (Nakfa 30,000) provided to the parents of EPLF martyrs could have been equitably extended to those who lost their lives under the ELF for the same cause. Additionally, declaring Veterans' Day in commemoration of the sacrifices made by freedom fighters for their country could have contributed to the healing process.

Not only did the regime fail to acknowledge the sacrifice paid by ELF fighters, but also refused to recognize even the members of the 1973 Menqa'e Movement as legitimate members of the EPLF. It was truly astonishing to come across group photos where the images of former EPLF fighters were intentionally erased. I vividly recall a specific photograph featuring the late Beraki (Wedi Fenkil), Mehari Ogbazghi, and the late Tewolde Iyob, each holding their AK-47 rifles. However, in one of the early 1990s editions of Haddas Eritrea daily newspaper, the image of Tewolde Iyob was deliberately blackened or obscured. This is reminiscent of the Soviet era when Joseph Stalin would erase former comrades from photographs using photo editing as a weapon in his great purge. Additionally, it was equally disheartening not to find any mention of Ogbe Abraha in an extensive video clip documenting the annihilation of WuQaw Commnad (ዉቃዉ እዝ), an Ethiopia military command defeated in North Eastern Sahel. Ogbe Abraha (currently languishing in prison due to his association with the G-15), was the commander of the front when this important milestone happened.

Establishing a warm and cordial relationship with its neighbors: Nations cannot choose their neighbors. Neighboring nations' fates are intertwined with each other. Change in the neighborhood will likely affect individual countries. Neighboring countries also encounter similar challenges. Climate change, refugees, countering extremism in all shapes and forms, and fighting drug and human trafficking, could be cited as examples.

Forging warm and cordial relationships with neighbors centered on the principles of partnership and respect for each other's sovereignty and territorial integrity are crucial to the stability of any nation. In addition to securing national security, this could also be the basis for a regional scheme that lays the ground for a stable and prosperous future for the countries in the same region. Where the region is characterized by volatility, it adds an extra layer to developing the capacity to navigate the situation and develop the art of resilience.

Eritrea's priority should thus have been to make an effort to understand global and regional politics and in tandem with it to frame a foreign policy that is aimed at ensuring regional harmony and a mechanism to absorb potential frictions. "Conduct dialogue for one thousand days rather than fight one day" Sun Tsu, the great Chinese military strategist, is believed to have said. The essence of the quote emphasizes the value of diplomacy, negotiation, and conflict avoidance over engaging in a direct military confrontation that is always destructive by nature.

Exerting smart diplomatic effort to garner international support and neutralize external threats: The world is intertwined like never before. Globalization has created a modus operandi that does not allow individual nations to survive let alone thrive. Either one understands the rules of engagement or one perishes. Gaining a comprehensive understanding of the rules of engagement and mastering the art of navigating the global system can be highly beneficial. The global setting is a platform aimed at promoting one's national interests without infringing upon the interests of others. By upholding some international standards and identifying common ground, nations can trigger regional harmony and stability, growth, and prosperity and create an avenue to learn from each other. Eritrea could have benefited from a policy that advocated for the aforementioned principles.

Framing a development program that centers people and is based on the principle of partnership: Sustainable growth requires stable and sound economic fundamentals at all levels, including a sound climate for investment and entrepreneurship in all sectors. This entails the development of a national poverty reduction strategy that focuses on national dialogues geared toward its fulfillment. It requires the formulation of appropriate macro-economic policy (including sound fiscal and monetary policy) that promotes entrepreneurship, encourages savings and investment, enhances exports, understands the need for strong trade relationships with neighbors and the outside world in general, and promotes regional cooperation.

When governments allow private competition in the domestic market, foreign investment has helped African countries scale up access to services, providing more flexible and innovative approaches than public sector monopolies. Mauritius has achieved international recognition for its exemplary private-public sector relationship. Kenya is often mentioned for its horticulture exports. Over a thirty-year period, horticulture exports have grown to become the country's second-largest foreign exchange earner.

The community-driven development approach should be promoted as communities are in a much better situation to know what their needs are and how to achieve them. However, the sustainability of these initiatives requires institutional change. Governments, thus, need to find ways to support public institutions to enhance accountability. This involves an effective decentralization of administration, resources, and political power backed by an accountability mechanism. India and Mauritius among the developing nations are good examples of this approach.

Diversifying the economy typically prevents nations from depending solely on one source of revenue, thus avoiding a single-economy status. It prepares them to absorb economic shocks. Mauritius has come a long way from a nation whose economy was based on the production of sugar to a more diversified and export-oriented economy. On the contrary, despite good economic performance, there are concerns that Botswana's economy might fall prey to fluctuations in the global diamond market. Argentina's economic failure is also attributed to a lack of diversification of its economy. It is therefore recommended that diversification is seriously considered as a development strategy[xxviii] (Liebenthal, 2006).

Eritrea's economic growth required collaboration with multilateral and bilateral financing agencies. Incentives for the private sector should have been provided to bolster the nation's economy. To thrive, Eritrea needed a strong economy, world-class diplomacy, positive relations with its neighbors and the international community, an innovative young population, and a thriving private sector.

Building institutions—separation of powers among the legislative, executive, and judiciary, ensuring rule of law, and defining government mandate (policy formulation, strategic planning, regulatory role, and research and training): Good governance is a critical ingredient of economic growth and a precondition for avoiding policy failures and market collapses. *Webster's Dictionary* defines governance as "the manner in which power is exercised in the management of a country's economic and social resources for development."xxix The World Bank describes governance as consisting of the traditions and institutions by which authority in a country is exercised. This includes the process by which governments are selected, monitored, and replaced; the capacity of the government to effectively formulate and implement sound policies; and the respect of citizens and the state for the institutions that govern economic and social interactions among them. The World Bank (WB) describes six dimensions of governance against which governance is measured. These include voice and accountability, political stability and absence of violence, government effectiveness, regulatory quality, rule of law, and control of corruptionxxx (Bank T. W., World Governance Indicators, n.d.).

In *An Introduction to Sustainable Development*, Peter Rogers and coauthors indicate that poor governance is a hindrance to development, distorts the process of development, and can have a disproportionately negative impact on the poor. They argue that adherence to good governance requires accountability, participation and decentralization, predictability, and transparency[xxxi] (Peter P. Rogers, 2009). Accountability involves holding officials accountable for their behaviors; decentralization enhances the manageability of participation by involving all the stakeholders in the decision-making process; strict adherence to sound policies, laws, and regulations ensures predictability; and citizens have to be informed on all government actions and policies in order for a system of governance to claim to be transparent[xxxii] (Peter P. Rogers, 2009).

According to Calderesi, economic growth can be achieved and foreign assistance works best where governments are already on the right track, establishing priorities, implementing policies, and developing key institutions for their own reasons rather than trying to impress people in foreign capitals[xxxiii] (Calderisi, 2006). Collier and Gunning, in an article entitled *Explaining African Economic Performance,* also indicate that there exists a negative relationship between economic growth and the amounts of Overseas Development Aid (ODA) for the great majority of African countries because of their weak policy environments[xxxiv] (Gunning, 1999). Paul Collier, in his famous lecture entitled *New Rules for Rebuilding a Broken Nation* (given at the State Department), also stresses the need for a clean government that promotes job creation for the youth and the provision of social services. "This", he says, "could lead countries in transition from the politics of plunder to the politics of hope[xxxv] (Collier, 2009)."

One of the nascent nation's main priorities was to address governance; to make an effort to frame its developmental strategy to be inclusive, to nurture homegrown policies that respond to the needs of its peculiar circumstances, to build strong and transparent institutions, and to develop standards of practice that will enable it to implement its policies and curtail behaviors of lawlessness.

A nascent nation has an obligation to delineate the government's mandate clearly, ensuring a precise understanding of its role in society. In general, governments possess specific mandates, whether they effectively implement them or not—an aspect deserving separate scrutiny. A government's success or failure hinges significantly on adhering to these mandates.

One of the pivotal responsibilities of any government lies in formulating developmental policies and elucidating the means to accomplish them. Governments define their mission statement, encapsulating their core values, goals, and objectives, ultimately charting the destiny of the nation. This mission involves delivering services to citizens, upholding the rule of law, fostering economic prosperity, guaranteeing the safety of citizens from internal and external threats, developing essential infrastructure for economic growth, providing education, healthcare, and various social services, nurturing positive relationships with neighbors and the international community for the common good, and more. Each of these facets must be articulated through policy documents deeply rooted in the socioeconomic context and extensively deliberated upon by the constituency.

Strategic planning stands as another cornerstone of any government's responsibility. The government must articulate how it intends to achieve these policy objectives. What approach will it adopt? How will it mobilize domestic and external resources? What role does the private sector play in this endeavor? What responsibilities do citizens bear in the pursuit of these objectives?

The third fundamental role of any government is establishing a robust regulatory system. According to the United Nations Economic and Social Commission for Asia Pacific (United Nations ESCAP), this system comprises a set of legal instruments, rules, procedures, and processes, alongside regulatory authorities vested with delegated powers. These mechanisms serve multiple purposes, including safeguarding public interests, defining technical, safety, and quality standards, and overseeing compliance[xxxvi] (ESCAP, 2008).

The fourth government mandate is to frame a policy on human resource development (HDR) to create the necessary human resource assets for national reconstruction and development.

The aforementioned mandates were monumental endeavors for a nascent Eritrea. The essence here was to begin with what you already possess and remain open and receptive to new ideas. It required the political will to embark on this path, as there was no alternative to achieving peace, stability, and prosperity but to follow this path.

Building a self-sufficient Eritrea has always been a long-term endeavor. To achieve this, Eritrea should have maintained a low profile, fostering positive relationships with its neighbors. Its strategic location along the Red Sea should have been leveraged for its own interests.

Maximizing Eritrea's human resource asset: Knowledge, values, and skills empower individuals, communities, and societies to enhance economic development. Educated people are more productive and contribute more to the economy. Investment in education yields relatively large returns in terms of individual earnings. Literacy and numeracy can increase economic growth by helping societies improve the quality of the workforce. Education is a key factor in raising the standard of living and lifting people out of poverty.

Education is key to economic growth. Economic growth and development require high labor productivity if the standard of living is to improve. This can only happen if there is a change in the quality of labor. Education and training are the only means to attain these ends[xxxvii] (James M. Cypher, 2004).

However, the quality of education provided by certain countries leaves much to be desired. This is especially true for developing countries. Education should come out of rote learning and be able to encourage critical thinking and respond to the ever-changing labor market needs (relevance). Hence, improving the quality of education should be the priority. In *Education for Sustainable Development Toolkit,* Rosalyn McKeown points out that education should focus on skills, values, and perspectives that encourage and support public participation and community decision-making. She argues that education should be universal and inclusive enough to attract the cross-section of a society[xxxviii] (McKeown, 2002). One OECD study indicated that HRD factors in four main elements. These are: educational attainment, workforce skills, population health, and employment policies that connect people to the labor market and provide opportunities to quickly adapt to new challenges structure[xxxix] (OECD, 2005).

Studies have demonstrated that increased application of human capital and knowledge to production enhances the economy[xl] (Dietz, The Process of Economic Development, 2004). The government should thus invest in people via education, on-the-job training, nutrition, health care, and sanitation to increase the quality of the employed labor force[xli] (James M. Cypher, 2004). Hence a sound human resource development policy is a requisite for development. As stated earlier, South Korea is one of the countries that succeeded in demonstrating rapid growth by making a huge investment in its human capital.

Investing in its people was pivotal in Eritrea. Highly educated Eritreans could have attracted world-class investments. The nation's vast coastline, spanning one thousand kilometers, could have been harnessed to develop a thriving tourist industry. There existed the potential for Eritrea to become a regional hub for the service industry and IT too.

Tapping on the potential of the diaspora—integrating the diaspora in national reconstruction: The WB estimated the number of Eritrean refugees at five hundred thousand in 1994[xlii] (Miovic, 1994). It is to be recalled that the diaspora organized itself into a mighty force and made a substantial contribution and paid a lot of sacrifice to the war of independence. The EPLF, through its mass organizations organized overseas, institutionalized the diaspora as a funding source following its fallout with/from the major political players (the West rallying around the US and Socialist Camp rallying around the former Soviet Union) in the international arena. In 1991, the government introduced a diaspora tax for all Eritreans living abroad, which stood at 2 percent of their annual income no matter whether it was derived from work or social welfare benefitsxliii (Hirt, 2014). The diaspora, in addition to becoming a major source of revenue to the front, also provided immense political support to the movement for independence. Through community diplomacy, it also served as the voice of the front on different international and regional political platforms.

After independence, the Eritrean embassies abroad have been active in amassing huge sums of money from the diaspora. In exchange, members of the diaspora were granted clearance enabling them to access government services, including the issuance of birth and marriage certificates, the ability to purchase land in Eritrea, the opportunity to operate businesses, and the option to obtain exit visas for elderly relatives[xliv] (Reich, 2015).

In hindsight, Eritrea could have capitalized optimally on its diaspora by pursuing a different approach. Instead of imposing a 2 percent tax on their salaries, it could have incentivized them to invest in their homeland thereby attracting massive foreign currency earnings to the nation which in turn could have set the nation towards a healthy growth trajectory. A united front, formed by diverse political entities, civic organizations, religious institutions, and the diaspora, could have paved the way for an all-inclusive government of national reconciliation. The worst thing that happened in post-independence

Eritrea was the polarization of politics within the diaspora initiated and deliberately nurtured by the regime.

Building a cohesive national entity: Communities that take pride in their culture, identity, history, values, and norms are likely to make sustained, albeit slow, progress. Identity is an effective instrument in rallying people around lofty ideals such as nation-building. Nation-building in Eritrea started way back in the late 1880s when Italy colonized Eritrea. Subsequent colonial administration—the British Military Administration—had a role to play in raising the once-suppressed political awareness. The federal arrangement with Ethiopia gave Eritreans the first opportunity for self-rule until the annexation of Eritrea by imperial Ethiopia in 1962. This gave birth to an armed struggle that rallied people from all walks of life for a common cause— independence. It is thus my belief that nation-building in Eritrea did start earlier on and reached its climax during the thirty-year war of independence.

The war of independence, regardless of its ups and downs, has galvanized a sense of strong national identity among Eritreans. Diplomatically isolated from both camps and in the absence of any support from the international community, the independence movements had no choice but to rely on their own resources—the Eritrean people. The path to independence was long and arduous, the enemy confronted was strong and sophisticated (supported by the Soviet Union and its allies), and the price paid was heavy, yet the movements for independence culminated in rallying the majority of their population around the noble cause. Imagine the sense of pride and national identity this has given birth to.

Post-independence Eritrea could have been built on this foundation to consolidate national identity. Apart from the thirty-year war that contributed to wielding national identity, other factors that could have been instrumental in taking it to the next level could have been building a well-developed economy, an educated population, modern infrastructure, good governance, respect for human rights, and the feeling among citizens of a sufficient amount of commonality of interests, goals, and preferences so that they do not wish to separate from each other[xlv] (Reich, 2015).

There was ample opportunity for the Eritrean regime to consolidate its gains and up its game to enhance national identity. A well-groomed new generation could have taken it to the next level once these values have been transmitted to it in the course of time.

Massive polarization of politics and public life was a roadblock to progress. Eritrea should have fostered an environment where people were encouraged to contribute to national reconstruction without fear of political repercussions.

Building a professional army: Wars or military confrontations between sovereign nations should be unequivocally avoided. The devastating toll of war spares no one, and its consequences are felt by all. The most effective means to prevent conflicts of this nature is through diplomatic dialogue and the pursuit of negotiated solutions. As an alternative, deterrence strategies can also be employed.

The establishment of a strong, professional military force is not aimed at initiating hostilities or engaging in warfare against neighboring nations. Rather, the primary objective is to serve as a deterrence and to safeguard national security. A highly skilled and professional military not only stands ready to defend the nation during times of crisis but also commands the respect and admiration of neighboring countries.

A modern, professional army—encompassing ground forces, naval capabilities, and an air force—was essential to counter potential threats from the south (Ethiopia as mentioned earlier), quell political or religious extremism, and stabilize the volatile Horn of Africa.

Drawing upon a wealth of experience amassed over three decades and harnessing the dedication and goodwill of its members and the population at large, the Eritrean government had a unique opportunity to create a streamlined, modern, and efficient professional military force capable of ensuring the nation's security. The establishment of a military academy dedicated to imparting contemporary military theory and practical knowledge tailored to the Eritrean context would have yielded a core cadre of military officers prepared for a lifetime of professional excellence in service to Eritrea.

Furthermore, the military academy, beyond its role in training career officers, could have also served as a valuable research and documentation center for the military history of the Eritrean Liberation Army (ELA) and the Eritrean People's Liberation Army (EPLA). This would have preserved the rich legacy of these organizations and allowed it to be passed down from one generation to the next.

Given Eritrea's relatively small size and limited resources compared to potential external threats resulting from its geopolitics, one might ponder whether the government could have explored the possibility of considering military alliances with larger and more powerful nations to counteract external dangers and potential military aggression. A relevant example to consider is neighboring Djibouti, a nation that was once a French colony. Djibouti, situated at the entrance of the Southern Red Sea, holds a strategic position as a crucial gateway for global trade. Historically, Djibouti has been seen as an essential maritime outlet for landlocked Ethiopia. Owing to its small population and vulnerability, Djibouti was susceptible to aggression from its neighboring countries.

What enabled Djibouti to command respect among its neighbors was its strategic military alliance and treaty with France. Of course, this alliance also benefited France's geopolitical interests in the region. From my perspective, Djibouti's government displayed astute geopolitical acumen by recognizing the importance of forging diplomatic and military partnerships to ensure its survival and establish itself as a prominent political player in the region. A close associate of mine, a former ambassador of Djibouti to Iraq in the late 1990s, once shared with me (while both were serving as board members of the International School of Baghdad) an insightful perspective. In those days, I had the privilege to serve the United Nations in Iraq. The former ambassador to Iraq believed that the most significant mistake made by the Kuwaitis was underestimating Saddam Hussein's threat to their sovereignty, despite Iraq's repeated claims that Kuwait was part of its legitimate territory. My friend emphasized, "We may be nomads, but we possess shrewd survival instincts. Without our alliance with the French, we might have easily fallen prey to neighboring nations like Somalia and Ethiopia. Unfortunately, despite Djibouti's repeated warnings, Kuwait did not heed our advice to invite the Americans or another Western power to establish a military presence. The consequences of their decision became painfully evident."

In contemporary politics, one can only imagine what the fate of the Baltic states could have been had they not joined the North Atlantic Treaty Organization (NATO).

Keeping up with innovation/s (ፈጠራ)—taking advantage of what the world could offer: Innovation is often linked with modern technology, and there is no denying that technology has profoundly transformed the world, as highlighted earlier in this chapter. However, its significance extends beyond technological advancements. At its core, innovation is about unlocking human potential by offering opportunities for growth. This necessitates an emphasis on education, especially for the younger generation, with the goal of cultivating a valuable human resource asset.

Innovation is synonymous with thinking outside the box and diverging from conventional thought processes. It encompasses the notion of adding value to goods and services, and it advocates for scaling efforts to maximize societal impact. Importantly, innovation requires the accumulation of capital. It is a multifaceted concept that not only reshapes technological landscapes but also shapes the way we approach the economy, education, creativity, and societal progress. The world underwent a profound transformation in the 1990s. It was during this time that the first-ever World Wide Web page and the browser application, which facilitated the circulation of vast information to users, were developed. This innovation ignited a revolution in communication technology, ushering in an era where people began incorporating cell phones and personal computers into their daily lives. The rapid dissemination of information significantly contributed to the acceleration of globalization.

Given these advancements, Eritrea had a unique opportunity to harness the potential of its young generation through advanced education and technology to support its developmental goals. With easy access to a wealth of information, the nation could have leveraged this knowledge to foster progress. Furthermore, Eritrea could have seamlessly integrated digital technology into its education system, thereby catalyzing advancements and nurturing a digitally literate new generation capable of meeting the demands of the twenty-first-century economy and diplomacy. In doing so, Eritrea could have positioned itself as a significant player in the globalized world.

Eritrea's resistance to a simple technology can be elucidated through a conversation I had with a former USAID Mission Director who operated in the region during the early 1990s. According to him, an American delegation visited Asmara to discuss bilateral relationships with the government. Among the topics discussed was the potential support for Eritrea in introducing mobile telephone technology. President Isaias's response was that he had more pressing priorities that took precedence over mobile technology. The delegation was awestruck to see their offer rejected.

According to the International Telecommunications Union, mobile-cellular subscriptions per 100 inhabitants (2021) were 50 percent in 2021. Households with internet access at home stand at 1.92 percent in Eritrea compared to Ethiopia (18%), Djibouti (52.6%), Kenya (24.1%), Sudan (16.2%), and Rwanda (18.5%) to name some[xlvi] (ITU, n.d.).

Overall, Eritrea had the potential to carve out a brighter future for itself and its people, but it required strategic foresight, wise leadership, and a commitment to long-term development through innovation.

5

CAUSES THAT TRIGGERED THE MOVEMENT FOR INDEPENDENCE

A N INDEPENDENCE MOVEMENT or any social movement for change finds its roots in the intricate dynamics of internal power structures. History bears witness to the recurrent emergence of such phenomena, where a desire for change becomes inherent within the subjugated populace, just as it is embedded in the subjugators' psyche to uphold the existing status quo, often resorting to coercion or manipulation.

The oppressors/subjugators, driven by notions of cultural and ideological superiority, actively seek to instill obedience and conformity among those they subjugate. They wield sophisticated institutional and military apparatuses, employing intimidation as a means to sustain their dominance.

Moreover, unforeseen external factors can exert influence on the internal political climate, further complicating the power dynamic. Inevitably, over time, the balance of power tends to shift—a law of nature.

Therefore, when analyzing the factors that contributed to the Eritrean movement for independence or self-determination, it is essential to view them through this lens or perspective, recognizing the interplay of internal dynamics, external forces, and the fundamental drive for change within the human experience.

Let us now look at what the internal and international factors looked like.

5.1. INTERNAL FACTORS THAT CONTRIBUTED TO THE MOVEMENT FOR INDEPENDENCE

Several internal factors played pivotal roles in shaping the movement for independence in Eritrea during a critical period of its history. These factors were instrumental in galvanizing the Eritrean people's desire for autonomy and self-determination.

History records instances of sporadic resistance to Italian colonial presence in Eritrea, particularly in response to Italy's attempt to designate land below a certain altitude as "Terra Dominiale." This policy and law denied peasants their rightful access to and use of land inherited from their ancestors. This, in turn, ignited anger within the peasant population, leading to various pockets of uprisings. One such revolt was led by Deghiat Bahta Hagos. Furthermore, there were Eritreans who, for ideological or religious reasons, held allegiance to the emperor of Ethiopia. Many of them joined the ranks of the imperial army and administration. However, it is important to note that, overall, a cohesive national movement challenging Italian rule was not prevalent during this period.

The political environment during the British Military Administration (BMA) of Eritrea was slightly unique in the sense that during the BMA, which followed Italy's colonial rule, Eritrea was exposed to a newfound culture of free speech and association. This marked a significant departure from its past, fostering an environment where political parties flourished and found a voice to express their views. These political groups seized the opportunity to express their distinct visions for the future of Eritrea through newspapers and various media outlets, initiating vibrant political debates that engaged the political elite and by extension the general public.

However, these developments were met with resistance from the Ethiopian imperial regime, which was uncomfortable with the burgeoning political activism in Eritrea. The Ethiopian government made considerable efforts to suppress these movements (or manipulate them to its own advantage) and created a challenging environment for those advocating independence.

Simultaneously, a domestic pro-unity movement started using religion, fear, and intimidation as its tool to weaken the call for independence. The Eritrean police resorted to violent repression against political dissidents, including students in an attempt to stifle the growing independence sentiment.

Haile Selassie, the Ethiopian emperor, employed strategic political maneuvers to gain the support of specific segments of Eritrean society, further complicating the path to independence. He leveraged the myth of Ethiopia's three-thousand-year history of independence and played on fears of Islam and the Arab world, especially countries bordering Eritrea, to entice the Christian highlanders to align with his cause. The Unionist movement, which supported unity with Ethiopia, was gaining momentum, posing a challenge to the proponents of independence.

Moreover, those advocating for independence found themselves at a disadvantage in comparison to Haile Selassie's diplomatic advantages due to their inexperience in dealing with the international community and international affairs in general.

The Eritrean people had high expectations following World War II, hoping for the decolonization of Eritrea similar to other Italian colonies like Libya and Somalia. However, these hopes were dashed when the United Nations Security Council decided to engage Eritrea in a federal arrangement with Ethiopia, contrary to the aspirations of a substantial segment of the population.

This federal arrangement imposed against the will of many Eritreans, ultimately led to its abrogation and further fueled the determination of those seeking independence. In sum, a complex interplay of internal factors, including political activism, repression, strategic maneuvering, and unmet expectations, fueled the Eritrean movement for independence during this critical period.

5.2 GEOPOLITICS

The nature of geopolitics becomes evident when examining the strategic significance of the Red Sea to the United States and its allies. During the Cold War era, the question of who would exert dominance in this region became a matter of utmost importance. Haile Selassie, seen as an ally of the Western powers, further piqued their interest in the area.

In the realm of geopolitics, the United States and its allies found themselves favoring Ethiopia over Eritrea for both geopolitical and strategic reasons. The influence of the United States and its allies extended to the international community, effectively silencing dissenting voices.

Ethiopia's standing in the international community was bolstered by Haile Selassie's popularity, which worked to the advantage of the Ethiopian regime. Notably, Ethiopia's land-locked status was a factor that demanded consideration in these geopolitical calculations. However, it is worth noting the diplomatic efforts made by both Eritreans and their limited allies to promote and package Eritrea's quest for independence on the international stage were not adequate.

6

Eritrea under the British Military Administration and the Ethio-Eritrea Federal Arrangement: The Forties and the Fifties

I T TOOK TWO decades for the independence movement to transition from peaceful protests to one that is characterized by a justifiable armed struggle that lasted thirty years.

6.1 The Forties
The forties were defined by the following characteristics.

Domestic Factors
The culmination of World War II marked a turning point as the scales tipped in favor of the Allied forces, comprising primarily of the United States, the United Kingdom, and the Soviet Union. As the dust settled, the defeat of Fascist Italy became evident, and one

of its last strongholds, Eritrea, witnessed the capitulation of its army to the British Army.

In the wake of this shift in power, the BMA assumed control, stepping in to oversee Eritrea. The BMA's presence brought with it a set of fundamental democratic rights for the Eritrean people, including the cherished freedoms of speech and association.

The role of newspapers during this period evolved significantly. They were transformed into vocal platforms of various political parties, becoming crucial conduits for the expression of ideas and ideologies. This transformation catalyzed the emergence of a nascent yet lively political landscape.

In response to the new democratic environment, political parties began to take shape, each aligning themselves either along political lines or, notably, along ethnic and religious lines. These parties, particularly the Pro-independence and Unity parties, sought to represent the diverse interests and perspectives of the Eritrean populace.

As newspapers continued to serve as the voices of these political organizations, a spirited and heated political discourse emerged, raising political awareness among the people of Eritrea. The exchange of ideas, debates, and discussions helped galvanize the population toward active engagement in shaping the future of their nation.

A significant milestone in this period of political ferment was the establishment of a common front or political platform that united all pro-independence parties and organizations. This unity marked a crucial step toward achieving the aspirations of the Eritrean people for self-determination and independence.

This decade is characterized by heated political debates, rapid political developments, fluid alignment of forces, increased political awareness of the general populace, moments of despair, moments of hope, moments of unity, and moments of chaos and political turmoil; all manifesting themselves in an evolving socioeconomic and political setting of the nation. This decade set the tone for political discourse in the decades that followed. It gave birth to an elite that foresaw the debacle that would haunt the Eritrean political landscape for decades. It also provided a golden opportunity for those who wanted to exploit the situation for their personal or group's ends. Leaders are born in situations inundated with rapid political changes of this nature. Eritrea was not an exception. People started rallying around charismatic leaders from across the political spectrum. People were curious to know who these people were, what they stood for, etc., before embracing them. Once they embraced them, they started idolizing them. Woldeab Woldemariam, Ibrahim Sultan, Abdulkadir Kebiré, Fessaha Woldemariam (Gandhi), and Deghiat Tessema Asberom (to name some) are the products of this decade.

INTERNATIONAL

The conclusion of World War II marked a decisive victory for the Allied forces comprising the United States, the United Kingdom, and the Soviet Union. In the wake of this triumph, Fascist Italy found itself on the losing side of the conflict, leading to the capitulation of its army in Eritrea to the British Army. With Eritrea under British control, a period of transition ensued. The BMA was established to oversee the governance of Eritrea. The fate of Eritrea and other Italian colonies (Somalia and Libya) was uncertain, and the international community, represented by the Security Council, embarked on a series of deliberations to determine their future.

Throughout these discussions, various options were considered for the disposition of Eritrea and the other former Italian colonies. Yet, amid the geopolitical complexities of the postwar era, it became evident that the interests of powerful nations held precedence over the desires and aspirations of the local populations. In this context, the will of the people often took a backseat to the broader strategic considerations of the world's leading powers.

6.2. CHARACTERIZATION OF THE FIFTIES

Eritrea and Ethiopia entered into a federal arrangement. This was dictated by the geopolitical interests of major powers, notably the United States. The Eritrean Constitution received parliamentary ratification. However, from the outset, there was a gradual erosion of this federal system.

In the wake of this slow erosion, Eritrean politics became increasingly polarized. Historians noted that this polarization extended beyond mere political differences, seeping into ethnic and religious divides. Sharp divisions emerged within the parliamentary members, with some aligned with the Independence Block and others with the Unionist Party. These rifts were widely known to the public, who were closely following political developments through newspapers and word of mouth.

Tensions escalated within the Eritrean Parliament, leading to student, worker, and nationalist groups' protests, which were met with police repression. The emperor's interference in Eritrean government affairs played a role in the resignation of the chief executive, Tedla Bairu, who was replaced by Biteweded Asfaha Woldemichael, the emperor's designated political appointee.

Andeberhan Woldeghiorghis describes the slow but corrosive tactics employed by Ethiopia as follows,

Ethiopia's disregard of repeated petitions and protests and heavy-handed interferences disaffected and alienated most Eritreans. While using the UP as the main instrument of intervention in the internal affairs of Eritrea to corrode Eritrean autonomy, Ethiopia disposed of, marginalized, betrayed, and alienated even its most loyal erstwhile collaborators in the UP (*Unionist Party*) and the MLWE (*Muslim League of the Western Province*), and turned them into staunch federalist who resisted its encroachment and defended Eritrea's prerogatives. Increasingly, Ethiopia's betrayal cornered its former unionist allies into open opposition, driving many to join the ranks of the emerging independence movement (Giorgis, 2014).

The emperor's viceroy, Lu'ul or Ras Indargachew Mesai, also became entangled in domestic politics, with Alemseghed Tesfai providing a detailed account in his book, "The Federation of Eritrea with Ethiopia—From Matienzo to Tedla 1951–55"[xlvii] (Tesfai, 2005).

Political repression persisted, with leaders facing police action, incarceration, and intimidation. Tragically, there were assassination attempts on pro-independence party members, including Woldeab Woldemariam and Abdulkadir Kebiré. According to some historians, Kebiré was assassinated in cold blood—by agents of the Unionist Party.

In response to the deteriorating political climate, several prominent figures, such as Ibrahim Sultan, Idris Mohammed Adem, Tedla Bairu, and Woldeab Woldemariam, fled the country and sought refuge in Egypt. The symbolic act of lowering or retiring the Eritrean flag loomed on the horizon.

Amid these tumultuous times, the Eritrean Liberation Movement ELM, known as Haraka, was born among diaspora Eritreans in Sudan. This movement swiftly established a presence in Eritrea, where patriotic Eritreans began organizing clandestine cells to advance the cause of independence. Its aim was to secure national unity (Tesfai A., 2016).

INTERNATIONAL
In the wake of World War II, the liberal Western powers emerged triumphant over the forces of fascism and Nazism. As a result, the postwar landscape brought about significant changes, particularly in the case of Italy. Italy found itself stripped of its colonies, including Somalia, Libya, and Eritrea.

Eritrea, in particular, faced a complex fate, as it was destined to enter into a federal arrangement with imperial Ethiopia. This decision was met with mixed reactions, seen by some as an unjust verdict against the will of the Eritrean people. It is a chapter in our shared history, whether one embraces it or not, and it is worth noting that a segment of the population desired union with Ethiopia.

This federal arrangement delineated that Eritrean internal matters would be under the jurisdiction of the Eritrean parliament, while foreign affairs and defense were entrusted to Ethiopia, with the emperor playing a pivotal role. Various other characteristics defined this federal system.

Regrettably, this arrangement quickly took a contentious turn, as Ethiopia began to interfere in the internal affairs of Eritrea, setting the stage for a complex and often turbulent historical relationship between the two nations.

6.3. WHAT DIFFERENTIATED THE FORTIES FROM THE FIFTIES

The situation in the forties and the fifties resulted in the creation of a political elite representing opposing viewpoints, with some advocating for Eritrean independence and others advocating for unity with Ethiopia, each fervently promoting their own agendas.

Both sides harbored apprehensions about the other's political intentions. The Unionist Party, which favored unity with Ethiopia, expressed concerns about the influence of Islam and the Arab world, while the pro-independence party feared the prospect of being governed by a feudal regime. Some members of the Unionist party held genuine concerns until they realized that Ethiopia's political agenda left much to be desired (Tesfai A., 2001).

Both decades were marked by a growing polarization within the political landscape. People's political awareness continued to evolve as they grappled with the complexities of the divided society, which often fell along both political and ethnic or religious fault lines.

The federal arrangement with Ethiopia emerged as a compromise solution to address this deep-seated division. Many believed it to be a more favorable option compared to Ethiopia's claim of immediate annexation of Eritrea or the partition of Eritrea as outlined in the Bevin-Sforza scheme. Another alternative was Eritrea remaining a trusteeship territory.

Throughout both decades, Eritrean society remained deeply divided, with these political tensions at the forefront. Foreign interests often took precedence over the desires and aspirations of the Eritrean people when determining the fate of the nation. Additionally, elements of violence and intimidation were unfortunately present during both periods, further complicating the sociopolitical landscape.

7

PHASE ONE OF THE ARMED STRUGGLE: THE SIXTIES AND SEVENTIES

7.1. THE SIXTIES

The domestic political landscape of the 1950s reached a climax marked by the complete dismantling of the federal structure. During this era, Eritrea found itself designated as the fourteenth province of Ethiopia, destined for complete assimilation into the Ethiopian Empire.

A year prior to the annexation and in response to the deteriorating situation, the Eritrea Liberation Front emerged in 1961, initiating an armed struggle against the Ethiopian occupation. Initially, the majority of its members hailed from the lowlands of Eritrea, primarily of the Muslim faith. Over time, Christian and Muslim highlanders joined the cause, but mistrust lingered between lowlanders and highlanders, between Christians and Muslims, and among various ethnic groups during the early years of this armed resistance. This being the case, one should note that those who enlisted in the cause were largely driven by a fervent sense of nationalism.

One notable deficiency was the dearth of political consciousness and the absence of a clear vision among the leadership. This leadership struggled to unite the people under a common banner, often grappling with internal divisions. The Front's rigidity in accommodating diverse perspectives also compounded the challenges it faced.

A sense of marginalization and sidelining persisted among Christian and Muslim highlanders and some other ethnic groups. Leadership based outside the country faced its own limitations, often disconnected from the realities on the ground. The prevalence of sectarian politics and its consequences could be traced back to the nation's socioeconomic structure and historical events (e.g., a substantial size of the highlanders siding with the Unionists in the forties and fifties).

Internal friction within the front further exacerbated matters, as conflicts often went unresolved in a democratic manner. Regardless of this friction, Ethiopia's repressive tactics, including the burning of villages, particularly in the lowlands, and mass migrations to Sudan and the Middle East, stoked bitterness and anger among the population, further fueling the flames of resistance.

The regional and international context of the decade in question is marked by the sweeping wave of decolonization that washed across the African continent. During this period, numerous independence movements of various types and sizes sprouted in different corners of Africa. Among the influential figures of this time was Kwame Nkrumah of Ghana, who championed the cause of Pan-Africanism, a movement that began taking root in the fertile African soil.

On the global stage, the world was organized into a bipolar structure, with the Soviet bloc on one side and the Western bloc on the other. This era was characterized by the principles of detente, deterrence, peaceful coexistence, and containment, which guided international relations during this period.

The Soviet bloc, in particular, launched a significant campaign against the colonization of Africa, aiming to win the hearts and minds of Africans in their struggle for independence. Concurrently, leftist ideology was on the rise across the world, giving rise to leftist movements in various regions.

In Africa, countries like Mozambique, Angola, and Guinea-Bissau, in their fight against Portuguese colonialism, declared Marxism as their preferred ideology, reflecting the prevailing fashion of the time. However, it should be noted that many of those who claimed to be Marxists often lacked a comprehensive understanding of the philosophy they espoused.

A notable literary work of this era was *The Wretched of the Earth* by Frantz Fanon, which gained widespread readership among African intellectuals in the 1960s, further fueling the intellectual fervor behind the decolonization movement.

The enthusiasm for decolonization continued to surge unabated during this period, inspiring various movements and ideologies. In the Middle East, Pan-Arabism, in all its forms and shapes, flourished, with Egypt's nationalization of the Suez Canal standing as a defiant act against Western influence in the region.

The regional and continental dynamics in Africa and the Middle East did not fail to exert their influence on the political landscape in Eritrea, shaping the course of its history and development during this transformative era.

7.2. THE SEVENTIES

Internal strife and conflict reached a boiling point, pushing Eritrea into the depths of civil war as the ELF clashed fiercely with the Eritrean People's Liberation Forces (EPLF), resulting in staggering losses on both fronts. What began as political disagreements soon became marred by personal egos and the unyielding pursuit of individual and group political ambitions, often cloaked in the guise of ideological differences.

The resounding mantra of the era became "Eritrea can- not sustain more than one front," echoing through the ranks of the ELF leadership. The toll of this relentless discord weighed heavily on the morale of both fighters and the local population, leaving scars that would last for generations. Suspicion and mistrust between the two liberation fronts deepened, with each side sowing seeds of divisive politics against the other.

The youth surged to join the ranks of the liberation fronts, reshaping their composition, which had previously leaned toward specific religious and ethnic groups. Regrettably, the leaders of both fronts seemed resolute in their refusal to entertain peaceful and democratic resolutions to their differences, dismissing such notions as an opportunity cost they couldn't afford.

Pressures mounted from both the rank and file within the fronts and the civilian population, demanding that their disputes be settled through peaceful and democratic means. I was elected from the rank and file of the EPLF to facilitate reconciliation efforts. The committee (ኣቀራራቢት ሽማግለ) comprised five EPLF members, including Beraki Ghebresellassie (currently languishing in the Ira-Iro prison along with the G-15), Hassen Mohammed Amir (martyred in 1978), Tesfay Temnewo (currently living in Germany), Amanuel Keshi (eliminated by the EPLF under the pretext of being a member of Yemin Movement), and me. The committee, though unable to meet with its counterparts (due to the ELF leadership citing the departure of committee members to attend ELF's Second National Congress in Barka), successfully visited ELF platoons in the highlands of Eritrea, La'ilay Barka, and Sahel. The reception from the ELF fighters, which included high-ranking ELF cadres and rank-and-file members, was very warm. The discussions took place in a cordial atmosphere, and the EPLF members of the committee observed the strong desire for unity among the ELF fighters. This productive tour spanned a duration of four to six months.

The dispute between the two fronts was framed as "ideological" when, in reality, it hinged on differing approaches to the goals of the independence movement—the New Democratic Revolution (NDR) versus a Non-Capitalist Path—despite the shared ultimate goal of achieving independence for Eritrea, centered around the principles of social justice.

Both fronts professed a commitment to "social justice," self-determination, the rule of law, economic freedom, respect for human rights, and fostering healthy relationships with neighbors based on mutual respect and equality. Strikingly, there were no significant ideological divergences between the two fronts; both held a leftist orientation and harbored clandestine factions within them, including the Eritrean People's Revolutionary Party, which later rebranded itself as a Socialist Party, and the Labor Party (within ELF).

Despite their internal disagreements, the two fronts seized an opportunity presented by the crisis in Ethiopia and liberated most of Eritrea's towns, with Asmara, the capital, surrounded by the joint forces of ELF and EPLF. However, an EPLF offensive on Massawa ended in a deadlock.

A very tragic incident happened in the chronicles of the history of the Eritrean war of independence in the early seventies. Some fearless fighters challenged Isaias Afewerki and the leadership team for their authoritarian practices. The EPLF leadership crushed the reformist movement—the Movement of 1973 later nicknamed Menqa'e—and consolidated its power. Tesfay Temnewo writes extensively about this in his book titled "ንኣርብዓ ዓመታት ዝተቐብረ ጉዳይ" (A case that has been buried for forty years—1972–2013)[xlviii]

(Temnewo, 2013). Members of this movement were mainly intellectuals or former students, to say the least. Basic demands of the movement included respect for the democratic rights of members of the front, the introduction of checks and balances, accountability, bringing an end to authoritarian practices, freedom of expression, bringing an end to the abuse of power by some veteran fighters on new-recruited members of the front, and so forth.

The movement was vilified, the ring leaders incarcerated and later perished, and the followers marginalized, emasculated, and humiliated. I happened to be one of the victims of this tragic history. I was appalled by Mesfin's statement in an interview with Dehai Eritrea, where he claimed that the death sentence of the ring leaders of the movement had to be executed immediately due to a lack of available holding facilities (Hagos, ኣብ መጽሓፍ ተጋዳላይ መስፍን ሓጎስ ዝተሞርኮሰ ሰፊሕ ዝርርብ! Interview with Mesfin Hagos on his book, 2023). This raises a serious question. Is one left to believe that the EPLF did not have holding facilities for hundreds of detainees who were held until their cases were investigated in the liberated areas? Very hard to believe! With all due respect to Mesfin, this is an insult to one's intelligence.

I was contacted by members of the G-15 during the heat of the political crisis in 2000–2001. During our conversations, it was ironic to hear from some members of G-15 that Isaias was going to use the same tactics (the Sahelian way) he used to destroy the 1973 Movement to wipe them out and break their souls. They were right. The irony was that they never stood up on behalf of their colleagues who languished in the front's security apparatus—Halewa Sewra (Guardian of the Revolution) in the seventies. Some of them were indeed accomplices in crushing the reformist movement.

Some members of the reformist movement (G-15) capitulated (or were compromised), some of them even supported the physical elimination of their colleagues, some of them were instrumental in portraying the movement as "destructive" (A'Enawi) and that their leaders were opportunists or power mongers or Awrjawian (members of the same Awaraja rallying around narrow Awraja interests). A session on "The destructive 1973 Movement" was dedicated during a three-to-four-month- long indoctrination of members of the front in EPLF's Cadre School. The ideologues of the school were Haile Woldetensae and Ahmed Al Qeisi.

My personal experience of the Reformist Movement of 1973 is captured in Chapter 13.

There was another group of EPLF members that comprised intellectuals and peasants who were labeled "Yemin" or "Rightists" by Isaias and his cronies and later liquidated by a unilateral decision made by Isaias and executed by Ali Said Abdalla without the knowledge of other members of the Political Bureau (Hagos M., 2023).[xlix] Iyob Ghegrelul—a geologist who studied in the Soviet Union—was vilified for maintaining there was no ideological difference between the ELF and EPLF. The same tactic—an extensive smear campaign—was used to vilify or demonize the group first before they were rounded up one by one and ended up in jail. These, amongst others, include Mehari Ghirmatsion, Ghebremichael Maharzghi, Iyob Ghebrelul, Haile Jebha, Solomon Woldemariam, Araya Semere, and Kidane Abieto.

In the late seventies, negotiation efforts between the Dergue regime and the two Eritrean fronts, each conducting their own talks with the mediation of Berlin, failed to yield any meaningful progress. Ethiopia, bolstered by support from the Soviet Union, East Germany, Cuba, and Yemen, regrouped and launched a massive offensive, pushing the liberation movements back to their base areas in Sahel and Gash Barka. EPLF referred to this retreat as a "strategic withdrawal."

In the Sahel region, heavy fighting raged on, marked by a series of offensives named numerically (First Offensive, Second Offensive, Third Offensive, Fourth Offensive, Fifth Offensive, The Initiative, etc.) with each resulting in substantial losses on both sides.

Outside factors were characterized by a popular uprising in Ethiopia that was hijacked by the military, diverting its momentum toward its own objectives. Concurrently, leftist factions like the Ethiopia People's Revolutionary Party (EPRP) and All-Ethiopia Socialist Movement (MEISON), as well as nationalist movements, including TPLF, Ethiopia Democratic Union (EDU), Oromo Liberation Army (OLA), and others, were steadily gaining prominence, each driven by distinct political agendas.

The regime of Haile Selassie was overthrown by a military junta, ushering in a period of turbulence. This era saw the onset of the Ethio-Somali War, a conflict that exacted a heavy toll on both nations. Interestingly, the Soviet Union shifted its allegiance to Socialist Ethiopia, offering substantial military and political support. Consequently, Somalia met defeat in the war, while Ethiopia capitalized on this victory for its political advantage.

The bond between the Dergue regime and the Soviet Union, alongside its allies, reached its zenith as they poured military and diplomatic backing into the Socialist Ethiopian government. Regrettably, the Dergue regime further fortified its repressive rule, culminating in the tragic Red Terror, which claimed the lives of tens of thousands of innocent civilians suspected of "treason."

8

PHASE TWO OF THE ARMED
STRUGGLE: THE EIGHTIES UNTIL 1991

8.1. CHARACTERISTICS

Internal features of the eighties were characterized by—a turbulent and tragic page of Eritrea's history—the failure of both fronts to resolve their differences through peaceful and democratic means. The impasse led to the re-ignition of a brutal civil war, inflicting colossal losses upon both sides and perpetuating a cycle of suffering.

As the ELF crumbled under the weight of external pressures (war with the EPLF) and internal discord, its members faced a mass exodus, dispersed to distant lands such as the Middle East, Europe, the United States, and Canada. Bitterness and anger festered among disillusioned ELF members, and they tried to emerge as a political opposition force challenging the dominance of the EPLF in the diaspora.

In the crucible of conflict, the EPLF ascended to unparalleled power, becoming the unchallenged political and military force on the Eritrean landscape. Amid shifting alliances, a pivotal moment arrived when a faction from the ELF, known as Saghem, officially

SEMERE SOLOMON

embraced the ranks of the EPLF during its Second Organizational Congress. This union followed years of dialogue and collaborative efforts, marking a significant shift in the Eritrean political landscape. The relentless war of attrition between Eritrean and Ethiopian forces raged on, ultimately finding its conclusion in the Sahel region. The pivotal moment arrived with the annihilation of the Nadew Command in Af"abet and its surroundings, signaling the beginning of the end for the Ethiopian Dergue regime.

Externally, in the tumultuous period of history, schisms within the upper echelons of the Dergue, Ethiopia's ruling military junta, began to emerge, ultimately culminating in an attempted coup d'état against the Mengistu Regime. The architects of this audacious coup were subsequently court-martialed, with General Mer'id Negusse emerging as the chief mastermind behind the ambitious plot.

During this time, an interesting development occurred on the geopolitical stage. The relationship between the EPLF and the TPLF was on the upswing. This flourishing alliance paved the way for joint military operations within Ethiopia, significantly impacting the ongoing conflicts in the region.

In a climactic turn of events, Eritrean forces stormed the capital, Asmara, in May 1991, a historic moment that marked the closing chapter of a tumultuous era in Eritrea's history.

Amid these dramatic events, the world witnessed another seismic shift as the Soviet Union imploded. This event marked the disintegration of the Socialist Camp and sent shockwaves throughout the international community.

As the geopolitical landscape continued to evolve, Mengistu Hailemariam, the long-standing leader of Ethiopia, found himself increasingly isolated. This isolation coincided with a new era known as "Perestroika," which was dawning in the Soviet Union. This period of reform and restructuring ultimately led to the collapse of the Soviet Union, bringing an end to the era of communism not only in the Soviet Union but also in Eastern Europe, where popular political uprisings were reshaping the political landscape.

8.2. FACTORS CONTRIBUTING TO ERITREA'S INDEPENDENCE

The primary credit for Eritrea's hard-fought independence belongs to the resilient people of Eritrea who, with resolute passion and determination, persevered until the very end. Despite their internal differences, which at times escalated into prolonged military conflicts, both the ELF and the EPLF served as the voices of the Eritrean people in their own rights. Nobody can deny the ELF its right to claim that it has contributed to the victory Eritreans inflicted upon Ethiopia's occupation. The brave freedom fighters from both organizations deserve commendation for their sacrifices, particularly the sacrifice of their youth. We must also honor our martyrs and war-disabled veterans, bestowing upon them the highest honors for laying down their lives for the cause. Above all, the people of Eritrea take credit for this enormous victory because had it not been for its support to the two organizations, the independence movement would not have triumphed.

The success of the war of independence should be viewed as the culmination of all the sacrifices made by every Eritrean, regardless of their political affiliation, both men and women.

It is also essential to recognize and remember those who lost their lives at the hands of their fellow comrades in arms due to various pretexts, such as the Reform Movement of 1973 known as Menqa'e, Yemin, Falul[l], perpetrated by the two fronts. As a veteran member of the EPLF, I find it reprehensible and criminal to execute schoolmates and young revolutionaries who should have been spared. I, as much as I want to give credit to the leadership for its contribution to the success of the war, equally and unequivocally condemn the atrocities committed by the EPLF leadership on innocent freedom fighters whose crime was nothing but harboring views different from those who were in power (i.e., the leadership). Dissenting views should have been accommodated or democratically resolved, and in the worst-case scenario, individuals should have been discharged from the ranks. Unfortunately, what we are witnessing these days has its roots in the war.

The 1973 Movement was aimed at reforming the EPLF and not destroying it— members of the movement were patriots who felt the EPLF could do better to safeguard the rights of its members. It was not a "destructive movement" as labeled by the leadership. Parents of these members of the front were not even notified under what circumstances they died. What a disgrace!!!!

The sacrifice made during the struggle for independence was immense, with an estimated 65,000 martyrs, according to the EPLF. This sacrifice goes beyond the loss of lives and extends to the economic opportunities that were missed, the displacement of the population caused by the prolonged war, the destruction of the social fabric, the fragmentation of the nuclear family, and the psychological trauma inflicted upon a significant portion of the population as well as former combatants who suffer from post-traumatic stress disorder (PTSD). Ironically, many former combatants do not acknowledge or believe they suffer from PTSD.

Additionally, the politics of division that was widespread among the diaspora Eritreans was a liability that is still haunting us.

Other factors that contributed to the success should not be underestimated. These include the changes in the power dynamic within the Dergue regime in Ethiopia, as well as the significant roles played by Ethiopian opposition movements.

As indicated above, global events and shifts had a significant impact on the struggle for independence, including the implosion of the Soviet Union (which was a major supplier of military equipment to the Dergue Regime), the fall of the Berlin Wall, and popular uprisings in Eastern Europe leading to the downfall of authoritarian regimes. In general, changes in the international political arena at large also played a crucial role in shaping the outcome of Eritrea's fight for independence.

8.3. COULD INDEPENDENCE BE A REALITY WITHOUT THE CLANDESTINE PARTY?

As has been discussed in the previous chapters, there existed a clandestine Marxist-Leninist party operating within the EPLF. As such, there are proponents of the view that without the leadership of this clandestine party (Eritrean People's Revolutionary Party (EPRP), subsequently rebranded as the Socialist Party), Eritrea would not have achieved independence in 1991.

I seek to contest this contention. For the following reasons: For a liberation struggle to triumph, it demands not only a righteous cause but also an adept political organization capable of unifying its populace behind that cause and harnessing its potential. In the case of Eritrea, the political landscape was so mature that the role of political entities was primarily meant to effectively convey the right message to the people and accordingly provide the required leadership.

The Eritrean experience indicates that such a political organization was lacking during the early years of the struggle for independence. It took time and numerous sacrifices to develop an organization or organizations capable of meeting the challenges of those times. Those formative years were marked by an excessive focus on exploiting socioeconomic differences to meet political ends rather than devising mechanisms to manage and ultimately resolve them.

After the formation of a robust political and military organization in the EPLF, driven primarily by the exigencies of war, it is reasonable to acknowledge that the circumstances may have necessitated a highly centralized and disciplined structure. But does this imply that an armed conflict inherently requires a totalitarian grip on power through a clandestine organization? Whether victory could have been attainable without such a totalitarian grip is a question that demands careful contemplation and not be taken for granted. These are matters deserving a collective reflection. Nonetheless, one fact remains clear: the current authoritarian practices that we see today did not materialize abruptly; their roots can be traced back to the days of the armed struggle.

What we observed in both the pre and post-independence era was the establishment of a political elite that deliberately utilized the clandestine party to enlist loyalists (not necessarily Marxists or socialists) to create a critical mass of followers who would not contest the political elite's way of thinking. This fostered a culture of conformity at the expense of independent and critical thinking. It contributed to the formation of a collective that was held captive to the will of a single figure. The EPLF, through the clandestine political party, formed a covert society that aggressively introduced a clear line of demarcation between its members and the rest (front members and the general population). It established a secret community that conducted its day-to-day affairs in utmost secrecy. This culture of secrecy and conspiracy continued unabated in post-independence Eritrea.

In retrospect, the party was established with the specific purpose of mobilizing loyalists (members who feel they are superior to others by virtue of their affinity to a mysterious organization within an organization) and using it as a control and coercion mechanism.

Members were indoctrinated to watch non-members with suspicion spending long nightly hours discussing how they behave (in meetings and outside meetings), who they associate with, what they say, how they respond to different circumstances, etc. Under circumstances of this nature, being a non-party member would expose one to rigorous scrutiny to the extent of losing self-confidence and undermining one's self-esteem. Criticizing a party member for any wrongdoing might also come at a significant cost.

Nearly three decades after the formal acknowledgment of the clandestine party within the organization, very few individuals are willing to raise the topic openly today. A code of silence, akin to omertà, continues in perpetuity. The most reprehensible transgressions committed under those shrouded circumstances are intended to remain concealed for all time.

Some party loyalists contend that the Marxist-Leninist party gave rise to war heroes and military strategists, suggesting that without them, Eritrea might not have gained its independence. I also wish to contest this narrative. Courage/bravery is not a product of Marxism; rather, it is an intrinsic quality of human nature. It simply needs the right setting—the battlefield—to foster it. The cultivation of courage necessitates the cultivation of a culture marked by resilience, unwavering dedication, and a profound commitment to one's beliefs. The cause at hand was the belief in Eritrea's inherent right to self-determination, and those who made the ultimate sacrifice did so in service of this cause. The last words of those who paid their life for this cause were "Victory to the Eritrean people" and not "Victory to Marxism." The tens of thousands of young people (from all walks of life) who joined the armed struggle did so for one simple reason— Eritrea's right to independence. Even Isaias Afeworki himself does not believe that Marxism and bravery are inherently linked. Here is why:

My late friend, Yemane Kidane (Jamaica), who served on the Central Committee of the TPLF, once recounted to me an incident when he, along with his colleagues, including the late Meles Zenawi, and Isaias, were sharing a drink in Asmara. This transpired during the golden days of camaraderie between the two organizations. As the evening progressed, and the effects of alcohol took hold, Isaias began to mock the TPLF leadership. He insinuated that they had established a Marxist-Leninist faction (the Marxist Leninist League of Tigrai) in an attempt to instill a culture of bravery, courage, and heroism. Isaias remarked, "Bravery cannot be cultivated. It is an inherent trait, one either possesses it or not. I consider myself brave because my great-grandparents were brave. It is in my DNA." Isaias was referring to his great-grandfather, Goshu Aba Dehen (buried in Yeha, Tigray). According to my late friend—Yemane—and close relative to Isaias Afewerki, Goshu (Aba-Dehen) came to Eritrea as one of the generals of Ras Alula (Aba-Nega). In the old days, leaders were mostly called by their horses, like Alula Aba-Nega and Goshu Aba-Dehen. This tells one that all the rhetoric propagated to mystify the invincibility and the relevance of the clandestine organization was a hoax.

To this day, former members of the party hang out together and are never at liberty to discuss issues of national concern with others. The inhibition still persists among them. A good example is the organization called Medreq which came into being at one point in the 2000s. It invited only (or at least the majority) former party members to their maiden meeting in Brussels, Belgium. These are former members of the clandestine party who deserted the regime but still felt they were the only ones who were capable of bringing about change in Eritrea.

In another instance, I encountered an individual—a former freedom fighter and member of a clandestine party—who happened to be in the US for personal reasons. Our conversation veered toward the deteriorating political, social, and economic situation in Eritrea. When I inquired about potential solutions, the response I received was that such matters were exclusively the domain of individuals like him, not for outsiders like me. It felt emblematic of an 'us versus them' mentality, a hallmark of a chronic and entrenched malaise.

Also, to justify the relevance of the clandestine party, certain party ideologues, like Ahmed Al Qeisi and Haile Weldetensa'e (Connell, 2005), contend that the party played a pivotal role in eliminating regionalism, or "Awrajawnet" (ኣውራጃውነት), from within the front. In my view, if we consider the post-independence era as proof, this assertion lacks credibility. On the contrary, it gave rise to warlords and exacerbated feudalistic tendencies and practices. Also, nobody could deny the fact that former members of EPLF who hailed from the Semhar Region (ቀዳማይ ወገን), have always taken political stances (against the 1973 movement, "Yemin", Sabbe, etc.) and in unison throughout the history of the EPLF. They were and still are closer to each other than they are with others.

While we are on the topic of regionalism (awrajawinet), I'd like to offer an observation on how the PFDJ interprets this concept. Allow me to illustrate with a few examples, and let readers draw their own conclusions.

1. The alumni of San Giorgio Secondary School, deeply moved by the state of disrepair in their alma mater, launched a significant fundraising campaign. Their goal was to renovate the classrooms and modernizing its library, laboratory, and other facilities. Extending their reach to alumni in the diaspora, the initiative swiftly gained traction, resulting in the mobilization of hundreds of thousands of dollars. However, the government expressed displeasure with this grassroots initiative. The committee overseeing the campaign was

instructed to relinquish control of the funds to the government, leading to an immediate halt to the initiative.

2. In 1992, the prosperous family – the Nesreddin family - originally from the vicinity of Mendefera (Debub Zone), undertook the commendable initiative of privately funding the construction of a state-of-the-art hospital in Mendefera. With the blueprint finalized, construction was set to commence in due course when the government unexpectedly intervened, abruptly halting the project. Unfortunately, no reasons were provided for the sudden cessation of this community-driven endeavor.

3. In the mid-2000s, Zemhret Yohannes initiated "DeQi Gezawtna," a project with the goal of bringing together individuals who shared a common upbringing in the same locality in Asmara. The initiative sought to facilitate conversations among these individuals, fostering collaborative efforts to support their respective former communities. However, for reasons shrouded in mystery, the project was abruptly halted.

4. In the framework of PFDJ's norms and politics, openly declaring one's origin from a specific village, woreda (district), or Awraja is almost considered taboo. What harm is there in expressing a genuine sense of belonging to a particular village, woreda, or Awraja, as long as such affiliations are not exploited for political ends? What is wrong with making associations with members of your village or individuals who shared a common upbringing with you? What harm does it cause if an individual wishes to construct a school in their village or place of origin, provided it caters to the needs of the community?

5. A few years after gaining independence, the map of Eritrea was redrawn with the intention of combating regionalism

(Awrajawnet). Did the architects of the scheme genuinely believe that altering the maps would effectively erase sentiments of regionalism from the minds of the people?

6. In my view, the most effective way to counter sub-national or narrow sentiments is through economic integration. This includes establishing a modern economy, a well-developed network of roads, railways, and air transport systems, an efficient communication infrastructure, free media, and an educated population. Simply redrawing a map cannot act as a magic solution to eradicate narrow sentiments. This process requires time and strategic efforts.

9

THE ERITREAN PEOPLE'S LIBERATION FRONT (EPLF) AND THE ERITREAN LIBERATION FRONT (ELF)

THE WAR OF independence featured two key players in its historical narrative. This chapter aims to illuminate and offer an analysis of the primary fronts that politically and militarily confronted the Ethiopian occupation from 1961 onwards. Numerous significant events transpired during those three decades, revolving around the power dynamics within each front and the broader political landscape of Eritrea (the power dynamic between the EPLF and ELF in particular), which has been extensively discussed in preceding chapters. This is not to insinuate there were no other organizations that took part in the armed struggle.

9.1. THE ERITREAN PEOPLE'S LIBERATION FORCES LATER RENAMED ERITREAN PEOPLE'S LIBERATION FRONT (EPLF)

Eritrea's history should be regarded as an ongoing continuum, intertwining the history of the EPLF with the broader struggle of the

Eritrean people for independence, characterized by their pursuit of self-determination in a backdrop of "aborted decolonization."

The emergence of the EPLF can be traced back to its roots within the ELF, representing a transformative offshoot. Moreover, the EPLF's formation was a complex amalgamation of various organizations, reflecting the intricate dynamics of its inception.

Crucially, the EPLF's genesis can be contextualized within the global wave of leftist movements that swept both developing and developed nations during the tumultuous sixties and seventies.

The EPLF, or Eritrean People's Liberation Forces, later rebranded as the Eritrean People's Liberation Front, emerged as a formidable political organization with unparalleled potential, qualities, and advantages to confront and navigate the constantly shifting political and military landscape in Eritrea since its inception.

The EPLF developed an exceptionally sophisticated and robust military apparatus, boasting a dedicated rank-and-file and a level of military discipline that surpassed many African nations' armies. The war gave rise to brilliant military strategists, many of whom had humble beginnings as ordinary citizens, hailing from diverse backgrounds such as peasants, students, intellectuals, workers, men and women, and individuals spanning the socioeconomic spectrum. It was a movement that united people regardless of their gender, ethnicity, or religious affiliation.

Leadership within the EPLF played a pivotal role in shaping the rules of engagement, defining the norms, and instilling values within the army. The EPLF's armed forces epitomized courage, displaying bravery in all its manifestations, acts of heroism, and a willingness to sacrifice for the cause of independence. This commitment extended beyond the battlefield to endure isolation from the international community, harsh living conditions, extreme temperatures, rugged terrain, shortages of weapons and ammunition, and a relentless propaganda campaign by the Dergue regime and the Socialist Camp aimed at isolating the EPLF from its population.

Resilience was a defining characteristic of the EPLA, with the front exhibiting unrelenting determination and tenacity in its pursuit of independence. It adapted to different obstacles and changing political landscapes through its flexibility. Within its ranks were creative individuals who consistently offered their best to the cause, proving the adage that "necessity is the mother of innovation." The EPLF's ability to innovate and adapt played a significant role in its ultimate success. As time passed, the front's influence organically expanded, encompassing a significant portion of the population through its mass organizations. It successfully generated substantial revenue and garnered support from Eritreans within the country and those in the diaspora. This support was instrumental in fueling its activities and boosting its morale.

Much like several liberation movements that emerged during the turbulent sixties and seventies, this particular movement adhered to a Marxist-Leninist ideology. Its core principles included advocating for the dictatorship of the proletariat, fostering an alliance between the working class and peasants, establishing a Socialist regime, nationalizing private property, and promoting solidarity with leftist movements worldwide.

The EPLF displayed a high degree of centralization, a trait often attributed to its military-oriented culture and mindset. Notably, it exhibited a marked intolerance for dissenting political views. This intolerance was evident during events like the 1973 Reformist Movement, the so-called Yemin Movement, and the suppression of sympathizers of figures like Osman Saleh Sabbe, or individuals with dissenting opinions, who were frequently labeled as Menqa'e or Yemin, even when such labels weren't entirely accurate.

Repression of this nature continued unabated after independence. Cases in point are actions taken against the popular 1993 uprising of

members of the front requesting basic subsistence salary, groups like
G-13, G-15, and the January 2013 movement also known as the Forto
Rebellion aimed at toppling the government.

The EPLF created a military echelon with unquestioned authority but with utmost loyalty to Isaias Afewerki. This group was left on
its own to amass immense power.

Dissension of any form or content had brutal consequences or
ended up in the physical elimination of the individual/s when other
options - such as discharging or expulsion from the front (Rftiya -
ርፍትያ) - were at the front's disposal.

Tragically, some of the EPLF's own members met their demise at
the hands of its leadership. To name some of the prominent ones, Mussie
Tesfamichael, Yohannes Sebhatu, Tareqe Yihdego, Habtesellassie
Ghebremedhin, Afewerki Teklu, Debessai Ghebresellassie, Dr.
Russom, Ghebreamlak Issac, Dr. Michael, Ghirmay Berhe, Tewolde
Iyob, Dehab Tesfatsion, Aberash Melke, Mesih Russom, Michael
Bereketab, Samuel Gheredinghil, Alem Abraha, Tecle Ghebrekrstos,
Goitom Berhe, and Haile Yohannesom[li] (Eritrean Human Rights
Electronic Archive, n.d.). Mesfin has the following to say about the
fate of some of the fate of these people,

> By far the harshest sentences were meted out to Habteselasie
> Ghebremedhin, Tewelde Eyob, Afewerki Tekhlu, Mussie
> Tesfamichael, Yohannes Sebhatu, Resom Zerai, Tareqe
> Yehdego, Aberash Melke, and Dehab Tesfatsion, who were
> sentenced to death (Hagos M., 2023).

Mesfin regrets that looking back, his fears and those of his leadership
colleagues, may have been exaggerated, their management of the crisis
may have been lacking, and their final decision may have been extreme,
but he supported the death penalty that a committee passed because he

believed Menqa'e had wreaked internal havoc and at a time when they could barely face off the ELF and Ethiopia (Hagos M., 2023).

The atrocities committed against dissenting freedom fighters were so heinous that they drove some individuals to mental instability, as evidenced by the case of Dr. Michael (a pharmacist by profession) or a suicide attempt by Dr. Haile Mehtsun while in detention.

Some intellectuals following coercion and intimidation, were willing to be compromised. Haile Mehtsun was one of them. He was allowed to join the clandestine party at a later stage and remained silent about his fellow comrades in arms. I myself shared a detention facility with Dr. Haile Mehtsun in 1976.

Others who softened their stance and joined the mainstream Isaias political line included Petros Solomon and Sebhat Efrem. Petros experienced the challenges of detention during his service in the Engineering Unit of the EPLF.

A relentless campaign of defamation against targeted individuals led to the complete isolation of many patriots, who were cast as enemies of the revolution and constantly viewed with suspicion. Some were entirely alienated from their fellow comrades, denying them the opportunity to contribute their best efforts. To name some: Isaias Tewoldeberhan (Wedi Finansa), Woldenkiel Haile, and Adhanom Ghebremariam.

The alienation and stigma that some experienced undermined their ability to play important roles despite their potential. Mesfin Hagos has the following stay in his book mentioned in an earlier chapter. He says,

> The association with Menka'e became a stigma on several members and undermined their capacity to play important roles until 1975. When a company political commissar was martyred, Sebhat Efrem was sent to take his place but could

not do so because the company refused to accept him due to his association with Menka'e (Hagos M., 2023)

I encountered incidents of this nature, and one illustrative incident took place in 1977 when I was overseeing the Mass Organization Unit (06) in the southern part of Asmara, stationed in the village of Adi Hawsha. At that time, Asmara was surrounded by EPLF forces, and my unit played a vital role in coordinating covert operations in the capital city. One of our primary responsibilities was gathering intelligence on enemy movements and plans within Asmara and coordinating operations, which I accomplished using an AN/PRC 77 Radio Set.

One bright morning, the Battalion Commissar of Battalion 23.3, Filipos Woldeyohannes, visited my operation center and requested that I surrender the radio I was using to him. Filipos explained that his radio set was malfunctioning, and it might take some time to repair it. In response, I politely declined, explaining that I could not hand over my radio as I had critical tasks to carry out with it. I suggested that he go to Dekemhare and request a replacement there.

However, he insisted that this was an order. I firmly reiterated that I would only accept orders from my immediate supervisor, who happened to be Woldemichael Abraha, a member of the Central Committee based in Dekemhare. As Filippos walked away, he insulted me, uttering the word "Menqa'e."

I vividly recall the day (immediately after I joined the EPLF) when I unexpectedly crossed paths with Ermias Debessai (also known as Papayo) in Ghereghr Asmara, where our cohort was undergoing military training and political indoctrination. Ermias appeared genuinely surprised to see me, and after exchanging a few pleasantries, he candidly inquired, "Why on earth did you decide to enlist?" (እንታይዲኸ ከትገብር መጺእካ), reflecting the evident frustration he was grappling with at the time. My association with Ermias dates back to my early childhood, as my elder brother, Bihon Solomon (martyred in 1978 in the battle of Barentu), had been close friends with him. Furthermore, Ermias's elder brother, Beyene Debessai, holds the role of my godfather. It is worth noting that my mother and his mother, both devout Catholics, shared a deep bond of friendship. Ermias later regretted what he told me (after he enlisted in the clandestine party) and asked me that I never mention our exchange to anybody. He feared for his political career and life.

Others suffered in EPLF's detention centers, where they experienced inhumane treatment. Some were left to rot in prison, enduring horrifying conditions. This relentless mistreatment resulted in the emasculation of some, destroying their egos, shattering their self-worth, and breaking their morale and spirit. In extreme cases, individuals were dehumanized or driven to commit suicide. Some freedom fighters even fled to Europe or the United States to escape these circumstances.

Furthermore, those who confessed to working against the front, whether through pressure or force, were often subjected to ridicule, mirroring the tactics employed by historical figures like Stalin during his reign of terror or Mao Tse-tung during China's Cultural Revolution.

Suicides were not uncommon within the EPLF, even among the leadership, with notable figures like Mohammed Ali Clay (Brigade Commander and member of the Central Committee of the EPLF), Habtemariam Debtera (in charge of the Intelligence Unit and a member of the Central Committee of the EPLF), Tekle Bahlbi (Wedi Lbi) in charge of intelligence, Southern Front, Dr. Mekonnen Haile, Wedi Zere (Ash'al), Alem Haile (Mass Organizations, Southern Zone), Dr. Be'imnet Ja'efer, and Wedi Haleka (Commissar, Brigade 4) among those who tragically succumbed.

The EPLF bore a striking resemblance to its leader, Isaias Afewerki, who possessed a set of distinctive characteristics. Isaias was obsessed with control. He had the desire to direct and manage every aspect of the organization. He was rather calculated, always weighing his actions and decisions, seemingly driven by a subconscious feeling of insecurity that made him fearful of his peers. His arrogance and narcissism knew no bounds, often leading him to assume a central role and consider himself the focal point of attention.

The EPLF's control extended into both political and ideological domains. It achieved this through the covert presence of a clandestine party within the hierarchy of the front, where dissenters faced severe punishments. Consequently, the EPLF became a breeding ground for authoritarianism, stifling any form of opposition or independent thought.

The EPLF utilized its Cadre School not only for ideological indoctrination but also for forcing individuals to confess to political mistakes they may or may not have committed. This brainwashing process aimed to mold front members into parroting the party's desired narratives and beliefs. To further consolidate control, the EPLF encouraged its fighters to spy on their comrades, particularly targeting educated members of the organization. Suspicions were rampant within the EPLF, particularly toward intellectuals and educated members of society. The organization showed no mercy to those suspected of entertaining differing views, subjecting them to various forms of coercion and repression.

The presence of a clandestine political party was affirmed during the PFDJ's Third Congress (and the last one) in 1994, but there has been no official mention of it since, as detailed in Connel's book. Connel notes that the EPLF was influenced by a hidden Marxist organization, known as the Eritrean People's Revolutionary Party, which offered a sense of direction and guidance to the front. This party played a pivotal role in influencing both the EPLF's evolution and in shaping the enduring political climate that characterizes the nation's post-independence political scene. A significant portion of the party's initial efforts were focused on shaping the EPLF into a unified political and social entity. This endeavor aimed to establish a model for revolutionary conduct, the promotion of fresh ideals, and the cultivation of national unity in opposition to divisive sectarian values. The People's Party came into existence as an instrument of political leadership; however, it inevitably became more of an instrument of control than one of political leadership (Connell, 2005).

Externally, the EPLF established a formidable propaganda machine with a global reach, disseminating its message across the Middle East, Europe, and the United States. Festivals, like the renowned Bologna festivals, served as platforms to romanticize the EPLF's revolutionary struggle, showcasing only the positive aspects while concealing the darker facets.

The EPLF divided its members into distinct categories, including democrats, patriots, and those with negative political tendencies or "deviants." The inner circle was dominated by the party leadership, followed by the rank and file of the party, and then the members of the front. Privileged individuals enjoyed easy access to information and various excesses, including positions of power, drinks, cigarettes, and even sexual favors. This hierarchical structure further reinforced the EPLF's control and manipulation over its members. The party apparatus closely resembled a security apparatus, with the distinction lying in the terminology used only. It was indeed a security apparatus.

The ideological foundations of the organization began to evolve after the Second Congress of the EPLF. There was a shift in the political discourse, focusing on moving away from socialist rhetoric and incorporating a more national perspective. I vividly recall a year-long effort during which approximately forty to fifty senior members (cadres) of the EPLF convened to deliberate on the content of political education within the organization (ሽማግለ ምስንዳእ ፖለቲካዊ ትምህርቲ). I had the privilege to be in that group. Two distinct schools of thought emerged:

The majority believed that socialism and, by extension, Marxism-Leninism should remain the guiding principle of the front.

A tiny minority, of which I was a vocal member, argued against Marxism and socialism as the guiding principles for the front. The minority maintained that while the Marxist ideology might have served its purpose up to a point, continuing to use it as the primary rallying ideology might not be the most appropriate course of action. The minority contended that the moment called for more inclusive guiding principles. It advocated for uniting people around the values of independence, patriotism/nationalism, democracy, social justice, tolerance as a way of political life, women's rights, respect for Eritrean culture and religion, and more. The tiny group that I was part of believed that this approach would yield more tangible results.

The minority also emphasized the importance of moderation, tolerance, magnanimity, national reconciliation, and reducing the harsh rhetoric directed at the ELF. Terms like "reactionary," "feudal," "power monger," and "tribalist" were discouraged, as it argued that the history of the armed struggle should be viewed as a continuum. The group maintained that the ELF, despite its vulnerabilities, should be seen as an integral part of Eritrea's independence movement, constituting our shared history. Whether we liked it or not, we felt the need to embrace it. I take pride in standing steadfast in those beliefs.

Some colleagues were particularly enthusiastic about Marxist philosophy, insisting that Dialectical and Historical Materialism should receive due attention in our revised political education manuals.

The discussion persisted for months, and with each new topic that emerged from the multitude, opposing viewpoints inevitably surfaced. Among our colleagues, there were those who staunchly contended that religion should be perceived as the opium of a society and hence be combated. Meanwhile, some fervent advocates championed the appropriation of private property in the vein of socialism. A few even pushed the envelope by advocating for the creation of a classless society. These arguments were not entirely unexpected, given the history of our colleagues' conformity with the front's ideology over the years.

A few colleagues and I remained resolute in our beliefs, thus, we occasionally endured intimidation from ardent party members. Some insisted that I temper my rhetoric. While some colleagues acted out of genuine concern for my safety, others questioned my faith. Some even suggested that a second stint in Halewa Sewra (prison) might await me. I recall very well Ahmed Al Qeisi (a member of the Central Committee of the front and the party) approaching me one evening in Himbol to let me know that I may need to tone down my principled beliefs. He mentioned that I might face retribution. Later, at the Secretary-General's directive, Ahmed Al Qeisi was detained.[lii]

I encountered Qeisi a few days after his release from detention in 1991 at Iteghe Menen Hospital. Qeisi was surprised to see me and, after exchanging pleasantries, he remarked, "I never anticipated encountering you again after the controversy you stirred at Himbol." He was alluding to my steadfast opposition to the teaching of Marxism-Leninism during the ongoing deliberations about revising the Political Education Manual of the EPLF.

A decision needed to be made, a declaration that would align with the front's core mission. Directives had to be issued, or else the debates threatened to persist indefinitely. The responsibility for this decision rested squarely on the shoulders of none other than the Secretary-General, Isaias Afewerki.

I vividly recall the evening when the Secretary-General of the Front came from his headquarters in Amberbeb, Sahel, to the venue where several senior cadres of the organization were convening. I was pretty sure that the Secretary-General of the Front had been briefed on what was going on. Nonetheless, the purpose of his visit was to listen to arguments from both sides and provide advice that he did.

The Secretary General delivered a clear and emphatic message to the group. He asserted that the time for change had come. His discourse extensively covered the topic of social justice and its implications. He recommended that the group tone down or soften its socialist rhetoric, specifically Marxism. He elaborated on a set of guiding principles that encompassed patriotism, democratic rights, tolerance, mutual respect, the importance of viewing history as a continuum, women's rights, and more. I, along with a few like-minded colleagues who shared these beliefs, were astounded by the Secretary General's stance. It felt like a vindication of our perspective, and I took pride in being one of the few voices advocating for change.

Interestingly, only one person (Petros Hailemariam) reacted to what the Secretary-General had articulated asking what would become of socialism. In a polite but firm manner, the Secretary-General conveyed that this might not be the right path to pursue.

You may wonder why the Secretary-General sided with me and the minority group during the then-ongoing debate on the nature of political education to be endorsed by the front. I can only assume that he himself was acknowledging the evolving circumstances in the world, perhaps wanting to present himself as a pragmatist. However, in my perspective, the core issue lies elsewhere. He seemed to have denigrated the cadre of loyalists, insinuating that they did not live up to the title he bestowed upon them, i.e., "loyalists," or that they were lagging behind events.

I distinctly recall a conversation with a colleague (whose name is withheld for safety reasons) regarding the late Romadan Mohamed Nur's reaction to the General Secretary's stance on this matter. Romadan confided in my colleague that Isaias's statement was akin to abandoning the socialist philosophy that he held in high regard. Romadan voiced reservations about the Secretary-General's position. Worth noting is that Romadan served as the Head of the Justice Department and was also a member of the Politbureau.

I have heard about similar reservations expressed by other Central Committee and Politbureau members too.

A few days later, Alemseghed Tesfai and I received an invitation to join the six-member Editorial Body, which comprised four members of the Central Committee of the EPLF, and the Political Education manual has been crafted in alignment with the fresh perspective.

In addition to overseeing the quality of other contributions to the manual, I was also tasked with writing on different topics.

Connel cites Alemseged Tesfai, who notes that the EPLF initiated a departure from strict Marxism in the late 1980s. In 1989, the EPLF designated a small group of cadres to revise their political education program to better correspond with contemporary circumstances. Ahmed Al Qeisi and Haile Menkerios spearheaded this endeavor, and during one of their meetings, it was determined that the new political education should steer clear of rigid Marxist ideology (Connell, 2005).

On another occasion, I had the privilege to be part of the Editorial Board of a political platform through *Harbegna (Patriot)*, the EPLF's internal magazine aimed at fostering political awareness and encouraging healthy political discussions among front members. This chapter in history was truly remarkable. I served on the editorial board and collaborated with individuals like Ahmed Al Qeisi, Alemseghed Tesfai, Zemhret Yohannes, Kidane Solomon, and Mahmoud Chirum.

The internal magazine delved extensively into topics such as democracy, women's rights, the conduct of high-ranking officials within the front, conformism, the role of intellectuals within the front, national unity, excesses, and various concerns voiced by members of the front.

The magazine showcased a variety of articles addressing significant topics such as the right to self-expression rooted in democratic principles, women's rights, the crucial role of intellectuals in raising political awareness, and the importance of national unity. I distinctly remember the magazine's remarkable impact, particularly when Ahmed Qeisi penned a lengthy article discussing veteran fighters who took great pride in their years of service on the front but were resistant to change. This article ignited a passionate and spirited discussion, evoking strong reactions from the readership.

I also penned an article about the issue of democracy within the front, drawing from interviews with numerous front members. Among those interviewed were the late Worku Zerai, Belainesh Araia, Hiwot Shigom, and Ghenet Tewolde, all women fighters. Their perspectives were resolute in highlighting the lack of democracy within the front and underscoring the imperative for significant enhancements. This article sparked a fresh round of feedback and discussions.

"The majority should exercise tolerance" ("እቲ ዝበዝሐ ክጸውር ኣለዎ") was another article that I authored. It specifically addressed Tigrigna speakers and aimed to convey a cautionary message, urging them to be mindful of the sensitivities of minority groups within the EPLF. I vividly remember illustrating this point with an example of a colleague who, despite being educated in Arabic, was perceived as illiterate by Tigrigna speakers because he couldn't read or write Tigrigna. My intention was to demonstrate that there are values and norms important to others that deserve respect by others. Upon reviewing the article, Ahmed Al Qeisi, the chair of the Editorial Board, agreed with the content but raised concerns about the potential controversy that this article could raise within the organization. Consequently, the article was never published.

Contributions from fellow front members poured in, astonishing many readers who couldn't believe that such spirited debates were taking place within the organization. The magazine quickly became a sensation and gained immense popularity. The pertinent issues raised ignited controversies that the leadership found challenging to tolerate. Ultimately, the leadership decided to permanently close the magazine. Its existence was brief, lasting less than two years. Dan Connell recounts about the popularity of the magazine in the following words,

> In the late 1980s, for example, a group of intellectuals associated with the Department of Political Guidance came together to develop a newspaper—*Harbenya* (The Patriot)—that was to carry both in-depth report- age and lively debates over pressing social and political issues of the day. Among those involved were Mohamed al Qeisi, Kidane Solomon, Semere Solomon (myself), Alemseged Tesfai, and Zemhret Yohannes. The experiment lasted a year and was reportedly quite popular among the forces before it was shut down and its participants dispersed by the department's top officials - Alamin Mohamed Saud and Haile Wolde'ensae (Connell, 2005).

I also distinctly remember an occasion when the Front's Secretary-General, Isaias Afwerki, convened a meeting of senior EPLF cadres to discuss the organization's political orientation and future trajectory. Once again, a few attendees, including myself, argued that there was a lack of free debate on various political matters within the organization and that forums for open discussion should be promoted. I was vocal during this debate. Regrettably, there was no follow-up to the meeting, except for repercussions faced by those brave enough to express their views. The team that ran the internal magazine, *Harbegna*, was disbanded and its members dispersed across different units of the front.

Finally, the Harbegna team was the one that came forward with the idea that the song "Eritrea" to be our national anthem.

9.2. THE ERITREA LIBERATION FRONT (ELF)

The nationalist organization in question, the ELF, held a significant role as the embodiment of the Eritrean people's collective voice and their resistance against the annexation of Eritrea by imperial Ethiopia. This resistance transcended the circumstances of its establishment and the identities of its leaders. The ELF managed to unite numerous progressive, patriotic, and dedicated individuals from diverse backgrounds in their pursuit of independence.

However, the ELF's journey was marked by internal divisions and schisms, some rooted in political disagreements, while others were drawn along ethnic and religious lines. In a later phase of its history, a prevailing belief emerged within the organization that "the field cannot support but one front."

To advance its cause, the ELF initiated military offensives against Ethiopian garrisons and troop movements. Despite facing overwhelming odds and limited access to weaponry, the front survived and made advances.

The front maintained strict military discipline during its formative years. Survival was a constant struggle, as the Ethiopian army had the upper hand, and the ELF had to rely on the local population for sustenance and supplies.

Initially confined to Gash and Barka Awrajas, the ELF eventually expanded its operations into other regions of Eritrea. Its early members predominantly hailed from the lowlands of Eritrea and were primarily followers of Islam. However, in the early 1970s, Christian and Muslim highlanders began to swell the ranks of the ELF.

The ELF served as a platform for a wide array of ideological perspectives until a group of progressive elements within the organization established the Labor Party, that professed Marxism. Herui Tedla recalls the moment when he was approached by certain members of the Labor Party, including Said Saleh, Ibrahim Ghedem, Omar Mohamed, Siraj Abdu, and Mohamed Nur Ahmed. They informed him about the existence of a Marxist-Leninist faction within the ELF and extended an invitation, which he willingly accepted (Bairu, 2016). In contrast to the EPLF, within the ELF, there was a comparatively more liberal atmosphere that encouraged members to express diverse viewpoints. This is particularly true during the 1970s.

I had the opportunity to engage with a significant number of ELF fighters in various parts of Eritrea while serving as a member of the EPLF Committee designated to foster closer ties between the two fronts (ኣቀራራቢት ሽማግለ ክልተ ውድባት) in 1975–76.

Within the ELF, a continuous clash of ideologies and opinions has persisted throughout its history. This ideological contention was not restricted to the leadership only. Prominent figures within the ELF frequently challenged one another, as did the rank-and-file members and mid-level cadres. As I served as a member of the committee, I bore witness to fervent debates among members of the ELF. These discussions revolved around topics like unity and various other issues of concern, often accompanied by an air of confidence that sometimes contradicted the positions held by the leadership. I have witnessed differences of opinion (that were tolerated) between the rank and fine and the leadership.

This hypothesis may warrant additional sociological research, nonetheless, I would like to present my conjecture on why the ELF exhibited a greater degree of liberalism internally compared to the EPLF, despite the shared ideologies between the two organizations. Both professed Marxism, and each had a clandestine party guiding their respective fronts. The EPLF might have adhered more strictly to discipline within its ranks. It appears that the crux of the matter lies in the socio-cultural composition and psychological make-up of their respective members (both leaders and the rank and file) which in turn contributed to the two distinctive organizational cultures.

Initially, the ELF was predominantly composed of lowlanders, contrasting with the EPLF's dominance by Tigrigna speakers. Tigrigna speakers began to significantly join the ranks of the ELF only after 1973.

The two organizations that amalgamated to form the EPLF [ቀዳማይ ወገንን ካልኣይ ወገንን or ህዝባዊ ሓይልታት ሓርነት ኤርትራን (The Group from Semhar) and ሰልፊ ነጻነት ኤርትራ (The group from Kebesa)] may have had equal influence at the outset. However, over time, the balance of power shifted to Selfi Netsanet Ertra (ሰልፊ ነጻነት ኤርትራ or ካልኣይ ወገን), solely due to the substantial influx of highlanders into its ranks. Over time, the Tigrigna culture gained increased prominence within the EPLF and continued to do so.

The Tigrigna society, and by extension its culture, exhibits a more hierarchical structure compared to that of the lowlanders. The Tigrigna-speaking highlanders had more distinct feudalistic structures and value systems than those in the lowlands, possibly influenced by their sedentary economic and social life. This hierarchical nature is further intensified by the infusion of an alien Marxist ideology within the EPLF that advocated conformism at all levels. The result was a fertile ground for the regimentation of ideas, creating a conducive environment for ideological conformity.

The lowlanders' more tolerant culture, characterized by a willingness to listen and accommodate diverse views, could be attributed to their socio-economic formation. The quasi-nomadic culture dictates a life of solitude, patience, tolerance, and resilience in the face of adversity.

For instance, how Tigre-speaking communities raise their children differs from the approach of Tigrigna-speaking highlanders. Colleagues raised in Tigre-speaking communities highlight that children's voices are valued and respected, akin to the treatment of adults. Children in these communities feel comfortable sharing their views in the presence of parents or elders and are even encouraged to do so. In contrast, Tigrigna-speaking highlanders emphasize respect for elders, where children are expected to refrain from speaking while elders are engaged in conversation.

I observed another cultural distinction where individuals from the lowlands exhibit a greater tendency to forgive each other compared to their Tigrigna counterparts.

I believe the above socio-economic, cultural, and ideological factors could explain the difference between the organizational cultures of the two respective organizations.

More than anything else, it appears to me that the ELF, due to the socio-cultural context mentioned above, accommodated several contending forces from within, each wielding varying degrees of political influence—particularly evident as of the early seventies

(ዝደፋፈሩ ግንክ ተመጣጣኒ ፖለቲካዊ ጽልዋ ዘለዎም ጉጅለታት). These forces shared a common objective: the pursuit of an independent Eritrea. In stark contrast, the political culture of the EPLF did not tolerate dissenting voices. Notably, when the Secretary General of the EPLF spoke, the entire organization echoed the words verbatim. This was a departure from the ELF, where the political environment allowed room for differing opinions, which were acknowledged and accommodated. Here I am speaking about the ELF of the seventies.

Unlike the ELF, within the EPLF, any opinion diverging even slightly from the tightly held views of the leadership, especially that of Isaias, faced severe criticism (ርእስኻ ዘይንን ነፋራታ), and in the worst-case scenario, individuals were ostracized. Labels such as "divisive," "destructive," or "deviant" (መቃቃሊ: ኣዕናዊ: ዝንቡል: ወዘተረፈ) were readily assigned to those expressing differing viewpoints; similar to how the current regime deems dissenting voices as Woyane, traitor, or CIA currently

Having said that it is paradoxical to witness contradictions being resolved violently within the ELF leadership. Suffice to mention the incident in Rassai, Sudan, when the ELF leadership met to assess their situation after the ELF was forced to vacate Eritrea in the early 1980s. Abdella Idris, a leading figure in the ELA, the army wing of ELF, ambushed the participants of the conference and arrested the leading figures of ELF. Melake Tekle, the head of security of the ELF, resisted arrest and was killed in the shootout that followed.[liii]

Ultimately, the ELF's internal divisions and conflicts played a more significant role in its disintegration than the external war with the EPLF.

I wish to underscore that there were no significant ideological disparities between the ELF and the EPLF. Both were led by clandestine Marxist-Leninist parties. The assertion made by the EPLF, which contended that its differences with the ELF were rooted in ideology, lacks substantial merit. I ardently maintain that the root cause of the devastating civil war was primarily a struggle for power among the contending factions within the Eritrea war of independence, exacting a heavy toll on the Eritrean people.

In this context, I recall a conversation with a colleague (whose name is withheld for security reasons), a former EPLF member, contemplating the authorship of the history of the armed struggle. He had been discussing the idea with close friends. One bright morning over coffee, I posed a question: "Could you please share your understanding of the difference between the EPLF and ELF?" He was caught off guard, taking a moment to ponder before responding, "This is a very interesting question. I have never thought about it." I expressed my belief that, despite the EPLF ideologues' assertions, there was little ideological difference between the two, and the primary cause of the rift was a struggle for power. I advised him to steer clear of this topic, cautioning that attempting to write the history of the armed struggle under the scrutiny of the PFDJ would likely hinder reaching an independent conclusion. I believe he postponed the endeavor indefinitely.

Alganesh Solomon and a friend visiting Sahel from Switzerland

An article on a Spanish newspaper covering the war (me in the middle)

The late Bahgu,Tesfasellassie, Atilla, Nkrumah, the late Worku,
I, Gual Signora in Sahel

Giving an interview to Simon Dring of BBC in 1977

I, the late Mekonen Gubtan, Habteab, Zemzem, Yodit, and Mulu

In North Eastern Sahel

Martyr Bihon Solomon

Martyr Alem Abraha (Wedi Giorgio)

Martyr Rufael Solomon

Me in North Eastern Sahel

Me briefing Spanish journalists in Alghena Front –
North Eastern Sahel

With Ahmed Al Qeisi and Zemhret Yohannes in Sahel

With Mehari Solomon - my younger brother - in Sahel

With the group that worked on the Political Education manual in Himbol
- Sahel

The late Worku Zerai and Kidane Solomon (my elder brother) in Sahel

Yitbarek, Tesfamichel Sherifo, Alemseghed Tesfai, and Tesfamichael Gerhatu

My late mother (Madalena Yosief)   My late father
(Blatta Solomon Abbai)

My late father (on the right) and the late Ato Habtu Engda
(his best friend) – maybe in the 1940th

10

PEOPLE'S FRONT FOR DEMOCRACY AND JUSTICE (PFDJ)

THE PEOPLE'S FRONT for Democracy and Justice (PFDJ) emerged as an evolution of the EPLF. Serving as an extended iteration of the EPLF, the PFDJ endeavored to present itself as a revitalized rendition of the EPLF, symbolizing a "fresh blood" for a "new era." This transformation was characterized by the appointment of new leadership and the unveiling of the National Charter.

In my January 21, 2001 write-up, I, under the pen name—Tedros Tesfai—described a complex series of events that culminated in the emergence of the PFDJ as the dominant political force in post-independence Eritrea, granting it considerable influence over the nation's destiny. The president of the Provisional Government of Eritrea officially declared that the PFDJ would be the sole political entity in Eritrea, firmly asserting that Eritrea would not become a battleground for various other Eritrean political organizations (ኣብ ኤርትራ ሓሽውየ ውድባት ኣይከነፍቅድን ኢና).

According to this article, shortly after achieving independence, the EPLF embarked on a significant effort to rebrand itself by claiming a new blood of leaders had taken over. This initiative was spearheaded by none other than Isaias Afewerki himself. This initiative involved a comprehensive overhaul of the organization, marked by a strong critique of the previous leadership as being "rotten."

In 1994, during the third organizational congress, a pivotal moment arrived when the EPLF underwent a profound rebranding, adopting the name "People's Front for Democracy and Justice" (PFDJ). No sooner did the PFDJ take shape than the inner circle led by Isaias drafted what is commonly known as the National Charter to demonstrate the PFDJ's commitment to change. This document was meant to encapsulate a range of lofty ideals, including democracy, social justice, the rule of law, and a free press, among others. Through the National Charter, the PFDJ articulated its vision for a nation where the Eritrean people would receive recognition for the sacrifices they had made to establish their country. (Tesfai, 2001)

Another significant development was the constitution- making process. While there was some level of consultation with the local community, a significant portion of the opposition was excluded from the constitution drafting process.

The PFDJ not only failed to fulfill its promises, as articulated by Tedros Tesfai in the same article but also took a disturbing turn after consolidating its authority. It became evident that the efforts put into creating a National Charter and crafting a constitution were deceptive maneuvers. The Front shifted from its original intent and morphed into an entity centered around a single individual, Isaias Afewerki. This transformation prioritized advancing his personal desires, ego, and notably, his megalomaniacal ambitions. Consequently, the Front evolved into a separate power structure within the state, with a core philosophy aimed at endorsing dictatorship. Tedros continues, and I quote,

Let me be very explicit at this juncture as to what I mean when I refer to the Party. I am referring to a person—Issaias - and a few of his cronies. It's about the machine created by him and for him whose main task is to suck out the EPLF of its substance and to deny the country of its soul. I am referring to the tool created by him to legitimize the "Privatization" of all the structures and thus of the Eritrean society. All the rest i.e., the elimination of historical figures is a reflection of this vacuum-cleaning act. Snatching away decades of collective effort for the glory of one; the ultimate ripping-off of the gallant people of Eritrea.

The situation deteriorated due to the senseless war with Ethiopia in 1998. The regime was ill-prepared and lacked the political acumen to effectively handle a crisis of such magnitude. Prior to this, there had been a similar conflict with Yemen over the disputed islands of Hanish and Zuqur, which ultimately resulted in a diplomatic disaster for Eritrea. Eritrea's relationship with Sudan also went through a comparable ordeal, culminating in the termination of diplomatic ties between the two nations.

It was obvious that the intricacies of geopolitics and the agenda of various international and regional powers were to play a significant role in determining Eritrea's survival. The country's ability to master the art of diplomacy and formulate astute policies was crucial for navigating the challenging political landscape in the region. This was an indisputable reality.

The PFDJ regime has, once more, demonstrated a profound misunderstanding of diplomatic language and the dynamics of international relations. It has failed to grasp the intricacies of navigating complex geopolitical landscapes, showing a lack of recognition of the importance of peaceful coexistence with its neighbors. Moreover, it has overlooked the fact that other countries also have their own national interests to protect, highlighting a crucial need to comprehend and embrace the concept of compromise. Consequently, the regime has inadvertently become a destabilizing force in the Horn of Africa.

What one practices in domestic politics usually reflects in its foreign policy. This aptly mirrors the situation in post-independent Eritrea. When a government employs a confrontational and authoritarian approach in its domestic affairs, it often translates into a similar stance in its external policy/relations. This pattern is notably evident in the policies of the PFDJ regime. This is characterized by a readiness to resort to force and intimidation when addressing disagreements related to national interests with neighboring countries. In essence, the PFDJ appears to apply the same language i.e., that of the barrel of a gun internally and externally, leading to a confrontational and aggressive foreign policy stance.

Eritrean domestic politics has been marked by the heavy- handed use of violence and coercive tactics to suppress dissent and quell differences. Examples include the rebellion of former freedom fighters in 1993, protests by war-disabled individuals, the incarceration of hundreds of Muslim lowlanders on the pretext of "Islamic Extremism," the abduction and continued imprisonment of prominent members of the ELF from Sudan, the relentless pursuit of ELF members in Ethiopia, and the ruthless suppression of the reformist movement led by the G-15 and the Forto rebellion. These incidents and how they were handled serve as stark reminders of the authoritarian nature of the PFDJ-led regime.

Under PFDJ rule, the nation exhibits political disarray, a decline in political standards, widespread human rights violations, autocratic governance, excessive centralization of authority, and a lack of tolerance.

PFDJ does not profess any ideology. I, under the pen name Zeineb Ali, wrote at length on this issue way back in 2002 (Ali, 2002).

The pretext: I am purposely avoiding concepts like philosophy, ideology, etc. I have carefully chosen the word "pretext" because it is deep in my belief that PFDJ has neither a philosophy nor an ideology of its own. It started with a seemingly leftist/nationalist one and ended up with none. Now let me tell you why it is behaving the way it behaving now.

It all stems from an inferiority complex; it emanates from ignorance of the world reality; it has its roots in arrogance, jealousy (envy) and hatred. Hatred for the people. Hatred for anything new and unPFDJ. Hatred for organized institutions. Hatred for democracy and pluralism. It originates from suspicion, uneasiness, and contempt. It emerges from hatred for alternative solutions. It all has to do with its very protective and closed nature. And whenever it is confronted and has no way of rationally defending itself, it reverts to its 'famous' pretext of 'uniqueness'. Everything is unique in Eritrea. The National Assembly doesn't convene on a regular basis because Eritrea's situation is unique. Parties are not needed; they are against the interest of the unique situation in/of Eritrea. The uniqueness that prevails in Eritrea today doesn't permit the existence of an independent press, democracy, pluralism, etc. The fact that Eritrea is multi-ethnic, multi-lingual, and the fact that its people profess more than two religions are also justifications for its uniqueness. Don't be surprised if one bright morning, PFDJ comes forth under the pretext of the size of the population and the varied topography and climate of the land as a justification for any forthcoming ulterior move. "Everything is unique. So PFDJ has the right to opt for unique solutions to problems". Solutions that have never been applied in modern human history.

On top of everything, Eritrea's "uniqueness" is strongly underlined when it comes to the fact that Eritrea's fate rests in the hands of one man, the "Honorable" President Isaias Afewerki. What an insult to the land of the GREAT HEROES!!!!!!!!!

Resorting to the most awkward: PFDJ has to resort to anything illogical, sinister, archaic, malicious, and conspiratorial because it has no vision. If there is any, it is destruction and destruction and destruction. Destruction of the Eritrean people's pluralistic entity, destruction of a historic and tightly knit social fabric, destruction of the would-be vibrant economy, and destruction of the deep-rooted culture. It is the destruction of anything that threatens its existence. It has to always resort to the 'pretext' of 'uniqueness' whenever the need arises with a view to destroying one of the above.

PFDJ's raison d'être revolves around instilling and perpetuating absolute fear. Any perceived threat to its authority, and consequently its very existence, is ruthlessly suppressed. Shortly after achieving independence, the front's initial move was to vilify the old leadership and prominent historical figures, branding them as "rotten." This was done ostensibly to pave the way for a new generation of leaders. The names of revered figures like Woldeab Woldemariam were strictly forbidden from discussion. Even when Woldeab Woldemariam returned from decades of exile, his arrival was deliberately kept low-key, according to Abdalla Jaber, a former member of the Executive Committee of PFDJ who now languishes in PFDJ prisons. There were explicit instructions from PIA (President Isaias Afwerki) not to publicize this event.

The regime also waged a relentless campaign against religious institutions. The Orthodox Church was subjected to direct government oversight, and its bishop was placed under house arrest. The Catholic Church, on the other hand, resisted complying with the front's demands and paid a heavy price. All of its assets, including schools, clinics, and health centers, were confiscated. Additionally, one of the four bishops in the diocese was detained for several months. The Islamic Council and the Lutheran church were similarly infiltrated and subdued.

The private sector was declared the primary enemy of the regime, leading to a deliberate effort by the government to create a hostile environment for investments of all sizes, whether domestic or foreign. Consequently, aspiring local entrepreneurs were driven out of the country, effectively paving the way for the monopolization of markets by PFDJ-controlled business enterprises, without the presence of effective checks and balances. Notable examples of failed projects include the Barka Sugar Factory and Massawa Airport.

The failure of the economy was extensively discussed in an interview PIA gave to Eri-TV on January 8, 2022. After painting a grim picture of the economy, the President categorically dismisses the existence of an economy in Eritrea, and if there is any he says it is a subsistence economy (ናይ ዕንጭሩ ቁጠባ)[liv] (Afewerki, 2022).

Eritrean entrepreneurs sought refuge in neighboring countries such as South Sudan, Uganda, Kenya, Angola, the United Arab Emirates, and others, as they fled the deteriorating economic conditions. This mass exodus ultimately resulted in the widespread impoverishment of the entire nation, as a self-sustaining middle class was and is often seen as a potential threat to any regime. The regime's strategy was, thus, designed to weaken the middle class deliberately, as it was perceived to pose a significant challenge to its grip on power.

An offensive was launched against traditional institutions, which were represented by the established administrative structures such as Awraja, Woreda, and Adi. These structures were then replaced by six

Administrative Zones that seemingly disregarded the deep-rooted Eritrean psyche, thought patterns, cultural norms, judicial systems, and the significance of watersheds, among other aspects that had evolved over centuries. This drastic transformation was carried out under the pretext of combating "regionalism," but it had profound implications for the Eritrean landscape.

This malevolent scheme also entailed a significant redrawing of the Eritrean map, a subject extensively discussed by Mesfin in his book titled *"The Revolution Reclaimed."* In his work, Mesfin offers a thorough examination of the consequences arising from the modified maps and the reorganization of conventional administrative units. Mesfin argues that, in theory, the administrative reorganization was aimed to promote economic growth and enhance administrative effectiveness. Nonetheless, in reality, it posed several challenges, particularly in relation to the management of water drainage systems, which resulted in people and land holdings falling under different administrative zones. Mesfin's conclusion is that the revised map did not achieve its intended goals of administrative efficiency and economic development as intended (Hagos M., 2023).

Wars perpetuated by the regime have taken a toll on the nuclear family, which is regarded as the most sacred institution in Eritrean society. The youth are fleeing the country out of fear, primarily to avoid being ensnared in the never-ending "National Service" and forced labor, as well as to escape persecution by the ruthless security apparatus and military. They lost faith in the government and their own future prospects. Due to these pervasive issues, many of the youth never return home.

Former French President François Hollande, speaking at a gathering of over sixty leaders representing both Africa and the European Union, highlighted that a significant portion of migrants hailed from Eritrea and Sudan. He stressed the urgency of applying "maximum pressure" on Eritrea's leadership to address this dire situation. He pointed out that Eritrea is facing a crisis that is causing its own population to flee, a predicament exacerbated by unscrupulous leaders who allow their people to depart without addressing the root causes"[lv] (VOA, VOA News, 2015).

The front's panic was glaringly evident when it dealt with the university students' protest enrolling in the summer program unless certain reforms were carried out. The request included better treatment from the government and consultation on matters that concern them (Human Rights Watch, 2001). Not only were the students detained in the most inhospitable and scorching region of the country (Wi'a), but the university as an institution was permanently closed. This serves as a stark reminder to anyone familiar with the history of the EPLF of how intellectuals and the educated segment of society were ostracized.

The youth also had to be tightly controlled. This segment of society was subjected to PFDJ's program of social engineering, which involved mandatory enrollment in an eighteen-month "National Service" program. The duration of this service remained uncertain. The objective was to reshape the youth into the image of a freedom fighter (ተጋዳላይ) and to expose them to the harsh realities of life during the war. This indoctrination aimed to manipulate the youth into adhering to prescribed norms, with the ultimate goal of asserting control over their spirits and independence. Additionally, they were often exploited as cannon fodder in PFDJ's military campaigns, including the recent and unwarranted intervention of the Eritrean Army in Ethiopia's internal affairs.

The Eritrean opposition, primarily based outside of Eritrea, has faced a relentless campaign of political vilification, intimidation, abductions, and unjust imprisonment as well as physical elimination of its members. Notably, the opposition has never been included in discussions regarding national reconciliation, even though it was essential to engage them in the process. This situation is reminiscent of the stance taken by the ELF in the early seventies, when it argued that Eritrea could not accommodate but one organization. Regrettably, the EPLF has succumbed to the same position by stating that Eritrea should not become a battleground for various Eritrean political organizations (ኣብ ኤርትራ ሓሽውየ ውድባት ኣይከነፍቅድን ኢና).

PFDJ exhibits a disdain for established institutions, particularly governmental bodies with defined mandates and policies. Ministries, once crucial components of governance, have been rendered ineffectual, impotent, and obsolete under the Front's rule. These institutions endure a constant lack of respect, often circumvented by party officials. The Cabinet of Ministers scarcely convenes, and even when it does, it operates behind a shroud of secrecy, keeping the public in the dark. Mesfin Hagos, in his book *The Revolution Reclaimed* recounts how the President gradually consolidated power within the Ministry of Defense to such an extent that Mesfin felt compelled to resign due to his frustration with the president's malpractices (Hagos M., 2023).

A friend of mine, currently residing in Eritrea and possessing significant knowledge of the power dynamics within the country, affirms that General Filipos Wodeyohannes, the Chief of Staff of the Eritrean Military, does not wield control over the entire army. Instead, the various units, including the Ground Force, Naval Force, Air Force, and militia, under his "jurisdiction," maintain a direct reporting line to the Office of the President and receive their orders directly from the president. It is worth noting that whenever General Filipos Woldeyohannes is approached by his subordinates seeking advice, he redirects them to the president himself.

Another critical issue threatening the PFDJ's continued existence pertains to the principles of checks and balances. To maintain its grip on power, the PFDJ has systematically undermined or disabled the three essential pillars of governance: the legislative, the executive, and the judiciary. For over two decades, the National Assembly, essentially reduced to a rubberstamp institution, has not convened. The judiciary's independence and its duty to uphold the rule of law were compromised with the establishment of the Special Court. Additionally, as previously mentioned, the ministerial cabinet barely holds any meetings.

PFDJ has consistently employed the "fear factor" to justify its continued hold on power, instilling a sense of dread in the general public by emphasizing external threats. The PFDJ has repeatedly employed the fear factor to excess. For instance, it often claimed that "bringing Eritrean life back to normalcy" was an insurmountable task while the TPLF (Woyane) held power in neighboring Ethiopia. Under this pretext, critical national initiatives such as the implementation of the constitution, ending indefinite conscription into the "National Service," launching development programs, and addressing human rights concerns remained unfulfilled.

Notably, as soon as the PFDJ "proclaimed" victory over the TPLF, it swiftly identified a new "vicious" enemy in the United States (Washington clique—ጀነዳ ዋሺንግተን). More recently, following an uprising by Eritrean youth in Israel, the regime, in one of its press releases, went so far as to accuse the Israeli Intelligence agency, MOSSAD, of being behind the unrest. Such excessive reliance on the fear factor to justify its actions raises concerns about the regime's transparency and its commitment to addressing the genuine concerns of the Eritrean people.

The futile acts of subversion—perpetrated through surrogate and rogue groups—are in essence sponsored by major intelligence agencies (including MOSSAD). Bewildered, as they are, by the indomitable resilience of the Eritrean people, they desperately seek to foment division within its ranks"[lvi] (Eritrea, Press Release, 2023).

The PFDJ rhetoric extends beyond the examples mentioned above. Amnesty International, the UN Human Rights Commission, and the Western media are all characterized as enemies of the Eritrean people and are therefore targeted. At one point, even the Intergovernmental Authority on Development (IGAD) and the African Union (AU) were branded as enemies.

The PFDJ has established a military hierarchy characterized by absolute authority and strong allegiance to Isaias. This select group has been given considerable autonomy, enabling them to amass significant power, engage in economic ventures devoid of accountability, and oversee prison facilities, among other responsibilities. Additionally, the regime has cultivated warlords, and corrupt Generals who are there to fulfill political objectives and missions.

Two seasoned former freedom fighters (names withheld for security reasons), engaged in a conversation revolving around the governance in present-day Eritrea. During their discussion, one of them expressed the view that how the generals were steering the country bore a resemblance to feudalism. According to him, the governance system seemed unequivocally feudalistic. Contrarily, the other colleagues hesitated to label the governance system as feudal. He remarked, "I am not sure whether we can categorize it as feudal. Feudalism entails distinct structures and a systematic approach. At least you know what you expect to get from feudalism. I believe the governance structure in Eritrea has not yet attained the level of sophistication one sees in feudalism." He was pointing to the absence of the rule of law, well-defined value systems, and structure.

The population is highly militarized, with all citizens up to the age of seventy obligated to enlist in the militia forces and undergo ongoing military training. They are also expected to keep watch over their neighborhoods at night.

This is what we call life under PFDJ.

11

THE PRINCIPLES OF MODERN-DAY AUTHORITARIANISM AND HOW THEY RELATE TO ERITREA

D R. STEPHEN KOTKIN[lvii] provides a succinct overview of contemporary authoritarianism in his lecture titled "Modern Authoritarianism and Geopolitics: Thoughts on a Policy Framework." He organizes these regimes into five dimensions that span across different authoritarian systems[lviii] (Kotkin, 2022).

The first method employed is the utilization of coercive mechanisms. All authoritarian regimes rely on the police, the military, and the security apparatus to enforce coercion. These regimes maintain a wide array of coercive mechanisms, uniquely tailored to suit each regime's specific needs. These units are often deliberately fragmented and sometimes set against each other to prevent any potential united opposition to the regime.

The Eritrean regime heavily depends on the security apparatus organized under the National Security (Hagherawi Dhnet). Additionally, parallel intelligence structures exist, reporting directly to the Office of the President. According to my sources, the latter are also tasked with monitoring the conventional security apparatuses that the public is familiar with.

The following anecdote illustrates how the traditional security apparatus has been marginalized by the regime and how it is perceived by the public. I had the opportunity to converse with a colleague (name withheld for security reasons) I had known for years, who currently works within the security apparatus. The colleague recounted a meeting chaired by Brigadier General Simon Ghebrednghil, the Chief of the Internal Security Department, where an officer with the rank of Colonel raised his hand to discuss how the public viewed them. He stated, "In the past when we entered a coffee shop, everyone would change the subject they were discussing out of fear of being overheard and reprimanded. Nowadays, as soon as we enter the coffee shop, people start raising their voices to continue their conversations, hoping to be heard what they've been talking about." The attendees of the meeting shared a collective laugh. My colleague also mentioned that the traditional security apparatus has become ineffective due to the emergence of a parallel structure reporting directly to the President's Office. He stated, "We don't have any cases involving individuals suspected of dissent that we can independently pursue. Instead, we're instructed to detain people whose cases we really know nothing about."

Furthermore, consider the presence of the most feared extrajudicial institution within the regime—the Special Court. This court was established through a Presidential decree, operates independently of the established judicial system, and offers no avenue for appeal once a verdict is rendered. Notably, the judges serving in this court are selected from the military and lack any formal legal credentials.

The military plays an active role in apprehending individuals attempting to evade military conscription. Those caught are typically subjected to indefinite imprisonment under deplorable conditions. While it is challenging to verify, there are believed to be a minimum of seventy-seven prison/detention centers operated by the police and the military throughout the country[lix] (UNITAR, 2016). Among these, the most notorious is the one located in Adi Abieto[lx] (PBS, 2021).

PBS describes the prison situation in Eritrea by quoting Sheila B. Keetharuth, the former U.N. special rapporteur on human rights in Eritrea,

> "Anything to do with facts and figures and actual statistics is very difficult to get in Eritrea. It all goes to the opaqueness of the system," Sheila B. Keetharuth, the former U.N. special rapporteur on human rights in Eritrea, said in Escaping Eritrea. "Any official prison system should be in a position to have a list of all those in their custody. This is not possible in Eritrea"[lxi] (PBS Frontline, 2021).

The second dimension revolves around revenue streams and cash flow, and Professor Kotkin asserts that authoritarian regimes rely heavily on these to maintain their grip on power.

Importantly, this economic lifeline isn't tied to the well-being of their populace or fostering economic growth; it's primarily focused on the extraction of valuable resources like precious minerals and hydrocarbons. This dimension is equally applicable to the authoritarian regime in Eritrea. Gold mining and, more recently, potash extraction represent the primary sources of revenue for the regime. Additionally, the various business enterprises under the control of the PFDJ, along with their covert and overt trade and financial activities, further contribute to their financial base. In an article featured in the Middle East Research and Information Project, Dan Connell describes Eritrea's economy as follows,

> Throughout these years, the economy has been dominated by the state and the PFDJ, which share ownership of the major financial and commercial institutions, utilities, services, communications facilities, and transport companies. In fact, the PFDJ owns or controls enterprises in banking, trade, construction, shipping, metalworks, auto repair, road surfacing, and well drilling, among others. It also holds controlling stakes in joint ventures with foreign investors for other large-scale undertakings, such as mining[lxii] (Connell, 2006).

Furthermore, the regime capitalizes on the diaspora through its persistent policy of imposing a 2 percent tax on their earnings. It's also called the "milking of the diaspora." This practice yields tens of millions of dollars annually, which are funneled into sustaining their coercive apparatuses. It is worth noting the irony that, unlike many other diplomatic missions around the world, Eritrean embassies prioritize the collection of funds from the diaspora and that of spying on their citizens, often relegating the traditional embassy functions to a lower priority. To compound matters, the regime has set a fixed exchange rate, irrespective of the local currency's actual value if allowed to float. This effectively amounts to extortion when it comes to remittances sent by the diaspora to support their families back home.

Another troubling facet was the regime's willingness to grant the use of the Assab airstrip to Saudi Arabia and the UAE as part of their efforts to quell the Houthi rebellion in Yemen. In return, the regime received substantial financial rewards, totaling tens of millions of dollars.

SEMERE SOLOMON

According to Professor Kotkin, the third dimension revolves around the control of life opportunities. In his sociological analysis, the professor asserts that authoritarian regimes exert dominance over various aspects of citizens' lives, such as employment, education, international travel, and property ownership. This essentially means that an individual's ability to survive or thrive within such a regime hinges on the goodwill of that regime. Any form of opposition to the regime by an individual may lead to the revocation of these privileges, with far-reaching consequences for their entire family.

How does this concept apply to the context of Eritrea? A All employment opportunities in Eritrea are either provided by the government or enterprises owned by the ruling party, PFDJ. Imagine the consequences for anyone who dares to voice dissent in such a tightly controlled environment. They may face repercussions ranging from being "frozen out," a fate experienced by numerous mid- and high-level civil servants, to being cast out onto the streets.

Travel to foreign countries is severely restricted under this regime. The screening process for those seeking to travel for medical reasons is stringent, and only those deemed privileged are granted permission. Housing is also under the complete control of the regime. Houses are allocated to individuals based on their degree of loyalty and proximity to the ruling party. Consequently, individuals have little choice but to conform to the regime's demands if they wish to retain their homes.

Last but not least, Kotkin delves into the themes of stories and narratives. According to the professor, these narratives primarily focus on both internal and external threats to the nation. They emphasize the historical glory of the past and the nation's greatness, all while operating an intricate propaganda machine aimed at shaping or brainwashing the mindset of the populace. This system thrives on high levels of censorship and information control, executed with remarkable cunning and sophistication. Eritrea exhibits all these characteristics.

The PFDJ's narrative centers around vehement anti-Woyane (TPLF)rhetoric, vilifying the West and particularly the United States for their perceived alignment with Woyane in their attempts to undermine Eritrea. This machinery romanticizes the hardships endured during the war of independence, idolizing the victories achieved against the Ethiopian occupation forces in key battles like Nadew, WuQaw, Mebreq, FenQil, and various fronts. It endlessly recounts the saga of the Ethiopia Offensive, spanning from the first to the sixth and including the Stealth operations (Selahta Werar).

Eritrea's calendar is punctuated by annual festivals, notably Independence Day, Fenkil, Women's Day, Workers' Day, Martyrs Day, and September 1, commemorating the start of the armed struggle. The period from July to September is dedicated to national festivals, observed both within the nation and among the Eritrean diaspora worldwide. One well-informed colleague (name withheld for security reasons) once shared with me that the preparations for the annual festivals at the Expo premises span almost a year. The administrative zones must initiate preparations for the upcoming year immediately after concluding the current one, creating a perpetual cycle of festivals designed to divert the population's attention from the pressing issues.

The roster of internal enemies encompasses opposition members, such as the ELF, the G-15, the Forto Rebellion, and G-13, among others. Much has been written and spoken about them, especially during the purges of 2001 (targeting the G-15) and 2013 (following the failure of a rebellion led by high-ranking officials within the PFDJ and the government). It was ironic to note the Sahelian tactics were used to first tarnish their names and reputations and later on were left to rot in the dungeons of Ira Iro. G-15 members were labeled traitors, Woyane collaborators, those who capitulated, and so forth. Members of the Forto Rebellion of January 2103 were labeled "Islamists." I want to emphasize a key point: irrespective of the individuals' ethnic or religious affiliations, members of the group who led the Forto Rebellion fulfilled what was expected of any justice-seeking Eritrean.

In conclusion, Professor Kotkin delves into the impact of the international environment on authoritarian regimes, highlighting how their anti-Western and anti-imperialistic rhetoric plays a crucial role in strengthening their hold on power and in misleading the populations they govern. The Eritrean regime's grudge against the West has been in its narrative for decades.

12

REFUTING THE EASILY REFUTABLE: THE SAGA OF CONFORMISM

C ONSIDERING THE CONTENT discussed in the initial chapters of this book and the country's experiences over the past three decades, it is difficult to fathom anyone in their right mind supporting the current regime. Nonetheless, it remains far from unusual to encounter assertions from the regime's proponents that Eritrea stands as an island of peace amid regional turmoil. Each time I engage with these individuals, they often bring up the persistent instabilities in Sudan, Ethiopia, South Sudan, and Somalia. They refer to the Arab Spring, recounting how the uprisings were suppressed and the devastating repercussions they unleashed across the Middle East. They also recall the African liberation movements that swept through Africa during the seventies and eighties, underscoring how these movements ultimately disappointed their respective populations.

I maintain a consistent stance that drawing such comparisons fails to do justice to the subject at hand. It is akin to comparing oranges to apples. Instead, I argue that the success of the Eritrean struggle for independence should be measured or evaluated against the specific criteria/goals set by the movement itself as discussed extensively in previous chapters. Assessing whether these goals have been attained or not is what matters. I emphasize the importance of asking whether the envisioned Eritrea characterized by the rule of law, good governance, a commitment to human rights, prosperity, peaceful and harmonious relationships with neighboring nations and the international community, a focus on maximizing its human resources, and an appreciation for diversity has become a reality or not. The answer is obvious. None of these expectations have been met.

In spite of the country's reputation for continued deterioration of different aspects of life (as discussed in previous chapters), there is still a segment of the society that wants to maintain the status quo. This chapter is dedicated to examining this unfortunate phenomenon.

There could be a few hypotheses that could be considered to discuss the phenomenon.

- It could be the narrative/stories that the regime has been disseminating ever since it came to power as described by Professor Kotkin, and people believe them.
- It could be fear. Fear for their lives. Given the coercive mechanisms perpetually used by the regime, people may have chosen not to react. The irony lies with the state of mind of many Eritreans in the diaspora. Could this also be due to the fear factor?
- Could it be due to the weakness of the opposition?
- It could also be the "Stockholm syndrome"—a unique psychological malaise that is exhibited by the captives in relation to their captors.
- Could there be other external factors?

Let us have a look at the aforementioned factors one by one:

12.1. NARRATIVES/STORIES

While it may seem counterintuitive, there are several compel- ling reasons why individuals conform to narratives disseminated by authoritarian regimes. One primary motivation for this conformity is the fear of retribution. People often adhere to the regime's narratives out of concern for their own safety and the well-being of their loved ones. This can be attributed to a fundamental survival instinct ingrained in human nature, as conforming with the regime's narratives may be perceived as a crucial strategy for self-preservation, particularly when non-conformity could result in severe consequences.

Furthermore, authoritarian regimes, as articulated by Professor Kotkin, typically exercise strict control over information and restrict access to alternative media and viewpoints. This can significantly limit people's exposure to diverse perspectives and narratives, leading them to accept the regime's narrative as the sole available truth. Moreover, it is not uncommon for authoritarian regimes to invest heavily in propaganda and indoctrination efforts to maintain a firm grip on the narrative. Also, educational institutions, media outlets, and other influential institutions often serve as platforms for propagating the regime's narrative (Kotkin, 2022).

In societies where conformity is the prevailing norm, individuals often harbor apprehensions about the potential consequences of deviating from the accepted narrative, such as the fear of ostracism or reporting to authorities. Some individuals may even develop coping mechanisms to rationalize their adherence to the prevailing narrative. Additionally, it is not uncommon for some to genuinely believe they are doing the right thing or else go to the extent of believing that change is impossible.

Professor Kotkin delved into the concept of "control of life opportunities"[lxiii] during the aforementioned lecture (Kotkin,

2022). People whose livelihoods are intricately linked to a particular regime may find themselves hesitant to challenge the prevailing narrative, as doing so could jeopardize their own economic and social well-being.

These challenges become even more pronounced when the opposition to the regime is marked by fragmentation and disorganization, making it exceedingly difficult for individuals to envision a viable pathway or an alternative toward effecting meaningful change.

It is crucial to recognize that adhering to the narratives of a repressive regime does not inherently indicate endorsement of that regime. Numerous individuals may conform due to the necessity of their circumstances or for survival, rather than holding genuine beliefs. As circumstances evolve and opportunities for resistance emerge, some of these individuals may eventually join movements dedicated to fostering change or reform.

In the context of Eritrea, as previously described, the prevailing narratives wield a powerful influence in fostering conformity among its citizens. The continuous dissemination of falsehoods and subtle insinuations can lead individuals to question their own intellect and instincts. At times, many might find themselves compelled to physically pinch themselves as if to verify the authenticity of the narratives they are exposed to.

Many long-standing members of the EPLF often create a cocoon of comfort within which they reside until their passing. Their daily exposure through official government media primarily revolves around tales of heroism and a glorified past. In the face of the perceived vulnerability of this relatively small and "enviable" nation to potential absorption by larger neighboring countries like Ethiopia or international powers such as the United States, there exists a prevailing sentiment that every conceivable sacrifice must be made to safeguard Eritrea's sovereignty.

In this environment, alternative media sources are virtually nonexistent, leaving the populace reliant solely on state-controlled outlets for information dissemination as internet access is next to nonexistent.

The civil service and business enterprises affiliated with the PFDJ constitute the primary sources of employment for the population. Access to essential food rations (bread, sugar, lentils, oil, etc.) is often contingent upon attendance at party meetings and participation in the militia forces.

Numerous anecdotal accounts further attest to the notion that, while two individuals may confide in one another on sensitive matters, the presence of a third party can abruptly halt such conversations. A colleague aptly notes that people have adapted to exist with a dual personality under these circumstances.

12.2. WEAK OPPOSITION

The opposition, in its current state, can be characterized as fragmented, disorganized, and unwieldy. It struggles to coalesce into a unified front with a clear minimum program—a situation that has persisted over time. Numerous opposition movements exist, their sheer number exceeding any conventional standard. These movements primarily find their bases of operation in the Middle East, Europe, and North America. Despite varying worldviews among them, they share a common objective: the imperative need for transformative change within Eritrea.

Within this diverse landscape of opposition, some have deep-rooted historical ties with the ELF, while others used to align with the EPLF. Many, however, operate independently of these established entities. The opposition takes various forms, with some functioning as political parties and others as civil society organizations.

Utilizing the power of social media, these factions utilize online platforms to disseminate their agenda. Regrettably, the discourse among them often takes on a personalized and occasionally acrimonious tone. It has also been used to sow discord and foster schisms among its various factions.

Recognizing the detrimental effects of such discord, a few social media outlets strive to promote more civilized discussions and interactions among the opposition movements.

Despite their shared objective of opposing the regime in Asmara, a significant portion of their energy is expended on internal conflicts and attacks against each other, rather than pooling their efforts for a unified political and diplomatic front against the incumbent regime. This absence of a common platform to combat the Asmara regime hampers their effectiveness, with some, inadvertently, causing more harm than good to the broader cause for change.

There is also the troubling possibility that the opposition may have been infiltrated by the intelligence apparatus of the ruling party, PFDJ. It is not unthinkable that this infiltration could have the capacity to compromise their effectiveness and unity.

Furthermore, many elements of the opposition seem content with remaining within their comfort zones, creating a complacency that can hinder the development of a more dynamic and responsive opposition movement.

Another source of division arises from schisms between the old and the young generations within the opposition. This generational gap has led to differences in priorities and strategies.

Last, there is confusion within the opposition regarding the Ethiopian crisis. Several members of the opposition become entangled in the intricacies of each military and political development in Ethiopia, losing sight of the broader perspective. Some align themselves either with Prime Minister Abiy or the TPLF. On the contrary, some view this as an internal Ethiopian matter, driven by political differences that should not have at all developed into a full-fledged war. This group believes the only solution lies in diplomacy, which should have been started and concluded at the negotiation table. Additionally, there is disagreement on whether external forces, including Eritrea, should be involved, with some arguing that such interventions not only worsen the situation but are irresponsible on the part of the regime. Others declared their allegiance with Eritrea's armed forces (or for that matter the regime) during their quest to eliminate the TPLF from the face of the earth. These conflicting views further complicate the opposition's ability to form a coherent and effective strategy for addressing the Ethiopian crisis.

In my opinion, internal Ethiopian matters should be exclusively managed by Ethiopians. If there is a role for Eritrea, or any other neighboring country, it should be a constructive one, for example, exerting pressure on both sides to facilitate a negotiated resolution. The Eritrean army's unwarranted military intervention in Ethiopia deserves unequivocal condemnation.

These internal divisions within the opposition provoke considerable anger, frustration, and, at times, even hopeless- ness among Eritreans residing within the country.

The general populace's conformity and lack of visible dissent can, in part, be attributed to the disarray and infighting within the opposition, which hinder their ability to present a united front against the regime.

12.3. THE FEAR FACTOR

Fear is a natural response to perceived threats or dangers, a universal instinct shared by all human beings. How individuals react to fear varies based on the nature of the threat or danger they perceive. In essence, people's responses to authoritarian regimes can exhibit significant diversity, with the level of fear and repression differing from one regime to another. Many individuals may opt to comply with the restrictions imposed by the regime or compromise their principles out of fear of potential punishment. Others may seek refuge in other countries or go into hiding. Some may decide to keep a low profile, intentionally avoiding drawing attention to themselves. In contrast, certain individuals may opt for silence, refraining from engaging in any form of activism or opposition due to concerns for their personal security and the safety of their loved ones. Conversely, others may become more nationalistic and rally behind the regime in response to perceived foreign threats. All the aforementioned factors apply to why the Eritrean people fear the regime. Several pieces of anecdotal evidence attest that a substantial number of the middle class has compromised its principles to mitigate the ramifications of their actions should they fail to conform with the established narratives.

The fear factor extends to a section of the Eritrean diaspora too. However, we are witnessing a situation we have never witnessed before - an Intifadah-like uprising by Eritrean youth that is organized around a worldwide movement called "Brigade NHamedu." They have chapters in different parts of Europe, the Middle East, North America, and Africa. This movement comprises young Eritreans who went through all sorts of predicaments. Some were shot while crossing the border into Sudan and Ethiopia to evade conscription from the National Service. Others have been subjected to forced labor, exposed to Bedewin's atrocities while crossing the Sahara Desert in search of refuge, risked their lives while crossing the Mediterranean Sea, and so on. These young men and women hate the regime that squandered their youth. They are rightfully bitter and angry and feel betrayed by the regime. They are also highly politicized and are fearless.

The rest of the diaspora fears the regime because some own property in Eritrea and want to mitigate the risk of confiscation. Others want to be able to travel home occasionally to visit aging parents, siblings, and close relatives. Many do not want to be labeled traitors, Woyane supporters or to face the risk of being isolated by their communities. They want to enjoy annual festivals organized by PFDJ because it allows them to connect with their fellow compatriots in a setting that reminds them of home – dancing (ጓይላ), connecting, eating injera, wearing traditional garb, and socializing.

I believe one group of the Eritrean diaspora is suffering from what is known as the "Stockholm syndrome"—a unique psychological malaise that is exhibited by the captives in relation to their captors.

Stockholm syndrome is a phenomenon wherein individuals who are held hostage establish a psychological connection with their abductors during their captivity. This syndrome typically arises in situations characterized by power imbalances, such as hostage-taking, kidnappings, and abusive relationships. Emotional bonds can develop between captors and captives even though such bonds may seem irrational considering the danger and harm faced by the victims. Stockholm syndrome leads hostages to develop feelings of loyalty and affection for those who detained them captive (Singh, 2022).

In 1973, an incident involving Jan-Erik Olsson, a parolee, occurred when he attempted to rob a bank called Kreditbanken, one of Stockholm's largest financial institutions, where he took four employees hostage, including three women and one man. Olsson enlisted the help of his friend, Clark Olofsson, who was in prison at the time, to assist him. The hostages were kept confined for six days inside one of the bank's vaults. Surprisingly, upon their release, none of the hostages testified against their captors in court; instead, they began raising funds for their defense (Singh, 2022).

Another notable case is that of Patty Hearst, the granddaughter of publisher William Randolph Hearst. In 1974, she was abducted and held hostage by the Symbionese Liberation Army (SLA), described as an urban guerrilla group. During her captivity, she publicly denounced her family and the police, adopting the name "Tania." She was even seen robbing banks in San Francisco alongside the SLA - expressing sympathy for their cause. However, when Patty Hearst attempted to use Stockholm Syndrome as a defense in her 1975 trial, it did not succeed, much to the disappointment of her defense lawyer, F. Lee Bailey. Eventually, she received a commuted seven-year prison sentence and was later pardoned by President Bill Clinton, with the understanding that she had not acted of her own free will[lxi] (Singh, 2022).

The aforementioned hypothesis could be applied to the ongoing relationship between a section of the Eritrea diaspora on the one hand, and the repressive regime in Asmara and its embassies or Interest Sections in other countries on the other. Members of this group of the diaspora will tell you about the abhorrent situation back home. They will not hesitate to talk about the prevailing poverty, persecution, forced conscription of the youth, economic downturn, frustration among the population, the never-ending war with neighboring countries, life in the Eritrean countryside, and so forth. But the more they stay associated with the regime that perpetrates this agony on the people, the more they sympathize with it, and in some cases, they become apologists of the regime. This is an interesting social phenomenon that requires further sociological and psychological research.

While the aforementioned suggestion to conduct a research initiative may provide insights, it is crucial to acknowledge the possibility that the sympathy with the regime might not solely stem from genuine beliefs; it could also be driven by other factors such as vice or addiction (ኣመል ወይ ወልፊ). In ordinary life, many individuals are aware of the harmful effects of tobacco and alcohol on their health but continue using them due to addiction regardless of the harm they cause. It seems that our fellow countrymen are grappling with this ailment

13

BEING AN OUTSIDER IN AN ORGANIZATION

13.1. THE CONTEXT

Experiencing political isolation, social seclusion, and character assassination represents an incredibly arduous ordeal for any human being. This challenge becomes all the more daunting when it unfolds within an organization born out of a worldwide liberation movement that has left a mark on numerous developing countries.

The alien ideology promoted by such movements lacks meaningful roots within the socioeconomic and political landscape of the society it seeks to influence. It is akin to trying to fit into a size 58 or 60 jacket when your correct size is a more modest 38 or 40. This forced adaptation and improvisation can lead to significant missteps.

According to this ideology, society is dissected into various classes—bourgeois, petty bourgeois, worker, rich peasant, middle-level peasant, and poor peasant. Yet, discerning clear distinctions between these categories can be exceedingly challenging. Moreover, the student population and the educated segment of society are often labeled as petty bourgeois, and treated differently (with caution). Interestingly, it is suggested that this petty-bourgeois class cannot be trusted until it "commits suicide as a class." On the other hand, rich peasants, known as Kulaks, are considered enemies of the people and the struggle.

In this perspective, religion is seen as the opium of a society. A belief in God is deemed reactionary and the church is viewed as a tool for spiritually subduing the oppressed. The overarching goal of the struggle is to establish a classless society. These liberation movements are integrated into the broader global Socialist Movement, and everything within these organizations is framed as a manifestation of class struggle.

Conformity to this ideology is imperative, and questioning it comes at a significant cost. There is little tolerance for new ideas or alternative political perspectives, which are considered deviations from the established norm, and dissenters face consequences for their divergence.

Within the context of the EPLF, an organization that framed everything through the lens of class struggle, dissent in all forms was ruthlessly suppressed. Those who entertained personal viewpoints outside of the accepted ones faced severe consequences, sometimes to the point of metaphorically being "buried alive." Even personal conflicts and disagreements were politicized, blurring the line between what did or did not constitute a class struggle.

The Reformist Movement of 1973 also called Menqa'e was branded as "reactionary," "corrosive," "destructive," and "divisive," among other labels, and the solution was to annihilate it. I joined the EPLF during a time of heated debate between supporters and opponents of this movement, while figures like Isaias Afewerki and his leadership team, including Ramadan Hamed Nur and Mesfin Hagos, striving to maintain the status quo.

Although I was not an active member of the movement, I had the natural inclination to associate and engage in conversations with its proponents, as they had been my classmates during high school and at Haile Selassie I University when I was attending the freshman program. However, as I went on to deploy to combat units following military and political training, I witnessed firsthand how supporters of the movement were subjected to acts of intimidation and coercion.

My ordeal commenced when I received a summons from the then chairman of the EPLF, Isaias Afewerki, shortly after the dissolution of the committee (also known as AQerarabit Shimagle) that was tasked with finding a common platform for the two fronts to work together and ultimately form a united front. At this time, I had already been assigned as Head of Department of Information, Culture, and Education within the organization.

Upon being summoned, Isaias Afewerki informed me that I needed to undergo questioning and might need to stay with the Security Team (ሓለዋ ሰውራ) until further notice or instruction. The Security Team, led by Solomon Woldemariam, was initially uncertain about the reasons why I was sent to the Security Team, and Solomon sent someone to inquire with Isaias, who reiterated that I should remain there under custody until further notice.

Several weeks passed without any new development. After this period, the late Dawit Habtu, a member of the Security Team, contacted me and handed me a handwritten note from Isaias Afewerki himself. It became apparent that this note contained a series of questions for which I was expected to provide clarifications. As I recall, the questions began with an exploration of my background as a prelude to the main issue and then delved directly into the core topic— the Movement of 1973, also known as Menqa'e.

I was asked about my opinion concerning the Movement of 1973 and where I stood on various aspects of that movement. Given this opportunity, I articulated my perspective and repeatedly conveyed the following in writing:

The political education manual of the EPLF outlines two distinct types of contradictions: primary and secondary. The primary contradiction exists between the Front and its adversary, Ethiopia. This is an irreconcilable contradiction and it is deemed necessary to address this through violent means. On the other hand, internal differences among EPLF members are classified as secondary contradictions and are recommended to be resolved through democratic dialogue.

The Movement of 1973 represents an internal contradiction among various front members or groups, reflecting the diversity of opinions within the organization. While these perspectives may vary significantly, it is essential to emphasize that peaceful and democratic dialogue remains the preferred avenue for resolving these differences. The Movement's objective is not to undermine the EPLF from within but rather to advocate for positive change.

I, therefore, do not support the incarceration or detention of colleagues involved in the Movement.

Following the initial exchange, there was a continuous exchange of messages between Isaias and myself, with the late Dawit Habtu consistently serving as the intermediary or messenger. Throughout these exchanges, I consistently reiterated the same viewpoints, steadfastly defending certain fundamental principles that held great significance to me, despite Isaias's insinuations that my assessment was incorrect.

This ordeal went on for months at the detention center before I heard back from Isaias.

My journey took an unexpected turn when, one bright morning, Isaias called for my presence, accompanied by the late Dawit Habtu. We convened in a small cave for this discussion. Isaias informed me that I was now free to leave, but on a different assignment: instead of returning to my former unit as the head of the Department of Information, Culture, and Education, I was directed to join the Mass Organization Unit located in the vicinity of Asmara. Ermias Debessai, also known as Papayo, led this unit. Before departing, I mustered the courage to inquire about the reason for my earlier detention, seeking clarification on the perceived wrongdoing. I specifically asked about the lessons I could learn from my detention and what specific mistakes I had made to deserve such a punishment. I wasn't supposed to pose such questions to Isaias, but I did, regardless of the consequences citing my youth and inexperience as an excuse.

Isaias proceeded to speak at length, although without divulging any substantial information. Ultimately, I was left with the vague message that I may have been a "victim of circumstances." I refrained from asking further questions, well aware of the potential repercussions. To this day, no one has had the guts to provide any explanation for my detention. In 2016, over a phone conversation, Ahmed Al Qeisi said that he was approached by Haile Jebha (in charge of the Security Team) to answer some questions about me (on my involvement in the 1973 Movement) while I was in detention. Haile Jebha was trying to make a case of my detention after I was detained. Maybe at Isaias Afeworki's instruction.

As a consequence of this experience, I found myself alienated from the party, branded as a "diviant" for the rest of my stay with the EPLF. The fact that someone had a history of being detained in Halewa Sewra (EPLF's detention center) automatically carries a stigma, and I was not an exception.

During the period spent at the detention center, the deputy chief of the Security Team, Haile Jebha, unexpectedly summoned me to his office one day. Without warning, Haile Jebha raised his voice, remarking that followers of the 1973 Movement were more harmful than Ethiopian spies, a statement that left me bewildered to this day.

Prior to the above event, I also recall a significant incident involving the late Romadan Mohamed Nur, the vice chairman of the EPLF, during the time when my batch was undergoing military training and political indoctrination when I first joined EPLF. He paid a visit, stayed briefly, and left, but his words have remained etched in my memory to this day. He referred to me as a "Menqa'e" or a follower of the movement as he walked by. It was striking to consider that such a statement came from a high-ranking member of the EPLF leadership, the second most prominent figure in the organization, addressing an enthusiastic young Eritrean who had left behind the comforts of my higher education studies to join the front in the remote wilderness of Eritrea. This incident left a lasting impression, eroding any respect I had for Romadan Mohamed Nur.

My batch at Ghereghir Asmara military training camp comprised Woldemichael Abraha, the late Teklai Hareka, the late Andemichael Kahsai, the late Yemane Kidane (Jamaica), the late Ghebremichael (Qeshi), and myself. Ghebremichael (Qeshi) tragically took his own life after fatally shooting Memhir Mehreteab in Kerkebet, Barka in 1980. Both Mehreteab and I were serving as Battalion Commanders in Battalion 27, where Ghebremichael (Qeshi) held the position of Platoon Commissar under our command. The distressing incident unfolded after a clandestine party meeting, during which Mehreteab and his group criticized Ghebremichael for perceived cowardice. Regrettably, while Mehreteab was taking a nap, Ghebremichael abruptly shot and killed him before taking his own life. At the time of the incident, I was just a few meters away, also during an afternoon nap under the shade of a tree. The tragic events of that day left an indelible mark on our shared history.

In contrast to Romadan Mohamed Nur's disheartening remarks, Tewolde Iyob and Woldenkiel Haile, distinguished veterans of the EPLF, took the initiative to visit me upon learning about my enlistment and military training in Geherghir Asmara. It was a delightful experience engaging in conversations with both of them on separate occasions. Their words of encouragement and valuable advice resonated deeply with me. During our formative years around Kidane Mehret Church, Tewolde Eyob and Woldemichael Haile (Wedi Haile) were revered as our local heroes and happened to be neighbors of my grandmother. I have not seen Tewolde since then.

Prior to independence, my last significant interaction with Isaias occurred in 1988 when I was serving as a member of the editorial board of the internal magazine *Harbegna*. During that time, I had been tasked with interviewing the Secretary- General of the EPLF about the issue of unity among Eritrean organizations. On the eve of the interview, I was invited to have dinner with a friend, Tesfamichael Ghebremedhin (Sheriffo), who was recently married and on his honeymoon. Isaias arrived late in the evening after Tesfamichael and I had already had dinner and he joined us for a drink. I do not recall whether Isaias asked for dinner or not. Isaias was accompanied by Naizghi Kiflu, and aside from them, Yemane Ghebreab was present, along with Tesfamichael's wife, Akberet - Gual Badre. Currently, Tesfamichael is languishing in one of PFDJ's dungeons. He was taken away by security agents in August 2014.

During the get-together, Naizghi Kiflu playfully teased Yemane Ghebreab about his past intention to form a Marxist Party along with Andeberhan Woldeghiorghis while they were in the United States.

Yemane's response was calm, merely asking to be left alone. Naizghi also started teasing me but Isaias consistently urged Naizghi to stop. However, the conversation took an unexpected turn. Despite my belief that Isaias was not drunk, Isaias began repeating, among other things, that he had been forced to kill his colleagues (ንብጸተይ ከም ዝቐትል ጊሮምኒ) who belonged to the Movement of 1973 (ኣዕናዊ ምንቅስቓስ ናይ 1973). This revelation left me utterly shocked, unable to comprehend why Isaias would make such a statement in the presence of someone (me) he had ostracized as far back as 1976. To this day, it remains a perplexing enigma for me.

13.2. WHAT IS IT LIKE TO LIVE A LIFE OF POLITICAL ISOLATION, SOCIAL SECLUSION, AND CHARACTER ASSASSINATION

Since my ostracization by Isaias, I was consistently regarded with suspicion by EPLF cadres. Regardless of the assignments I received, people were informed that I was one of the remnants of the Movement of 1973 and should, therefore, be under surveillance. The weight of this suspicion and scrutiny on an individual who was deeply committed to his country and willing to make the necessary sacrifices cannot be overstated. Character assassination campaigns became the norm. In 1978, a prominent member of the Central Committee— Habtemariam Debtera— told a close friend of mine that he should stay away from me. My friend told me about this after independence.

After my discovery of the clandestine party, every party member knew about my awareness, and they were instructed to closely observe my movements. Despite the caution exercised by party members, I occasionally stumbled upon members having secret meetings while I was serving in the capacity of Battalion Commissar in Brigade 31. In my role as Battalion Commissar with Brigade 44 Battalion 1, I found party correspondences that were negligently left on the desk by my colleague, Ali Manjus (Battalion Commander). While I read these correspondences, I chose to remain silent. Stumbling on party members' meeting was also not uncommon. They usually meet at odd hours.

Newly recruited party members were encouraged to work against me as a means to demonstrate their loyalty to the party. I did not enjoy the same level of access to information as privileged party members did. Any attempt to seek information or ask questions was seen as tantamount to challenging the party's position and was sometimes perceived as deliberate defiance, leading to its own set of consequences. Regardless of these practices, I never refrained from expressing my viewpoints on different issues.

On certain occasions, clandestine party meetings are held bringing together all party members within the Battalion. During these events, I found myself assigned to lead reconnaissance missions, often with a small unit, along the enemy or behind enemy lines. The objective seemed to be to keep me occupied and away from the meetings in session. One such instance occurred in the Barka region while we were actively engaged in military skirmishes with the ELF. Others happened while serving in Brigade 44.

One day (this was after 1991), Tesfamariam Tekeste (Wedi Bashai) and I were engaged in a casual conversation over coffee at Bar Royal, Asmara. We had been very close at one point. Abruptly, he asked me if I knew why I had not been endorsed as a party member when my name was submitted to one of the clandestine party's cells. I expressed my lack of awareness regarding this development. In response, he said, "One peasant mentioned that Semere Solomon does not believe in Marxism and, therefore, does not qualify to be a party member."

Another incident occurred during the intense internecine war between the EPLF and ELF in Barka in 1980. I found myself in the midst of this unfortunate conflict, witnessing brothers turning against each other for reasons that seemed to solely serve the egos of our leaders. Amid the military skirmishes, I collaborated closely with one of the Battalion Commanders, a member of the artillery unit as well as the clandestine party whose name was Wedi Teka. He was deeply impressed by the speed, agility, and courage displayed by the battalion under my command. Our camaraderie grew, but during a casual conversation, he inquired whether I was a member of the clandestine party. I brushed off his question, feigning ignorance. However, a few days later, he began to avoid me, and our closeness diminished. I suspected he must have learned I was not a party member. Bringing up our conversation with his colleagues could have jeopardized his life and most likely he chose not to do so.

One evening shortly after gaining independence, Ahmed Al Qeisi graciously invited me and two other colleagues (names withheld) to his home for dinner. Our gathering delved into an intimate conversation about the political landscape of the time. As the night progressed, one of the two colleagues (whose names are withheld) confided in me about the animosity he harbored towards me during the war of independence. Upon inquiry, he revealed that he had clear directives from the party to hate me (ውድብይ ከምኡ ስለ ዝበለትኒ). I couldn't help but express my disbelief, stating, "So you hated me simply because the party instructed you to do so?" His unwavering confirmation was disheartening, and he made it clear that he held no remorse for his actions. Disappointed, I confronted him, highlighting my disdain for individuals like him who had invested 19 years in education (12+5+2) yet blindly adhered to the party's counsel without granting the person in question, namely myself, the benefit of the doubt. In response to his arrogant stance, I asserted, "One day, your party will betray you." I was so upset (by the whole conversation) that I abruptly stood up and left Qeisi's place. True to my prediction, the party indeed betrayed him. He and I became good friends at a later stage.

Criticizing party members had its own repercussions. An incident comes to mind when the leadership of Brigade 4 failed to fulfill its obligations during an offensive unleashed against the Ethiopian army in North Eastern Sahel. I considered raising this issue during a broader meeting and consulted with my Brigade Commander (Breray) on the incident, but I was informed that the matter had already been resolved, seemingly aimed at protecting certain party members that belonged to Brigade 4.

During my tenure with Battalion 27, I worked hard to optimize the battalion's resources and enhance efficiency by introducing committees—literacy/education, cultural activities, and Trenches' committees—organized at the battalion and company level. This approach was scaled up to the North Eastern Sahel front and later on other fronts like the Nakfa front. Before I was transferred to Brigade 44, Teklai Habtesellassie, the Commander of Brigade 31, commended my high-level organizational skills and bravery. However, he mentioned that I had been a solitary person. That was not without a reason (he and his party colleagues were the ones alienating me) and he knew it. My acquaintance with Teklai dates back to 1975 when we both served as rank-and-file members in Berhe Tsada's platoon in 1975.

In this Orwellian reality, one exists in a constant state of surveillance, my every move meticulously observed. Party members gang up, forming a formidable force in meetings, ready to pounce on any uttered word, subjecting the speaker to a relentless barrage of scrutiny and criticism. Even those who were innocent members of the front were cautioned against associating with me.

People questioned my associations with any member of the front. One day, Teklai Habtesellassie, our Brigade Commander, summoned me to his office and inquired about my relationship with the late Adhanon Ghebremariam. The late Adhanom had previously held the position of Brigade Commissar in Brigade 23, and we used to spend time together during a two-week- long cartography course. I explained to Teklai that I enjoyed being around Adhanom because it was fun to hang out with personalities like him and that the conversations were intellectually stimulating. Teklay advised me to maintain some distance from Adhanom, as he was not well received by the organization and its leadership.

However, I never refrained from talking to Adhanom, despite Teklay's advice. After independence in Asmara, I shared this incident with Adhanom while he was serving as the prosecutor general at the Ministry of Justice.

Contrary to Teklai Habtesellassie's attitude towards me, Adhanom would often tell me that the late Gherezgabiher Andemariam (Wuchu) always held me in high esteem. Adhanom recounted instances where, during Brigade Commanders' meetings, Teklai Habtesellassie would speak negatively about me, and Gherezghiher Andemariam would consistently rise to my defense. He would assert, "ሰመረ ሰሎሞን ጅግና እዩ። ብዘዕብሉ ሕማቕ ምዝርብ ተብዘሑ ኢኻ," which translates in Tigrigna as, "Semere Solomon is a brave commander; you are too tough on him." Perhaps it stemmed from my intimate collaboration with his Brigade during the joint offensive against the Ethiopian army in 1979. At that time, Tekle Manjius, now Brigadier General, served under the command of Wuchu in Brigade 4, holding the position of Battalion Commissar, just like myself. He consistently expressed praise and admiration for my Battalion and its commendable performance throughout the offensive.

Furthermore, on various occasions when Major General Wuchu interacted with my younger brother, he expressed, "ሓውኻ ጅግና እዩ። እንታይድም ገዲፉና እንዶ ከይዱ።" This translates to, "Your brother is brave;

SEMERE SOLOMON

it is a pity that he left us." This was after he heard that I left to join the UN.

Chapter 9 bore witness to my stand against several party members regarding the formulation of the new political education manual. The crux of the matter rested upon defining the front's philosophical underpinnings, an ideological tug-of- war between Marxism and social justice, and Marxism vis-à-vis nationalism or patriotism. My staunch political views and principles were not well received by the majority of party members in the committee until high-level intervention by the Secretary-General himself.

One day, I remember rejoicing after hearing the news that the Romanian dictator, Nicolae Ceauşescu, had been overthrown. I truly meant it. A few days later, someone reported this to the Secretary General's office in Amberbeb. These incidents may appear minor, but the underlying message is that my statements were under close surveillance.

My life unfolded in a perpetual state of insecurity, solely because of advocating for the resolution of secondary contradictions through democratic dialogue and opposing incarceration of the followers of the Movement of 1973 as a viable solution.

This dystopian existence extends its invasive tendrils into the personal sphere, where every aspect of one's life is meticulously monitored—from friendships to dating choices (this is not an exaggeration). It was a life where tireless dedication to a cause was met with continuous skepticism, a never-ending interrogation of one's beliefs and actions. In this world, conformity is demanded, dissent is punished, and individuality is a dangerous liability in the relentless struggle for ideological dominance.

If you closely followed Brigadier General Tekeste Haile's interview with Antonio Tesfay on TV Sened Ertra, you would be intrigued to discover how Ghebrehiwot (Wedi Hambir) and Tekeste were recruited into the clandestine party. The late Major General Gheberegziabher Andemariam (Wuchu) individually summoned them, expressing that both had demonstrated loyalty to the organization ("ውድባዊ እምነትኩም ተረጋጊጹ."), the EPLF. At the time of their enlistment, they had each dedicated over seventeen years of service to the organization, with Wedi Hambir and Tekeste Haile joining the EPLF in 1972 and 1973, respectively.

In addition to their long-standing commitment, they had also risen to significant positions within the military hierarchy. Both were told they had demonstrated loyalty to the organization "ውድባዊ እምነትኩም ተረጋጊጹ." One cannot help but ponder the weight of such a pronouncement. Could you fathom being informed that all the sacrifices made before joining the clandestine party were seemingly in vain? Wouldn't such a revelation evoke contemplation for an honorable suicide? This was tantamount to adding salt to injury to say the least.

Consider the challenging life that the late Worku Zerai and individuals of her kind had to endure over the years. Upon their release from prison, they found themselves consistently being the subject of political indoctrination at the Cadres' School of the EPLF. Every member of the organization was compelled to learn about their perceived "betrayal" and relentless efforts to undermine the EPLF from within. One can only imagine the reluctance of others to approach them after such indoctrination.

The news of the passing of our esteemed Worku Zerai in January 2024 was truly disheartening. May her soul rest in eternal peace! Worku lived a life that mirrored my own in many ways. While the sentiments she harbored and the wounds she endured may have been buried with her, nobody would dare deny her resilience, her dedication to her country, and, above all, her defiance against the regime and PFDJ.

13.3. THE CHOICES

I faced a series of six stark choices during a challenging period in my life. These choices were as follows:

First, I could have succumbed to the overwhelming despair and suffering that many had faced and opted for the tragic path of suicide, as a distressing number had done before me.

Second, I could have allowed the relentless pressures of my circumstances to push me to the brink of insanity.

Third, I might have chosen to surrender to the enemy, giving in to the demands and pressures they imposed.

The fourth option was to escape the turmoil of my homeland by fleeing across the border into Sudan, with aspirations of eventually making my way to Europe or North America.

The fifth option, perhaps the most poignant, was to meet my fate on the battlefield, risking death while serving my country. Despite being constantly exposed to this peril, I did not opt for it recklessly.

The sixth option entailed demonstrating remorse by denouncing the Menqa'e movement. This would have potentially paved the way for my reinstatement as the Head of Information, Culture, and Education, granted me access to the clandestine party, and eventually offered a clear path to becoming a member of the Central Committee. However, I made a conscious decision not to pursue this option. Accepting the incarceration (and later on the harsh death sentence) of my colleagues was a moral compromise I simply could not take, as it would have left me with a heavy conscience. Such a choice would have cast a long shadow over the remainder of my life.

Instead, I made a decision that defied all these choices. I opted not to take any of them. Instead, I resolved to persevere and continue the fight, regardless of the monumental sacrifices it might demand. I steadfastly held onto my beliefs and remained unwavering in my commitment. I chose to stay the course and, against all odds, was fortunate enough to live long enough to pen this memoir.

After Eritrea's independence, several of my colleagues came forward to apologize for their past behavior toward me during the war. Some explained that they had acted the way they did because they were instructed to do so. Some said it was fear for their safety that drove them to keep their distance from me. Others acknowledged that I had been gravely misunderstood, facing a unique set of challenges. Some of them marveled at my resilience and tenacity in enduring multiple psychological wars. One colleague said, "You went through hell but never capitulated. I admire your strength and resolve; I would have considered suicide or fleeing the country at the very least had I been in your shoes."

Even a dedicated member of the party expressed regret, stating, "You had foreseen the fate of the EPLF. I wish we had followed your lead or, at the very least, listened to your advice." These expressions of regret and admiration highlighted my integrity and determination and the extraordinary path I chose to follow in the face of adversity.

People may question how I endured this harrowing experience. Someone enduring years of isolation, character defamation, and social isolation is at risk of succumbing to despair, experiencing psychological distress, or surrendering to the pressure. A colleague said that emerging from such a nightmarish ordeal, with one's sanity intact, is a remarkable feat, warranting exploration as a compelling research topic for experts in the field of psychology.

There could be several factors that contributed to my mental sanity.

Being a person who handled situations of this nature with composure might have been one of the reasons. In retrospect, I still wonder how this was possible. Could this be a gift or blessing from God?

My ability to withstand the pressure might have been a result of the immunity I developed over the years. People respond to external stimuli in various ways, and perhaps this was my natural reaction.

The third reason stemmed from my commitment to patience. I firmly believed that, with time, the truth would inevitably come to light, circumstances would shift, and even the most enduring political honeymoon periods would ultimately wane. I never lost sight of this overarching vision. I remained resolute in my conviction that I could contribute to the cause as a dedicated nationalist without resorting to pseudo-leftist tactics to curry favor with the leadership. This steadfast approach ultimately proved to be a wise choice, and I believe it paid dividends.

The fourth reason stemmed from my deep love and passion for books. As a voracious reader, I sought solace within the pages of books during times of distress and despair. My literary journey encompassed the entirety of Russian classics, including the works of Tolstoy, Dostoevski, Sholokhov (And Quiet Flows the Don), Chekhov, Gorki, Gogol, Pushkin, Pasternak, and Solzhenitsyn. I also delved into Marxist literature, immersing myself in the writings of Marx, Engels, Lenin, Stalin, Mao Tse-tung, General Giap, Afanasyev, and Enver Hoxha. My curiosity extended to authors like Basil Davidson, Erlich Haggai, George Orwell, Robert Lamb, Robert Kaplan, Conti Rossini, Alberto Pollera, Tekeste Negash, Nawal El Saadawi,

Tesfatsion Medhanie, as well as Be'alu Girma's "Oromia," Richard Punkhrust, and John Spencer. Giovanni Boccaccio's *The Decameron*, Mario Puzzo's *The Godfather*, Kafka's *The Trail*, Naguib Mahfouz's *Children of Gabalawi*, Tarrant's *The Red Orchestra*, and Ngugi's *Petals of Blood* also found their places in the list of books read among many more. I even ventured into Amharic, even amid combat and while relaxing in the trenches.

For me, reading was akin to a religious experience, and I often pondered what might have become of me in the absence of books.

It might also be attributed to the fact that I had a circle of close friends with whom I could confide. These were friends I could trust, individuals who wouldn't divulge my secrets or use them for their own political gain. These were people who wholeheartedly believed in me.

Last but not least, I firmly believe that my tenacity, resilience, and confidence have not only enabled me to survive but also to thrive in life. However, this does not at all insinuate that I was a perfect person.

It gives me immense pleasure to have survived and to narrate this on my behalf and on behalf of hundreds (if not thousands) like me.

14

My tenure at the Ministry of Education: Tapping into domestic resources while enhancing international collaboration – a case study

14.1. 1991–1998

I was fortunate to support the nascent nation to stand on its own feet by serving as Director General of Planning and Development, at the Ministry of Education, from 1991 to 1998 until I faced the predicament of other senior government officials "froze/sidelined." I believe these were the golden days of the ministry and hence worth dedicating a chapter on it.

The education sector in Eritrea was characterized by low enrolment rate, poor quality, irrelevant curriculum, and rundown infrastructure in 1991. An IMF working paper records 36 percent enrolment rate at the primary level, 20 per- cent at middle school, and only around 12 percent at the secondary level (Zuzana Brixiova,

2001). According to the report, the destruction of infrastructure and the disintegration of the social services during the war caused deterioration in the quality of education, and as a result, female and male illiteracy rates were about 80–90 at the end of the war, respectively (Zuzana Brixiova, 2001). The Net Enrolment Rates—(NER)—were 22.4, 7.0, and 8.4 for elementary, middle, and secondary levels, respectively[lxiv] (Ministry of Education, Eritrea, 2003).

Although data is not available, the percentage of qualified teachers at the elementary level stood low in 1991. Textbooks were in short supply. The content of the curriculum mirrored that of Ethiopia; a different socio-economic context. It was neither culturally relevant nor did it align with the provisional government's new education policy that promoted the use of local language as a medium of instruction at the elementary level. This meant the ministry had a daunting task to shoulder and numerous challenges to address. This was compounded by the fact that the coffers of the government were empty; hence, lack of resources.

A sector analysis had to be conducted to provide insight into the current state of the sector concerning various access and quality indicators. Subsequently, an education policy needed to be formulated, pending ratification by the provisional national assembly. The ministry also had the task of clearly defining its role within the framework of the national education policy and in alignment with the overarching government policy of national reconstruction.

Additionally, a comprehensive curriculum overhaul was necessary to ensure alignment with the new national education policy. The organization of the school structure was slated for revision to see whether transitioning from a 5-2-4 structure to a 6-2-4 was a possibility. Simultaneously, there was a need to create a budget and establish a medium-term strategic plan.

Resource availability posed a significant challenge, as previously mentioned. Therefore, a strategy had to be worked out to forge partnerships with both local and international stakeholders.

Between 1991 and mid-1998, I had the privilege of serving the Ministry of Education in the role of Director General for Planning and Development. During this time, I played a pivotal role in shaping the ministry's direction and progress.

Major accomplishments included spearheading the drafting of the sector analysis (which culminated in the drafting of a paper "Prospects for Education in Eritrea" in 1991), the development and implementation of the sector policy, organizational structure (along with the mandate or scope of work of all the departments, divisions, and zonal education offices), and the drafting of medium-term strategic plan. My colleagues and I defined the ministry's four critical responsibilities. These included (i) the formulation of the national policy for education, (ii) the formulation of a strategic plan, (iii) the formulation of a regulatory framework to ensure quality and standards (this comprised the accreditation of all the education programs that the ministry provided and how they are assessed), and (iv) the training of education professionals (teachers and other professionals) and research.

In addition to this, I was entrusted with the crucial task of coordinating all donor support that flowed into the ministry. This encompassed working closely with various international organizations and funding agencies, such as the World Bank, Danish International Development Agency (DANIDA), United States Agency for International Development (USAID), Finnish International Development Agency (FINNIDA), Swedish International Development Cooperation Agency—(SIDA), Department for International Development (DFID), Japan International Cooperation Agency (JICA), Norwegian Church Aid (NCA), Agence Française de

Développement (AFD), Cooperazione Italiana, and other bilateral funding agencies. My portfolio extended to liaising with organizations like UNICEF, UNDP, UNFPA, WFP, Peace Corps Volunteers, VSO, Dutch volunteers (TVET), the Dutch government, and many more.

I also witnessed the release of the first Education Statistical Handbook developed by the Ministry of Education in 1991–92. This served as the basis for all planning undertakings by the ministry. The ministry never missed issuing this statistical bulletin ever since.

I was fortunate to attend a one-year Graduate Program on Educational Planning and Administration at the International Institute for Educational Planning (IIEP), a UNESCO institute, in Paris, France. It was an enriching experience, and I was proud to be recognized as one of the top 10 percent of his batch. Dr. Jacques Hallak, the Director of IIEP at the time, even honored me as the best among my peers during the graduation ceremony held at the prestigious IIEP premises in Paris. Students from forty to fifty countries, holding first and second degrees, attended the program.

Throughout my career, I actively participated in regional and international conferences, furthering my knowledge of the sector and my commitment to the field of education and development. These experiences have not only enriched my knowledge but have also allowed me to contribute significantly to the advancement of education policies and initiatives, both nationally and internationally.

I took on the role of Chairperson for the Ethio-Eritrea Joint Technical Committee, a significant responsibility tasked with harmonizing the education policies, curricula, the organization of the school system, and accreditation of educational credentials of the two sovereign countries—Ethiopia and Eritrea. Under my leadership, the Joint Committee also successfully launched a student exchange program, fostering collaboration between higher education institutions in the two countries. Eritrean students had the opportunity to pursue studies in fields such as Medicine, Pharmacy, and Engineering in Ethiopia, while Ethiopian students attended the College of Marine Resource and other faculties in Eritrea. Unfortunately, this collaborative effort was disrupted by the outbreak of war between the two countries in 1997.

Furthermore, I played a pivotal role in leading a ministerial committee focused on drafting a Memorandum of Understanding (MOU) with our Kenyan counterparts in the field of education. This effort aimed to strengthen ties and cooperation between the two nations in the educational sphere.

In addition to these responsibilities, I extensively traveled to negotiate bilateral collaborations between Eritrea and various other countries, reflecting a commitment to fostering international partnerships in education.

14.2. NOTABLE PROJECTS/PROGRAMS NEGOTIATED AND EXECUTED UNDER MY OVERSIGHT

Various organizations and entities played significant roles in the development and support of education in Eritrea. DANIDA, for instance, contributed by supporting school rehabilitation and construction initiatives, sponsoring teacher training programs, assisting in curriculum development, and printing millions of textbooks for pupils under a project spanning five years.

Another key player in the educational landscape was DFID, which provided technical assistance to support the development of English language curriculum in schools. Additionally, DFID extended scholarships to ministry officials, allowing them to pursue undergraduate and graduate programs at prestigious universities in the United Kingdom.

The Salesians of Don Bosco, operating through the Catholic Church, established the Don Bosco Technical School in Dekemhare. This institution offered training in various trades to young boys and girls, including automotive, metalwork, carpentry, and more. Students also received education in information technology and academics. Each trade program lasted two years, culminating in a national exam. Unfortunately, the government seized control of this technical school in August 2022 after twenty-three years of service.

Norway's Redd Barna played a pivotal role in Eritrea's education sector by sponsoring the construction of the Teacher Training Institute extension in Asmara and a boarding school in Asmat. It also facilitated the donation of sports materials to Eritrean children through Norwegian Winter Sports Gold medalist Johann Olav Koss.

The Lutheran World Federation contributed to the education system by supporting the construction and rehabilitation of numerous schools throughout Eritrea.

Collaborating with LWF, we developed a significant program aimed at supporting school rehabilitation in Eritrea. LWF submitted the proposal on behalf of the Ministry of Education, and following a competitive process, it was selected for an award by the Government of Sweden. The funds, amounting to millions of kronor, granted by the government, were utilized to rehabilitate multiple schools in the western lowlands of Eritrea. Aster Solomon, a senior technical staff member of my department, played a pivotal role in leading the design process and bringing it to a successful conclusion.

The LWF World Service began its involvement in Eritrea in 1992 through the signing of an agreement with the Eritrean government and the Evangelical Church of Eritrea (ECE). Initially intending to stay engaged until the mid-2000s, the primary focus of the initial phase was on revitalizing the ECE's Development Department and providing training for its staff. Unfortunately, this plan faced disruption in mid-1995 when the Government of Eritrea issued a proclamation. This proclamation prohibited churches and affiliated entities from conducting relief, rehabilitation, or development programs, abruptly interrupting the transition period from an international to a national church partner.[lxv]

Furthermore, the ministry collaborated with UNICEF on projects related to school rehabilitation, construction, teacher training, girls' education, and curriculum development.

UNDP played a crucial role in capacity-building programs, including sponsoring my scholarship for a graduate program in Paris, France.

The World Food Program (WFP) supported school feeding programs, ensuring that students had access to nourishing meals.

One notable effort involved my team and I working for over two years to develop a cooperation program between the World Bank and the Government of Eritrea. This initiative aimed to create a Technical and Vocational Education and Training (TVET) program, scheduled for implementation within five years. However, the government unexpectedly canceled the program just two days before its scheduled signing in Washington, DC, leaving me baffled by the decision and its abrupt termination.

My team and I initiated several interesting programs during my tenure, one of which was the Institutional Linkage Program with Bristol University in the United Kingdom, generously sponsored by DANIDA. Dr. Teame Mebrahtu, my counterpart at Bristol University, eloquently described this pro- gram in an interview conducted by the Centre for Comparative and International Research in Education (CIRE) at Bristol University on August 8, 2017. Dr. Mebrahtu shared:

> A third area which gave me great satisfaction whilst serving the University was the immense effort and sacrifice I made to build bridges between my alma mater in my second home, the UK, and the Ministry of Education in my country of birth, Eritrea. The Bristol-Eritrea Link Program which was sponsored by the Danish Organization DANIDA, resulted in the production of 1 PhD and 48 M.Ed. degree-holding Eritreans on-site in Bristol and in the professional upgrading of 250 School Directors, Supervisors, and District Education Officers over a period of three, in-service summers in Eritrea. Designing these tailor-made in-service modules and teaching and running them in Asmara were by no means easy tasks. The professional and financial benefits of this Link Program, which lasted for about a decade, were also of immense significance to the University of Bristol. Another area of activity recognized by many national and international educators as an accomplishment were the four International Conferences I organized on topical professional issues[lxvi] (Mebrahtu, 2017).

Another program of a similar nature was established at my initiative, forging a linkage between the Ministry of Education and the International Institute for Educational Planning and Administration (IIEP, UNESCO). This initiative provided opportunities to several Ministry officials to study in France for a year-long graduate program in Educational Planning and Administration, aimed at enhancing their capacity to manage education systems. Once again, DANIDA provided crucial sponsorship.

Additionally, IIEP, UNESCO and the Ministry of Education collaborated on a tracer study of Technical and Vocational Education and Training (TVET) graduates, made possible through the sponsorship of the Japan International Cooperation Agency (JICA). It was aimed at assessing how effective the program was and what the graduates ended up doing after graduation.

Furthermore, a select group of ministry colleagues attended analogous courses at the National Institute of Educational Planning and Administration (NIEPA) in New Delhi, India. NIEPA, situated in the heart of India's capital, is renowned for its research-focused approach to education.

The Ministry also collaborated with IIEP to organize a weeklong regional training program on monitoring the quality of education following the experience accumulated under the South African Consortium for Monitoring Education Quality (SACMEQ). Representatives of several neighboring countries were represented in the session.

The Hacin Foundation, a Swiss nongovernmental organization (NGO), played a pivotal role in establishing a computer laboratory at Barka Secondary School and funded a project to sink a well at Tsada Krstian Secondary School. The concept note for the establishment of the computer lab was developed by a highly skilled information technology (IT) expert and entrepreneur in the person of Tecle Abraha and was expected to be scaled up once it proved itself to be effective. The computer lab was set up but it was unfortunate the Ministry did not scale it up to other secondary schools after I left. Nor was Tekle given the opportunity to pilot the concept that was so dear and close to his heart. And he offered to do it pro bono.

Under my oversight, various volunteer programs were implemented, including the Peace Corps, Volunteer Service Overseas (VSO), and a similar initiative in the Netherlands. Peace Corps was suspended in June 1998, and all the forty-nine volunteers were repatriated to their country[lxvii] (Corps, 1998). These dedicated volunteers played a crucial role in teaching English, Sciences, and other technical and vocational skills in numerous schools. Beyond English instruction, they also provided valuable training to Eritrean teachers on fluent English communication and effective English teaching methodologies in the classroom. The rehabilitation of elementary schools received essential support from the Norwegian Church Aid (NCA).

Another significant achievement was the establishment of Eritrea's first UNESCO National Commission following my return from my studies in Paris at the IIEP/ UNESCO.

During my tenure at the ministry, I was involved in negotiations with the Catholic Diocese of Eritrea. Led by Bishop Zekarias Yohannes, the team sought the return of schools formerly owned by the church before they were confiscated by the Dergue. In return, they offered to compensate the Government of Eritrea by constructing new schools if granted suitable land. Notably, this included premises such as Comboni College Asmara and Lasalle among others. Despite these negotiations, an official response to the Catholic Church's request was not provided.

Initiating a school twinning program, my team and I collaborated with the Europe Desk of the Ministry of Foreign Affairs, under the oversight of Teame Tewoldeberhan. We crafted a user-friendly format for school profiles, intended for completion by Zonal Education Offices. Ghirmai Haile – a senior technical staff member of the department - played a crucial role in translating these school profiles into English. Subsequently, we extensively distributed them to Eritrean Embassies in Europe, aiming to explore the potential to engage schools interested in the school-twinning program.

I took the initiative and worked to reactivate the Eritrean Scouting Association after discussions with Mr. Beraki Ghebresellasssie, who, at the time, held a ministerial position at the ministry following independence. Launching a consultation process involving both freedom fighters and civilians, particularly former members of the Scouts Association, was crucial in understanding how to smoothly set things in motion.

I vividly remember meeting with Dr. Michael Ghebrehiwot Nebaray, a veteran physician, EPLF member, and former Scouts Association member, seeking his insights on the matter. His advice remains etched in my memory; he emphasized the Scouts Movement's three principles: "Duty to God, duty to others, and duty to self," boldly enshrined in the Constitution. He cautioned against compromising these principles, alluding to the potential challenges arising from former freedom fighters with varying beliefs in God. Impressed by his words of wisdom, we adhered to this guidance.

After laying the groundwork, I established a committee comprising former Scout Association members, developed a comprehensive scope of work, and set the task in motion. Following thorough preparations, Eritrea swiftly inaugurated its Scouts Association.

Right after gaining independence, my colleagues and I recognized the importance of acquainting high school students with their society and actively contributing to its well-being. I formulated the initial concept note for the Students Summer Program, which received official endorsement from the Ministry of Education after thorough deliberations with ministry staff and Regional Education Offices. Kidane Solomon, my elder brother, played a crucial role in refining the concept note. Since its approval, the program has remained consistently active.

The scarcity of reading materials in Eritrea was evident, prompting my colleagues and me to recognize the necessity of initiating a children's magazine to foster a reading habit among children. Taking the lead, I assembled a concept note and submitted it to UNICEF, seeking funding for its publication. I approached four prominent Tigrigna language experts, namely the late Abraham Sahle, Amanuel Sahle, Tekie Tesfai, and the late Ghirmai Ghebremeskel, inviting them to manage the project. With their consent, a comprehensive scope of work was developed.

The subsequent step involved setting the Editorial Board in motion, with the late Abraha Sahle serving as its chair. "Qolahta" children's magazine gained popularity among children. Grateful for the contributions of these four literary giants, the magazine successfully became a reality.

After gaining independence, we were confronted with the challenge of navigating and leveraging a distance education program that had been established during the Dergue regime. This radio program was designed for the adult population of Eritrea. However, with the EPLF assuming control, uncertainty loomed regarding how to effectively utilize both the facility and the personnel managing it. I was given the responsibility to conduct an assessment and provide recommendations for its upcoming use.

The consultation process with the program's experts proved to be time-consuming, but with their assistance, I gained a comprehensive understanding of the program's objectives and how we could best make use of it. Following extensive deliberations, we collectively decided to target teachers, aiming to enhance their mastery of subject matter and teaching methodologies. Subsequently, my recommendations were formally submitted to the Ministry, received endorsement, and a dedicated budget was allocated to sustain the program. This pragmatic approach was the most feasible given the prevailing conditions at that time. The consultation process added a touch of magic.

According to a study conducted by the International Monetary Fund (IMF), the gross enrollment rate[lxviii] experienced significant growth from 1991/92 to 1997/98. Specifically, the rates increased from 36% to 51% at the elementary level, 20% to 36% at the middle school level, and 12% to 16% at the secondary level during this period. (Zuzana Brixiova, 2001).

Eritrea: School Enrollment Ratios, 1991/92-1997/98

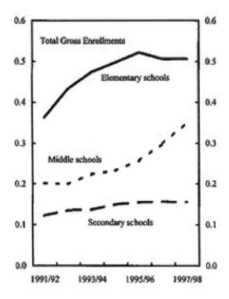

Interventions in the internal affairs of the ministry by external groups, notably PFDJ, were not uncommon. I recall a specific incident in which a businessman sent by the PFDJ approached our office, requesting exclusive rights to manufacture and distribute chalk to all schools. Another group also approached the ministry seeking a monopoly on the distribution of educational materials. In response, I affirmed that all procurement processes would be conducted openly and competitively. These responses did not fly well with PFDJ.

I vividly remember another instance when a consulting firm was tasked with conducting remote sensing of a plot of land for the construction of an educational institute in Halhalé, Debub Region. Despite our reservations, the consulting firm was awarded the contract without a competitive bidding process.

An equally noteworthy event was the introduction of religious education into all schools. This decision was made during one of the sessions of the Provisional National Assembly without prior consultation with the Ministry of Education and without any supporting research. We proposed conducting a comprehensive study to assess the validity of this policy. The study that we conducted could not identify any compelling reasons for introducing religious education into our school system. Nevertheless, the policy was implemented.

The termination of the ministry's collaboration with the World Bank was another significant development, as discussed earlier.

Furthermore, an unusual practice was observed, where civilian members of the Ministry of Education were not afforded the same treatment as former freedom fighters. On occasion, the minister would convene meetings to which civilian members were not invited, even when no confidential matters were being discussed. I raised this concern with the minister, and thankfully, it was not repeated. There were moments when civilian members of the ministry would visit my office to inquire whether I was a former EPLF member. In confidence, two ministry employees on separate occasions remarked, "You are different from the rest of your colleagues."

As the Director-General of Planning and Development, I used to accompany Minister Osman Saleh to numerous cabinet meetings. This was particularly routine during the government's formulation of sectoral strategies. The series of brainstorming sessions, presided over by the President himself, aimed to establish sectoral policies, mission statements, ministerial mandates, sectoral strategies, and the corresponding programs needed to achieve them.

These exercises proved to be valuable. Participating in discussions about the sector policies, strategies, and priorities of other ministries allowed for a comprehensive understanding of where the country is headed to. It was also aimed at ensuring coordination between sectors that was crucial to achieving the ultimate goal of national reconstruction.

During these meetings with Osman, I took on the responsibility of preparing all the relevant documents, including position papers, briefing notes and talking points for discussions. When permission was granted, I could express my opinion in these meetings. As a keen observer of the prevailing dynamics, I made adjustments to our presentations and plans as deemed necessary or is subsequent ministerial meetings.

I encountered some challenges at the outset before actively participating in these sessions. The guidance provided by Minister Osman Saleh regarding the expectations from the President's Office was initially unclear. There were instances when the requirements differed from what we had prepared for the presentation. Reflecting on this initial experience, I began seeking insights from colleagues in other ministries to gain a clearer understanding of the expectations, which I found challenging to obtain directly from the minister.

With all due respect to the minister, it seemed he faced significant challenges in grasping the requirements accurately. Additionally, despite thorough preparation through briefing notes, he often displayed nervousness in meetings and tended to veer into unnecessary details rather than articulating the main points succinctly. Sometimes, you would feel like grabbing the microphone and talking on his behalf.

In a particular session, I was tasked with presenting background data and information to justify the rationale behind our strategy and related programs. I began by sharing key indicators that were relevant for measuring progress in education. These indicators encompassed gender-disaggregated gross and net enrollment ratios, transition rates between different education levels, pupil-to-teacher ratio at the different levels of the school system, the proportion of education budget as of the overall recurrent budget of the government, etc.

I provided a comparative analysis with Sub-Saharan African countries, highlighting, for instance, that the allocation of the education budget as a percentage of the overall recurrent budget was at 4 percent, significantly below the Sub-Saharan average of 11 percent. Ghebresellassie Yosief, the then Minister of Finance, contested my argument, suggesting that the ministry could secure a larger budget if requested. The President dismissed this by remarking on the government's historical operation without strict adherence to budget (እንታይ ኢኻ ትዛረብ ዘሎኻ፡ ኣበይ ዘሎ ባጀት እዩ፡፡).

Another critique of our presentation came from Yemane Ghebremeskel (Charlie), who asserted that measuring education progress using indicators had become a fashionable trend imposed by international NGOs. This statement seemed to reveal a lack of understanding or ignorance on his part, as indicators play a crucial role in objectively assessing and gauging progress in education.

At one juncture, we discussed the role of the private sector in expanding access to education. Specifically, we were reflecting on the pre-Dergue era and how private schools contributed to expanding access to education and the provision of quality education. However, the President did not endorse the proposal, dismissing it by emphasizing that we were not reverting to the pre-Dergue era. The message was clear: private schools, especially those affiliated with religious denominations, were not to be encouraged.

Amidst these deliberations, some ministers presented amusing arguments. I recall Gherghis Teklemicahel, the former Minister of Transportation, suggesting the closure of all private driving schools (autoscuola) and being replaced by government-run ones. His reasoning was the prevalence of numerous car accidents. Gherghis is the individual with a poster in his office featuring a quote from President Isaias, stating, "We will never rest until the urban areas and the countryside of Eritrea are on equal footing." ("ከተማታትን ገጠርን ክሳብ ዝመዓራረዩ ኣይክድቅስን ኢና"). He proudly shares this sentiment with visitors to his office.

14.3. WHAT THESE OPPORTUNITIES MEANT TO THE RECONSTRUCTION OF THE NASCENT ERITREA

The collaborations described above held immense potential for Eritrea, fostering an atmosphere of genuine partnership that transcended traditional power dynamics and embraced the principles of equality, mutual respect, and reciprocity. In these collaborative efforts, all parties came together with a jointly developed common goal, valuing and respecting each other's perspectives, expertise, and contributions.

Within this environment, ideas were freely exchanged, and decisions were made collectively, nurturing trust, openness, and a commitment to innovation. This collaborative spirit promoted shared responsibilities and the pursuit of sustainable solutions, offering the possibility of transformative change and meaningful progress toward inclusive and lasting development. Furthermore, Eritrea had an opportunity to build its internal capacity by articulating its needs and priorities effectively.

The collaboration possessed the potential to mobilize both domestic and external support, drawing clear rules of engagement from the outset. By advocating for transparency when working with development partners and giving due attention to capacity building, such as the training of ministry officials, Eritrea made significant strides toward self-reliance and self-sufficiency.

However, there prevailed a substantial level of missed opportunities. It was lamentable that, at a later stage, Eritrea's Ministry of Education failed to fully utilize opportunities presented through collaboration with regional and international organizations. The Ministry also stagnated due to lack of exposure to what international development could offer to improve the quality of education and other best practices. One prominent government official recently confided in me saying that the Ministry was in a state of chronic paralysis.

Much could have been done by providing exposure to ministry officials and other education practitioners to understand and take advantage of best practices in the field of education. Annual conferences like the Comparative and International Education Society (CIES) bring together global education practitioners, development workers, and financing agencies to discuss crucial matters related to improving education worldwide. While these events attracted participants from across the globe, Eritrea's Ministry of Education's presence was notably scarce, with only one sporadic attendance.

It is essential to note that this observation does not suggest an emphasis on overreliance on foreign assistance. Instead, it underscores the importance of understanding the reality of a rapidly changing, globalized world. Technology advances swiftly, and new research continually reveals innovative approaches to enhancing education quality and access. Collaborations and experience exchanges represent the path forward offering invaluable opportunities that Eritrea can take advantage of. Regrettably, thanks to its self-imposed isolation, Eritrea did not stand to benefit from them.

I would also like to acknowledge the pivotal roles played by visionary individuals such as the late Aynalem Marcos, Berhane Demoz,

Yeshi Haile, the late Mehret Iyob, Ghirmai Haile, Aster Solomon, Paul Highfield, Temesghen Tekie, and others. Their exceptional skills and knowledge were instrumental in driving positive changes, yet the full extent of their potential contributions remained underutilized.

In conclusion, the collaborations described in the aforementioned context could have contributed to the development of a more prosperous and progressive Eritrea, grounded in genuine partnership, self-reliance, and a commitment to harnessing the collective wisdom of the global community for the nation's well-being and development. I consider my tenure at the Ministry as a case study of success.

While our collaboration with international organizations, both bi-lateral and multi-lateral funding entities, taught us a lot, it is also important to acknowledge the challenges we encountered. It is worth noting that there were instances where we categorically turned down certain aid packages due to misalignment with our policy and national priorities.

At times, we found it difficult to tolerate lectures from so-called "senior international experts" who lacked a deep understanding of our country's political economy and the challenges we faced. I vividly remember an incident where UNICEF's Country Office invited an expert (without consulting us) with a mission to instruct us on "what to do." The expert did not even have the courtesy to inquire about our policy, strategic plan, priorities, or the circumstances under which we operated. Instead, he dived directly into his lecture. We seized the opportunity to teach him a lesson he would never forget for the rest of his life.

15

MARGINALIZATION - MDSKAL
(ምድስከል): A REWARD FOR EXCELLENCE

IN PROFESSOR KOTKIN's nuanced analysis, the third dimension of authoritarian regimes is intricately linked to the control of life opportunities. Through a sociological lens, the professor reveals that these regimes exert influence over diverse aspects of citizens' lives, spanning from employment and education to international travel and property ownership. Essentially, an individual's ability to thrive or succeed within such a regime depends on the goodwill of that very regime. Any expression of opposition by an individual could lead to the revocation of privileges, with far-reaching consequences for their entire family.[lxix]

My personal background attests that I was not perceived to be a loyalist as measured against a set of criteria used by the ruling party. Consequently, I was not expected to find favor with the regime for higher-level assignments within the state apparatus. If there was any, the government chose to do so because it could benefit from my expertise. Otherwise, I am likely to be dispensed at any time.

Navigating an environment characterized by the regimentation of ideas as the norm, and where dissent against the government's behavior or its leaders is discouraged, requires a persistent commitment to conforming to the established status quo. One must conform to the narrative, refrain from questioning, and remain focused on adherence to the norms.

The philosophy or intent behind political marginalization can vary, often serving as an instrument employed by those in power to maintain control. By suppressing specific groups or individuals, authorities can sustain their influence unopposed. Factors such as the political convictions of individuals or the absence of loyalty to the government may be utilized to perpetuate this practice. "Mdskal" or to be frozen out or sidelined represents one form of political marginalization.

The impact of "Mdskal" can be profound on individuals and their mindsets. The state of mind of those who experience "Mdskal" can vary widely based on the context and the individual's resilience. It is crucial to note that individuals respond to "Mdskal" in diverse ways, and resilience can play a significant role in shaping their mental and emotional well-being. Additionally, societal and systemic factors contribute to the overall state of mind, with common outcomes being feelings of not being valued or respected.

Moreover, "Mdskal" negatively affects trust between colleagues and with the broader society in general. This practice can lead to emotions of exclusion, isolation, and powerlessness, creating a sense of alienation and frustration that impacts psychological well-being. This can contribute to a feeling of being trapped in a quagmire or conundrum, resulting in diminished self-esteem, affecting confidence and self-worth, and even leading to apathy and a lack of interest in politics. This experience can be compounded when members of your community believe that the government may have had a reason to sideline you or put you in that situation.

Individuals may experience a sense of disconnectedness from the wider community, fostering social withdrawal. In clinical terms, although I cannot claim I am an expert on this subject, those undergoing this ordeal may be more susceptible to anxiety and depression due to stress and a pervasive sense of exclusion. Despite these challenges, some individuals exhibit remarkable resilience and empowerment in the face of political marginalization.

"Mdskal" can result for various reasons in the context of Eritrea. In my case, the reason was political – I was deemed untrustworthy by the government despite years of exemplary service to the nation. During the war, while serving as Head of the Department of Information, Education, and Culture, I faced isolation and subsequent detention for expressing my view that internal contradictions should be resolved through dialogue. This refers to the 1973 Menqa'e Movement. This belief did not fly well with the leadership who relied on the peasantry and a handful of opportunists to crash the reformist movement.

On another occasion, I was transferred from the armed forces to the Department of Mass Administration due to my awareness of clandestine party activities and thus being perceived as an obstacle to the clandestine party's smooth operations. Despite being assigned to the Department of Administration, my focus on essential tasks was constantly disrupted, and I was repeatedly deployed to the frontlines – four–five times.

My last role as Brigade Commissar endured for over 4-5 months before being sent back to the Department of Mass Administration. Despite limited substantive tasks, I seized this opportunity to share (after being given a teaching assignment) my knowledge of the Eritrean society making reference to a book - The Indigenous Population of Eritrea - authored by an Italian historian and translated by the late Abba Isaac Ghebreyesus. More than a hundred combatants attended the two-week-long program.

Upon being relieved of the Ministry of Education without a new assignment, I recognized a familiar pattern – a déjà-vu. It was a method of marginalization, aimed at humiliating me and breaking my morale and spirit.

In this system, individuals are expected to beg for reinstatement into the civil service by appeasing the ruling party, and "by behaving themselves" to regain favor. Once sidelined, one is left to languish and wander the streets.

When submitting my resignation to Mahmoud Sheriffo, the Minister of Local Governments, he ironically advised me to add another sole to my shoes, signaling no immediate change in my status. I did not at all like the statement although he said it jokingly.

Although the norm was to accept reality and vegetate as a human being, I chose rebellion to complacency, I chose to defy the system, tendered my resignation, and refused to accept my salary.

My decision shocked many, and well-wishers urged me to be cautious for the safety of myself and that of my loved ones. A few colleagues provided friendly advice to not say anything about my situation or curse the government. Despite an offer by the minister of education to serve as an advisor, I declined, expressing my disappointment and loss of trust in the government. Determined to assert my right to lead an independent life in Eritrea, I was also planning to withdraw my membership from the ruling party – PFDJ.

I chose to convey a simple message to the ruling party and by extension to the government that says, "As an Eritrean citizen, the least I expect from the government is to be left alone to lead my own life the way I chose. Should I feel the need to stay away from politics and the civil service, so be it."

While awaiting a response from the government regarding my request to be relieved from the civil service, General Filipos invited me to meet for coffee, and together we drove to Aguadu (a restaurant on the way to the airport. During our coffee session, he inquired about my decision to tender my resignation. I elaborated on the reasons behind my choice. Filipos, known for his shrewd behavior, said, "I appreciate the bold move you've made. It could exert pressure on the government to reassign you elsewhere swiftly, considering the valuable contributions you can offer. However, exercise caution and don't push it to the end; you might not make any progress." At that point, we weren't exactly friends, but Filipos enjoyed our conversations. I sensed his eagerness to hear my perspectives on various issues.

On a different occasion, Filipos and I were sharing a casual drink in a bar in Gheza Banda Tlian, sitting in his car. During our conversation, I remarked that he seemed like the type who could stage a coup d'état in Eritrea. He was taken aback but responded in jest, stating that revolutions, like the one in Eritrea, typically don't culminate in a coup d'état. I cited the example of Cambodia and the post-revolution outcomes to illustrate my point. He laughed and said that we refrain from continuing the conversation. "ኣቲ ወዲ ይኣኽለኪ" was what he said in his peasant-tinted Tigrigna.

In a last-ditch attempt to secure my release from civil service, I sought an appointment with the President's Office. I reached out to Zewdi, The President's executive secretary, who graciously agreed to grant me an audience. On the scheduled day, I arrived punctually and was asked to wait while she consulted with the President. After a moment, she returned with the news that the President was unresponsive. She told me that she had been told to leave him alone.

Days before this encounter, I had been sitting in Zewdi's office, hoping to secure an appointment with the President. Yemane Ghebremeskel – Charlie (Head of the President's Office) noticed my presence and invited me to come over to his office. Having already seen the resignation letter carbon-copied to the President's office, he inquired if that was the reason for my visit. Confirming his suspicion, he expressed disapproval, suggesting that such requests were not totally acceptable. He recommended that I withdraw the letter. I declined any unsolicited advice and instead, I asked him to simply convey my message to the President and promptly exited his office.

Facing silence from the government, I took control of my fate, planned it well, and left the country. I never regretted that life-changing decision I took.

After leaving the country and joining the United Nations in Iraq, it was fascinating to learn about the conversations that unfolded between a couple of people.

Adhanom Ghebremariam moved into the house my family and I had vacated upon departing from Eritrea. Major General Teklai Habtesellassie was my neighbor and Adhanom automatically became his neighbor. According to Adhanom, Teklai shared that he wasn't surprised by my departure. "After all," Teklai remarked, "Semere was working for the CIA. I used to see him associating with the international NGOs on a frequent basis." The irony was palpable, as he was referring to my collaboration with various international development partners—a necessity in my role at the Ministry of Education in the role of DG, Planning and Development. If my engagement with international development partners leads to being labeled a CIA, how would Major General Teklai perceive the Minister of Foreign Affairs interacting with various foreign dignitaries on a regular basis?

Victims of "Mdskal" include Mesfin Hagos, Ghebremichael Lilo, Tsadu Bahta, Berhane Abrehe, Berhane Tsehaye (Brigadier General), the late Ghirmai Ghebremeskel, Rezene Sium, Teame Beyene, Andeberhan Woldeghiorghis, Fessahaye Haile (Afro), and many more.

16

FROM THE BUSHES OF ERITREA TO INTERNATIONAL DEVELOPMENT: A SNEAK PEEK INTO MY EXPERIENCE

16.1. FITTING IN INTERNATIONAL DEVELOPMENT

I have more than three decades of steadily advancing senior-level experience in the realm of education and civil society programs, with a pronounced focus on education policy and systems enhancement. My managerial and supervisory capabilities span the domains of strategic planning, service delivery, project management, and research. This expertise has been honed through the orchestration of multifaceted initiatives on behalf of reputable organizations such as USAID, the United Nations (UN), and during my tenure as a senior civil servant within the Government of Eritrea.

Additionally, I exhibit proficiency in a range of complementary areas, including interdisciplinary collaboration, business development, proposal formulation, system strengthening, policy advocacy, and the launching multi-million dollar projects.

After leaving Eritrea, I embarked on a distinguished career, serving as a senior program manager for UNESCO-Iraq and the United Nations Office of the Humanitarian Coordinator in Iraq (UNOHCI). In this role, I led initiatives focused on educational assessments, data collection and synthesis, and the development of sectoral and multi-sector policies to support vulnerable families. This impactful tenure spanned five professionally fulfilling years, from 1998 to 2003.

For the past two decades, I held senior-level, in-country leadership positions at Creative Associates International for diverse USAID-funded programs. These years represent the pinnacle of my career as an international development practitioner. This valuable experience connected me with numerous development practitioners, both local and international, from whom I gained a wealth of knowledge. I deeply treasure the friendships cultivated with these seasoned professionals during those long years of working together.

The roles I held include serving on the Revitalization of Iraqi Schools and Stabilization of Education (RISE) project in Iraq, as well as the USAID/Nigeria Community Participation for Action in the Social Sector (COMPASS) project in Nigeria. As the Regional Representative, Senior Education Planner, and Grants Manager under RISE, I effectively coordinated all activities in the Northern Region of Iraq, overseeing critical areas such as grant management, materials distribution, and accelerated learning and outreach initiatives aimed at out- of-school youth.

In my role as the Senior Education Advisor at COMPASS, based in Abuja, I demonstrated exceptional leadership by overseeing the education component of the COMPASS project, which included primary education, in-service and pre-service teacher training, community mobilization, school health and nutrition (SHN), and sub-grant activities. My pivotal contributions played a significant role in enabling the project to surpass all of its USAID targets. My ability to establish ministerial and LGA-level ownership within COMPASS can be attributed to my skillful cultivation of a robust network of stakeholders and my commitment to working as genuine partners with host state governments.

In my most recent role as Senior Director of Growth Strategy, I played an important role in laying the groundwork for the formulation of a comprehensive growth strategy for Creative Associates International. These include market research and data analytics, strategic partnerships with local organizations, countries of interest, trends analyses, etc. Before assuming this position, I held several distinguished roles, including Senior Director of the Africa Regional Center, where I led the successful implementation of the Regional Strategy.

In my capacity as Senior Director at the Africa Center, I was responsible for a wide range of key functions. I spearheaded the implementation of the regional strategy, conducted in-depth market research to inform both short and medium-term planning, established essential regional priorities for business development and operational platforms, provided recommendations for Countries of Interest and supervised their activities, meticulously crafted a region-centric and prioritized business plans, actively contributed to regional knowledge management and learning initiatives, pinpointed potential roles for regional initiatives such as Prosper Africa, and meticulously identified and developed plans for various marketing activities.

Furthermore, I served as the Senior Project Director for the Northern Education Initiative Plus (The Initiative) based in Washington. From 2007 to 2015, I successfully oversaw various projects in several countries, including Nigeria (Education Crisis Response and Northern Education Initiative), Zambia (Read to Succeed (RTS) and Makalidwe Athu), Pakistan (Pakistan Reading Project—(PRP), as well as projects in Kyrgyzstan, Tajikistan, and Turkmenistan (Quality Learning Project—(QLP)). In addition to these accomplishments, I also simultaneously held significant high-level responsibilities within the Division of Education for Development as Practice Area Director for the Africa Portfolio.

In these roles, I fostered a close, collaborative, and results-oriented partnership with in-country staff and USAID Missions, ensuring that projects met all contractual targets and deliverables. I also engaged in effective communication with USAID missions, taking part in corporate business development initiatives as the technical lead in Practice Area activities and contributing to other strategic decision-making processes. I have extensively traveled to implement multimillion-dollar projects across the globe.

My portfolio included overseeing projects from a technical, operational, and financial standpoint. These encompassed tasks such as providing technical assistance, facilitating annual work planning workshops, closely monitoring project progress, skillfully negotiating necessary adjustments with host governments, and managing expectations. These international assignments took me to a diverse range of countries, including Nigeria, Zambia, Namibia, South Sudan, Ethiopia, Pakistan, Iraq, Afghanistan, Jordan, Tajikistan, Kyrgyzstan, Turkmenistan, the UK, Mexico, and Canada.

I demonstrated my commitment to sharing insights in international development by extensively writing white papers and blogs on best practices.

My dedication and contributions to international development were recognized through awards, including the prestigious Best Employee of the Year award. Additionally, the projects I managed received notable accolades, with three of them earning the distinctive Project of the Year awards, and one project achieving exceptional

CPAR (Contractor Performance Assessment Report) results—an unprecedented achievement in the company's forty-six years of history.

I possess an advanced diploma in Educational Planning and Administration and a master's degree in Sustainable Development and Diplomacy (MSDD).

16.2 WHAT THIS MEANT TO ME AS A DEVELOPMENT PRACTITIONER

Having a twenty-five-year career in international development is a significant journey by any standard. It offers a profoundly gratifying and enlightening experience, enriching your global outlook by immersing you in a diverse array of worldwide concerns, encompassing poverty, inequality, health disparities, and environmental challenges. This endeavor enabled me to cultivate a more comprehensive perspective of the world and to recognize the intricate interdependencies among global issues. It provided me with valuable insights into the functioning of complex systems, whether it is economic, political, or social, at both the domestic and international scales—crucial for tackling systemic problems.

The experience I accumulated enhanced my cross-disciplinary expertise by necessitating collaboration across diverse domains, including education, economic growth, governance, public health, and other social services thus enabling me to acquire a wide spectrum of knowledge and skills.

International development usually requires one to operate in demanding and unpredictable settings and necessitates the demonstration of adaptability and flexibility in unfamiliar cultural contexts and work environments. Moreover, it helps you acquire robust problem-solving skills as one confronts intricate and real-world challenges.

International development necessitates the exploration and discovery of innovative solutions to tackle urgent challenges. Collaborating across various countries and diverse communities nurtures cultural sensitivity and awareness. It fosters a profound respect for and appreciation of diverse customs, traditions, worldviews, and approaches to development.

Effective communication plays a pivotal role in international development, and this experience equips you with the ability to convey ideas clearly and collaborate with others, even if they speak different languages.

International development projects often entail collaborating with diverse stakeholders, constrained budgets, and stringent timelines. Navigating these complexities can significantly enhance your project management skills, spanning the entire spectrum from initial planning and budgeting to seamless implementation and rigorous evaluation to achieve results.

Furthermore, international development often intersects with the political realm i.e., policymaking. Engaging in this field enhanced my political acumen, potentially leading me to participate in advocacy endeavors aimed at shaping policy adjustments. Additionally, I accrued valuable expertise in monitoring and assessing the outcomes of my initiatives, which is pivotal to the effectiveness and sustainability of development efforts.

International development can be a highly transformative experience that not only does it contribute to positive global change but also fosters personal and professional growth. It can also expose you to a diverse array of challenges and opportunities for learning and collaboration.

16.3. RETHINKING INTERNATIONAL DEVELOPMENT AND WHAT IT MEANS TO ERITREA AND OTHER DEVELOPING COUNTRIES

The concept: Development is a dynamic process that presents an opportunity to lead a secure life with basic needs met. It fosters the potential for creating and innovating, opening doors to build a better future for everyone. Crucially, development should be a locally-driven initiative, embraced by the people and their elected leaders. While international partners play a role in supporting development by sharing technology, technical expertise, and providing financing to encourage sound capital allocation, it is imperative to recognize that this support cannot replace the essential efforts and sustained commitment of local communities and leaders.

Development takes place when robust and efficient institutions are in place, and good governance is practiced, allowing both developing and developed countries to effectively manage their expectations and foster partnerships in a sustainable manner.[lxx]

A nation thrives when the talents and energies of its people are permitted to flourish within the framework of a stable society, where sound governance ensures that productivity and production are maximized.

Development manifests in individuals leading healthy and prolonged lives, with creativity at the core. It assumes active engagement from people in shaping and benefiting from its outcomes. Both as individuals and groups, people should take the initiative in determining their future. Consequently, equity and sustainability serve as the foundational principles of development.[lxxi]

The 2011 Human Development Report by UNDP places equity and sustainability at the forefront of any developmental process. It emphasizes the intricate connection between sustainability and the fundamental issues of equity, encompassing social justice and broader access to an enhanced quality of life. The report contends that sustainability involves "how we choose to live our lives, with an awareness that everything we do has consequences for the 7 billion of us here today, as well as for the billions more who will follow, for centuries to come.[lxxii]

Basic principles on how to conduct development work: Societies inherently strive for positive change and progress in their lives, and achieving this is more likely through active participation in a consultative process to shape their aspirations. Each society is unique and diverse, choosing its own distinct paths or strategies to realize desired changes. These pathways are determined at their own pace and aligned with specific homegrown aspirational goals.

Social transformation is a complex process, and there is no one-size-fits-all solution that can be universally applied. Solutions must be context-specific and tailored to the particular needs and circumstances of each society.

Societies are more comfortable utilizing their structures, both traditional and contemporary, along with their beliefs and value systems to guide the development process. In other words, the internal dynamic matters.

The better one understands and supports the needs and priorities of a society, the more likely it is to contribute to relevant and impactful outcomes. By doing so, development partners can contribute to the sustainability of initiatives and fulfill their responsibilities as partners. In essence, the objective of development initiatives is to empower the inhabitants of a country, within their specific circumstances, to attain and bring to fruition the future they have envisioned for themselves. (Runde, 2023)

International development must wholeheartedly acknowledge culture as a vital ingredient in shaping collective narratives, fostering a sense of community pride, and embracing diversity as a key factor for long-term sustainability. Understanding the transformative power of culture is critical in building a sustainable future that benefits all. To achieve this, the approach towards international development should be culturally sensitive, respecting and valuing the unique traditions and customs of each community. Contextual appropriateness is critical, as it allows tailoring development initiatives to suit to the specific needs and aspirations of the people international development aims to assist. By integrating cultural considerations into its strategies, it can strengthen the impact of development efforts and ensure they resonate more profoundly with the communities they serve. Ultimately, embracing culture in the approach not only fosters inclusivity but also empowers communities to take ownership of their development journey, paving the way for a more sustainable and prosperous future.

Institutional change stands as a fundamental requirement for the success of any development effort. To achieve this, host governments must proactively seek ways to transform public institutions, enhancing their accountability to the most vulnerable members of society. This necessitates effective decentralization of administration, resources, and political power, supported by a robust accountability structure.

The practice: International development initiatives encompass efforts, strategies, and programs dedicated to enhancing the economic, social, and political wellbeing of developing and developed countries as this entails active collaboration between or amongst partners. While this is not always the case, it should ideally be carried out in the spirit of partnership. In one of my white papers, I contend that true partnership does not involve patronizing or dictating terms based on resource control or forcing or imposing or restricting or dominating or monopolizing. Instead, partnership embodies the essence of collaboration, where all parties work together in the spirit of equality, mutual respect, and reciprocity, united by a jointly developed common goal (Solomon, 2023).

I emphasize that in such a dynamic partnership, each party's perspectives, expertise, and contributions are not only valued and respected but also celebrated. This fosters an environment where ideas flow freely, and decisions are collectively made. Furthermore, I assert that when implemented correctly, this genuine spirit of partnership cultivates an atmosphere of trust and openness, which in turn promotes innovation, shared responsibility, and the pursuit of sustainable solutions. By transcending traditional power dynamics and embracing authentic partnership, the partners unlock the potential for transformative change and take meaningful steps toward inclusive and enduring development (Solomon, 2023).

International development initiatives contribute to poverty alleviation through initiatives aimed at granting access to education, healthcare, clean water, and economic opportunities. These strategic interventions have the potential to elevate the living standards of individuals in developing nations and mitigate poverty rates. These often entail the construction of vital infrastructure such as roads, bridges, schools, hospitals, and utilities. This enhanced infrastructure can stimulate economic growth, generate employment opportunities, and augment the overall quality of life in developing regions. Moreover, international development initiatives can bolster healthcare systems, facilitate the distribution of essential medicines, and provide training for healthcare professionals. Consequently, this can result in improved access to healthcare, reduced disease prevalence, and enhanced public health outcomes.

Developing countries can reap significant advantages from international development initiatives that prioritize the enhancement of educational access and quality, the strengthening of educational systems, and the empowerment of education professionals.

A well-educated society contributes substantially to both economic growth and social development.

International development efforts also play a critical role in alleviating humanitarian crises by delivering essential and life-saving assistance. Numerous nations have reaped significant benefits from this vital support. In conflict and post-conflict situations, the approach must center on local and first responders who are already present on the ground. These local entities encompass communities, local civil society organizations, religious and traditional groups, and others. Their intimate knowledge of the situation, their agility, and their swift action make them indispensable during crises. Local responders are often the first to step up to the plate, displaying a profound understanding of power dynamics and the specific needs of the affected population, surpassing that of any external entity ready to offer support. Moreover, their dynamism allows them to adapt swiftly to ever-changing circumstances.

While local responders might lack some of the expected sophistication and compliance skills required by funding agencies, their effectiveness in responding to crises cannot be underestimated. Therefore, the approach should prioritize forging partnerships with local responders, aiming to bolster their responsiveness and efficiency. Supporting these local structures is crucial for providing timely assistance to the population in need.

The several years following Eritrea's hard-won independence— during my tenure— the Ministry of Education in Eritrea experienced the benefits of international development. That period stands as a testament to the transformative potential of such efforts.

A proposal for Eritrea: While international development can bring significant benefits to Eritrea, it is critical to recognize that it requires careful planning, coordination, and long-term commitment. Success often depends on local ownership, sustainability, and a focus on the specific needs and priorities of Eritrea. Additionally, institutional change stands as a fundamental requirement for the success of Eritrea's development efforts. To achieve this, Eritrea must proactively seek ways to transform its institutions, enhancing its accountability to the most vulnerable members of society. This necessitates effective decentralization of administration, expertise, and resources supported by a robust legal infrastructure.

I do not advocate for Eritrea, or any other developing country, to become dependent on foreign assistance, whether in the form of loans, grants, or any other mechanism of assistance that does not align with its priorities or needs. Furthermore, it is key that the host country maintains ownership of the programs initiated with foreign assistance. Sustainable assistance should always be rooted in local communities.

A nation's development also hinges upon the strength and robustness of the private sector. Developing countries can graduate from aid recipients to becoming global players through mutually beneficial commercial partnerships. Powerful economies like the United States can promote attractive investment ventures in developing countries and host governments can create a favorable environment for investment partnerships (Solomon, 2022).

Developing countries possess untapped potential that can lead to thriving economies. Unlocking this potential necessitates the right combination of well-crafted local policies and a strategy to attract foreign investment and technology, which can help unleash the full potential of private-sector engagement. This should be executed on purely business terms, thereby fostering mutually beneficial commercial/business partnerships, that involve a diverse array of stakeholders.

By nurturing private-public partnerships and supporting investments in strategic sectors, one can facilitate sustainable economic growth and promote prosperity and better livelihoods in developing countries. This kind of synergistic approach aligns the interests of various stakeholders, unleashing the immense potential for transformative development outcomes.

Eritrea's historical failure to harness the benefits of international collaboration can mostly be attributed to its self-imposed isolation. The six to seven years following independence serve as a testament to how engagement with international organizations can significantly contribute to national priorities.

Eritrea or any other developing country for that matter needs to understand that in this interconnected world, one cannot even survive in isolation. One needs to engage with others and find a win-win solution for everybody. This approach encourages cooperation and negotiation, as opposed to a zero-sum game. It emphasizes the need to work together to find solutions and it is often the most effective way to navigate the complex challenges of a globalized society.

Flaws in the practice of international development requiring further reflection: In the course of my extensive engagement in international development over the past twenty-five years, I find it imperative to shed light on certain inherent flaws prevalent in the practice.

It is not surprising that numerous host governments occasionally exhibit reluctance to collaborate with international funding agencies. This warrants a sincere contemplation on the part of these funding agencies. Several disconcerting realities demand thoughtful consideration:

I have borne witness to projects financed by both bilateral and multilateral funding agencies, conceived without meaningful consultation with the host country and forcibly imposed upon them. In such instances, governments often remain uninformed about the true nature and purpose of these projects resulting in undesirable outcomes.

Projects that fail to align with the priorities of the host government are not uncommon. In my perspective, this is due to a lack of consultation and, at times, a failure to understand the socio-economic landscape. Occasionally, it is associated with an attitude of arrogance, stemming from the belief that "We know what is good for you." This attitude finds its origins in the patronizing behavior of certain donors, resembling that of a colonial mentality.

While the project-based approach to development has its merits, it also possesses inherent flaws. Certain endeavors require a timeframe exceeding three or five years to manifest tangible results. For a project to exert a lasting impact on a community, it must establish the groundwork for sustained growth rather than fostering dependency syndrome. Furthermore, it should pave the way for the discovery of local solutions to local problems, utilizing innovation and the available resources within the financial constraints of the communities involved.

Projects should also help host governments and communities to graduate from aid and not to let it go in perpetuity. This was the end goal of the Marshall Plan and it worked (of course under totally different circumstances that I am not going to delve into in this chapter).

The procurement procedures prove to be intricate and cumbersome, necessitating an extensive amount of paperwork and conditionalities as an end result. Additionally, the reporting requirements are both sophisticated and highly demanding. While host countries still have challenges coping with these mechanisms, the initiative to be responsive to this demand still remains unfulfilled.

Regrettably, host countries are at times treated as junior partners, compelled to comply with directives under the looming threat of funding withdrawal. The focus also tends to shift toward contractual deliverables, to the detriment of the well-being of communities or beneficiaries.

I have encountered instances where projects are entirely managed by the headquarters of implementing partners, sidelining the input of local counterparts. Work planning exercises are conducted behind closed doors, excluding the crucial participation of host country counterparts. It is not uncommon to witness situations where host government counterparts lose track of what is going on and how progress should be measured simply because they are not kept abreast of developments.

A troubling pattern emerges where junior expatriates, and at times fresh graduates, assume the role of lecturers and dictate their terms on seasoned local experts. It is critical that young development practitioners listen and understand the local political economy before they try to make themselves heard.

Exorbitant budgets are laden with overhead and fees. The deployment of Short-Term Technical Assistance (STTAs) by home office staff, often without genuine need, is another observation.

Furthermore, the unsettling practice of contracting officers' representatives (COR) from bilateral agencies running projects from the comfort of air-conditioned offices without ever setting foot in the field is not uncommon.

In some instances, implementing partners' home offices are seen to exert a lot of pressure on project teams urging them to focus on spending rather than results. The more money spent, the greater the accrued overhead and direct and indirect fees charged to the client.

Practices often prioritize images over substance, favoring expatriates in the assignment of Chiefs of Party roles. It is also disheartening to witness that expatriates from developing countries receive disparate treatment in terms of salaries and benefits compared to their Western counterparts, despite possessing equivalent credentials.

In my view, the operational approach of the Millennium Challenge Corporation (MCC), the Development Finance Corporation (DFC), and the Global Partnership for Education (GPE) appear to be models that international development could adopt with slight adjustments. These agencies engage directly with host governments through a well-defined process, entrusting, in the majority of cases, the implementation responsibilities to the host governments themselves. USAID, in accordance with its recently released policy on locally-led development, seems to be aligning with this practice as well. However, the focus should go beyond channeling funds to local organizations and underscore collaboration based on the principles of partnership and local ownership.

These realities collectively underscore the urgent need for introspection and reform within the realm of international development practices.

A session with a community in Northern Nigeria

At a Congressional Hearing with Congresswoman Frederica Wilson

Family photo - 2015

In Sweden with Yousuf Hassen, Berhane Asghedom, ad Kidane
Ghebremichael

My wife and I - 2023

With Creative Associates work colleagues in Washington, DC

With James Stephenson - USAID Mission Director - Iraq

With my project team in Iraq

With my project team in Bishkek, Kyrgyzstan

Our basketball team, YMCA
Standing: L to R – the late Ghirmai (Voce), me, the late Ghetachew, and
Hagos
Sitting: L to R - Abraham, Lema, the late Awate, Araya, and Ghere

With teachers in Erbil, Kurdistan - Northern Iraq

With Tun Myat - Humanitarian Coordinator in Iraq

With USAID Mission Director - Michael Harvey - and Nigerian counterparts

Working on my book from home

17

THE PERSON/FACTOR ISAIAS

I SAIAS AND INDIVIDUALS of his breed are the by-products of the left-wing movement that swept across the world during the 1960s and 1970s. This ideological wave, however, failed to consider the unique socioeconomic circumstances of developing nations.

These societies were plagued by low economic development, widespread poverty, alarmingly high illiteracy rates, and more. Moreover, they clung to deep-seated sub-national sentiments, with religion often holding a sacred place in their collective psyche. The economies of these regions were predominantly agrarian, with a significant portion of the population comprising peasants. The stage was set for discord in attempting to apply a foreign ideology crafted to address the needs of industrialized nations to these developing nations.

During my youth and time as a student, I was exposed to this ideology and, like many at that age, became an idealist.

Among the ranks of young leftists, anyone could have ascended to a position of leadership, but not necessarily to eventually become a dictator.

The Isaias factor in the revolution must be viewed through this lens. One should not romanticize him as someone born with qualities such as invincibility, exceptional survival instinct, or vision. He was an ordinary fighter, who, by what could only be described as a historical coincidence, rose to a leadership position distinguishing himself from his peers through certain advantages he possessed. These advantages might have included his status as a former university student (although his classmates such as Woldeyesus Ammar maintain that he dropped out), his reading habits, his imposing height, his prowess as an orator (until he started sounding like a broken record), his writing skills, his rapid acquisition of the Arabic language, and quite significantly, his ambition and insatiable thirst for power. As Mesfin aptly put it, "Power did not transform Isaias into something he was not; it merely revealed his true self, and none of us harbored any illusions regarding his ruthlessness and the very real physical danger we faced when challenging him" (Hagos M., 2023). I cannot agree more.

Isaias despises being challenged. Rarely did he face opposition, and when he did, his response can be characterized as a ruthless display of brute force. Unyielding and unapologetic, he shows no hesitation in annihilating those who stand against him. As noted by Tedros Tesfai in his article, Isaias does not acknowledge adversaries; he perceives only enemies, and enemies are to be eliminated. (Tesfai T., 2001)

Numerous significant challenges have crossed Isaias's path throughout his political career, including the fate of the 1973 Menqa'e Movement, G-15 group, the Forto Rebellion, and the 1993 rebellion of EPLF members. Each posed a threat to his authority and was met with unrelenting backlash.

Consider the case of Ahmed Al Qeisi (a member of the Central Committee of EPLF), who was detained on Isaias' orders for standing up against him and calling him "Pinochet." Except for Ibrahim

Totil (another member of the Central Committee), no one dared to inquire about his whereabouts.

Isaias wielded power in such a way that nurtured a culture of subservience. Speaking out against his behavior, on a personal level, was unthinkable, and those who did paid a steep price for their defiance.

Suspicion and ambition were ingrained in Isaias's operandi. He was ruthless, readily resorting to vindictive measures and divisive tactics to maintain his grip on power. Manipulation was his weapon of choice and his fragile ego was inflated by his proxies. The whole propaganda machinery revolved around one man—Isaias the infallible—and his grandiose ideas. He was supposed to be the center of attraction, a belief that permeated the ranks of the organization.

Despite his occasional miscalculations, Isaias never expresses regret for his actions. He is often described as insecure by colleagues close to him. He withholds information from his peers, using them as tools whenever it suits his agenda, and occasionally resorting to blackmail. Isaias possesses a cunning ability to sow discord among his colleagues, pitting them against each other.

I will share a few anecdotes illustrating how Isaias fosters discord and mistrust among his immediate colleagues. One instance involves a driver taking Isaias from Arerib to Amberbeb accompanied by another Politbureau member. Passing by Hishkib, where Mass Administration and Security departments were located, the Politbureau member suggested stopping by the late Ali Said Abedella's Office (Ali was the Chief Security) for dinner. Isaias promptly dismissed the idea, stating, "Forget it, why would I waste time entertaining a drunkard," referring to Ali Said's drinking habits. On a different occasion, the same driver chauffeured Isaias and another Politbureau member to the same location. When his colleague proposed visiting Sebhat Efrem's place, Isaias, in a similar tone, rejected the idea, saying, "Why would I waste my time with someone who plays double standard?" He used the phrase "ክልተ መልሓሱ" to describe his colleague, Sebhat Efrem.

A colleague (name withheld for safety reasons), once a significant figure, shared a story with me from the early 90s. During an appointment with Isaias, upon Zewdi (Isaias's secretary) confirmation of his arrival, he entered to witness a compelling scene. Isaias was passionately reprimanding someone in his office, questioning, "When are you going to stop lying? When are you going to stop playing double standard?" The person being scolded was none other than Sebhat Efrem.

I also recall another time when a colleague (name withheld for security purposes) informed me that during Askalu Menkerios's visit to Asmerom Ghebreighziabher's office in Amberbeb, she witnessed Isaias yelling at Asmerom. He emphatically declared, "I am your patron, I will always be your patron." The Tigrinya phrase "ሎሚ ጎይታኻ ጽባሕ ጎይታኻ፡፡ ሃለዉለዉ ኣይትበል" was used to convey his sentiment.

Adding to these accounts, during the Menqa'e Movement in 1973, it was raised as an issue that Isaias humiliated the late Temesghen Berhe (Brigadier General) by slapping him in the face.

Another weak character who was subjected to Isaias's humiliation was Romadan Mohamed Nur. It is widely known that Romadan experienced an embarrassing departure from the PFDJ during the Third EPLF Organizational Congress in 1994. Even after this unfortunate incident, Isaias didn't cease to hound him. As disclosed by a high-ranking PFDJ official (identity withheld for their safety), Isaias would occasionally blackmail Romadan by inquiring about the origins of the funds that were used to construct the house he had started building shortly after independence on the shores of Massawa. Isaias, well aware that Seghen Construction was responsible for building the house, would bring up this topic during casual gatherings, often over drinks.

I would like to share accounts of instances where Isaias exhibited harsh treatment towards his subordinates within the military hierarchy as well. According to reliable sources, Major General Teklai Habtesellassie endured years of ostracism by Isaias (to the extent that Isaias would not even acknowledge him). Major General Ghebrezghabiher Andemariam (Wuchu) stepped forward voluntarily to act as a mediator and attempted to facilitate a reconciliation between them. My sources revealed that Wuchu pleaded with Isaias to forgive Major General Teklai. "You've already punished him. Kindly spare him; any more could push him to the brink of insanity." ("ቀጺዕካዮ ኢኻ ሕጂ ግን ይኣክሎ ናብ ጽላለ ከየይሀበሉ") was what he told him.

Regrettably, Major General Haile Samuel (China) passed away a lonely man under somber circumstances. Having been isolated and sidelined from the inner circle for an extended period, he was stripped of all his privileges as a General. His health rapidly declined, and he eventually succumbed to his ailments, living out his final days in solitude.

In the EPLF, fitting in with the peasants and concealing one's identity is essential for acceptance. College students raised in Asmara would even alter their accents to integrate into the peasant culture, fearing any association with the petty bourgeois.

In a striking incident (after Eritrea's independence), the late Major General Ghebrezghabiher Andemariam (Wuchu), dismissed rebellious university students in Wia, labeling them as irrelevant. He controversially stated that the liberation of the country had been accomplished by fourth-grade students (ራብዓይ ክፍሊ ዝወድኡ እዮም ነጻነት ኣምጺኦም), underscoring the deeply ingrained culture of conformity and subservience, juxtaposed with a prevailing attitude of disdain towards the educated. Such a statement is profoundly perilous.

The EPLF fostered a culture of disdain for the educated, earning Isaias the nickname "Pancho Villa" after the Mexican peasant revolutionary. Unlike the ELF of the 1970s, the EPLF was consistently governed by a single, authoritative figure. Isaias maintained an unassailable grip on power.

Going back to the EPLF, the unique circumstances in Eritrea cultivated a culture of blind allegiance to one individual, Isaias. This gave rise to an atmosphere of obedience. This distinctive situation also led to the emergence of an opportunistic elite that prioritized loyalty to Isaias Afewerki over loyalty to the broader cause.

The EPLF was shaped in the image of a single figure—Isaias, as mentioned earlier (ከምቲ ሰብ ብኣርኣያ ስላሴ ዝተፈጥሩ፡ ህዝበዊ ግንባር ብተምሳል ኢስያስ እዩ ተሃኒጹ). Regimentation within the organization reached such an extent that virtually everyone, including members of the Political Bureau and Central Committee, began to mimic Isaias in speech, dress, mannerisms, and even body language. Imitating his behavior became the standard.

One another occasion, while serving as a member of the Harbegna team, Alemseghed Tesfai and I were assigned the responsibility of covering the EPLF's major offensive on Af'abet, which led to the annihilation of Nadew Command (ናደው እዝ) of the Ethiopian forces. Alemseghed and I sought a briefing from Mesfin Hagos, who was in command of the Nakfa front. He provided a comprehensive overview of the offensive, including details such as the zero-hour, division responsibilities, and the military tactics the front intended to pursue:

After leaving Alemseghed in the Nakfa Front, I drove to join the late Wuchu's Division (Division 85) in Northern Eastern Sahel. I accompanied Wuchu, observing firsthand while he was commanding his troops during the offensive. The late Wuchu proved to be a brilliant military commander. Upon successfully completing the mission, Wuchu and I relaxed on the outskirts of Af'abet, perched on a large rock.

As we enjoyed our moment of respite, we heard an announcement by the TPLF over the radio. They were expressing their pleasure and excitement about this milestone and their desire for future collaboration. It was noteworthy that the EPLF and TPLF had been estranged for over four years at that time. In response to the TPLF's statement, I remarked, "This announcement from the TPLF is indeed a very positive development. The EPLF may need to reciprocate." Wuchu sharply criticized my statement, emphasizing, "Are you aware that the TPLF labels us undemocratic? Why should we reciprocate?" I told him that I was talking from a pragmatic point of view and that we should consider the potential benefits of collaboration. Unfortunately, the conversation came to an abrupt end.

Alemseghed Tesfai and I returned to Arerib (our base area) following the fall of Af'abet. Alemseghed penned an article titled "A Freedom Fighter's Heart," drawing inspiration from a poignant encounter with the remains of a fallen comrade. Using this experience as a metaphor, he eloquently captured the essence of martyrdom. His literary piece left a profound impact.

In parallel, I contributed an article titled "What's Next after Nadew." Delving into the complexities that accompany victory, I discussed the challenges ahead for the organization and outlined strategies for effective handling. Both articles garnered positive reception among the members of the front, resonating with the shared experiences and aspirations of our people.

A few days after TPLF's radio announcement, the EPLF, acting under the directive of the Secretary General, made an announcement supporting the TPLF's statement. Everyone, including Wuchu, began echoing the EPLF's position. This marked the re-birth of a full-fledged collaboration between the two organizations, a partnership that endured until the downfall of Mengistu Hailemariam in 1991.

The personality that Isaias had carefully crafted for himself during the tumultuous period of war, was about to face a series of rigorous tests in the newly independent Eritrea; in times of peace. The challenges that post-independence Eritrea encountered, though formidable, were not insurmountable, providing that one possessed the right attitude, principles, policies, and a clear roadmap.

Tests after independence: First and foremost, there was the test of coexisting harmoniously with neighboring nations. Eritrea had to navigate the complex political landscape of the region and the broader global arena. Furthermore, the question of interacting with both bilateral and multilateral organizations arose, bringing with it the need for diplomacy and negotiation.

The situation also required a strong desire to enforce the rule of law and ensure accountability, emphasizing the importance of good governance. Moreover, it demanded openness to institutionalize consultations with people at every level of the administrative hierarchy, recognizing that the input and involvement of the population was the key to success.

Eritrea also faced the challenge of jumpstarting its economy by mobilizing resources from both internal and external sources. There was a science behind it and failing to have a firm grip of this science was tantamount to running blindfolded.

In terms of governance, a system of checks and balances was necessary. It demanded a political will to understand and engage with institutions and believe in their efficacy.

All of these challenges collectively served as a litmus test for Isaias (as a personality). It was during this time that his true character was exposed, revealing his inability to adapt, lead, and make decisions in the face of complex and multifaceted obstacles.

Isaias strongly disapproves of institutions and the institutional approach to governing. This disdain is evident in his decision to render ministries obsolete, as illustrated earlier in the case of the Ministry of Defense. An anecdote circulating in Asmara humorously captures Isaias's aversion to well-functioning institutions. In contrast to his general stance, he saw that the Municipality of Asmara was operating smoothly, thanks to its established culture that dates back to the 1950s and 60s. Determined to dismantle it, he chose Major General Romadan Awlyay to accomplish this task and by appointing him as the Governor of Zoba Ma'ekel, Romadan Awlyay executed the job perfectly.

The mishandling of relationships with neighboring countries, the self-imposed isolation the country endured due to his isolationist and aggressive foreign policy, his approach to the private sector and international investment, and his tendency to operate above the law, all served as defining characteristics of Isaias and foreshadowed his eventual legacy. These are the factors that any sensible person would use to measure his successes or failures. The answers seem obvious.

Could this situation have been avoided? The answer is a resounding "yes." The consolidation of Isaias's power occurred because he was granted carte blanche to act with impunity. The absence of colleagues at his level, who could assert themselves, played a significant role in allowing him to become the dictator that he has become. His dominance in the political arena was a consequence of the opportunities he was given to shape the course of Eritrea's history, ultimately overshadowing the collective interests of the EPLF, its members, and the people of Eritrea.

Isaias became more and more delusional by the day. This demeanor becomes evident during his interviews with

EriTV – Eritrea's sole official TV station – particularly on the occasion of the new year. His discourse spans a wide array of topics, including the economy, regional and international politics, domestic affairs, human resources, climate change, infrastructure, energy, and water resources, among others. Throughout, he presents himself as an authority on virtually every subject. Whether discussing complex economic strategies, climate expertise, agricultural insights, political acumen, geological knowledge, or mastery in economics, President Isaias appears to assume roles beyond his actual qualifications.

He expounds on ambitious ideas for constructing a new international development order, outlining strategies for its achievement and proposing programs, along with considerations on resource mobilization. His vision extends to creating a better world for all. However, what eludes him is the stark reality of his nation's plight.

Eritrea continues to operate on rationing, with citizens queuing daily for basic necessities like bread, sugar, cooking oil, and lentils. President Isaias seems oblivious to the fact that his people are grappling with such hardships.

The mass exodus of youth fleeing the country further underscores the erosion of Eritrea's valuable human resources.

In his seemingly utopian mindset, President Isaias resides in a dream world, detached from the harsh realities and hardships faced by his people. His visionary rhetoric contrasts sharply with the tangible struggles experienced by those living under his authoritarian grip of power, revealing a stark dichotomy between his perceptions and the lived experiences of the Eritrean populace. This reveals the typical mindset of any dictator as discussed in previous chapters.

18

WHO IS ZEINEB ALI?

ZEINEB'S RISE TO prominence occurred between 2000 and 2021, marking a significant era in her journey. This period could be aptly described as a phenomenon of the early 2000s, a testament to her impact on the times. While some critics may argue that concealing one's true identity is an act of cowardice, Zeineb had a deeper purpose in mind. She chose to protect the identities of those individuals who courageously provided her with timely and valuable information during those days. Their safety was of the highest priority to Zeineb, underscoring her deep commitment to safeguarding their well-being.

This political turmoil unfolded in the wake of a significant crisis that gripped the nation following the 1998–2000 conflict with Ethiopia.

Eritrea found itself amid a turbulent political storm as it entered the 2000s. The years from 2000 to 2001 were marked by an exceptionally volatile political landscape.

During this period, several influential figures within the government dared to challenge the President, who was widely criticized for his disregard for the rule of law.

SEMERE SOLOMON

These government dissenters bravely emerged as vocal critics, expressing their legitimate concerns regarding the regime's handling of a wide array of issues, including political, economic, social, and security matters. Their bold actions sparked an unprecedented level of public discourse and debate among the various segments of Eritrean society, pushing the boundaries of political engagement and discussion to new heights.

The Open Letter, signed by the G-15, advocated for the rule of law, and the immediate implementation of the constitution. It addressed various issues, including the mishandling of the economy, the lack of transparency and accountability in PFDJ-run business enterprises resulting from a failure to follow legal procedures, a lack of clear policies, and a deficiency in professional administration, the absence of a Board of Trustees, and a lack of audit procedures among others. The Open Letter opposed the interference of the Front in government affairs and the incapacitation of the legislative and executive bodies, with the aim of establishing a one-man rule. Furthermore, the Open Letter emphasized the need for ensuring regional harmony, peaceful coexistence, and dialogue to resolve conflicts with neighboring countries. It defined what Eritrea's role and place should be in the region and the international community. The signatories of the Open Letter included Mahmud Ahmed Sheriffo, Haile Woldetensae, Mesfin Hagos, Ogbe Abrha, Hamid Hmd, Saleh Kekya, Estifanos Seyoum, Berhane Ghebreghzabhier, Aster Feshatsion, Mohammed Berhan Blata, Petros Solomon, Germano Nati, Beraki Ghebreslassie, Adhanom Ghebremariam, and Haile Menkerios.[lxxiii]

Two contending forces, the G-15 on one side and the President's supporters on the other, found themselves embroiled in a fervent political debate. This clash evolved into a direct confrontation, a head-on collision about worldviews and policies. The PFDJ, in its pursuit of silencing the G-15, resorted to the manipulation of state institutions and the use of official media channels to vilify and tarnish the reputation of these dissident individuals. In addition to these overt methods, unofficial platforms were also employed to besmirch the names of G-15 members.

The G-15 found themselves with limited avenues to express their concerns, and their sole recourse was through the nascent local newspapers. These publications became the platform for interviews featuring prominent politicians who were willing to challenge the status quo. Notably, this marked the time when local newspapers covered the dissenting voices of influential figures in Eritrea Prominent journalists, including Sium Tsehaye (freelance), Amanuel Asrat (Zemen), Yusuf Mohamed (Tsigenay), Dawit Isaac (Setit), Said Abdelkader (Admas), and Fesshaye "Joshua" Yohannes (Setit), demonstrated great courage; thus, were detained on September 18, 2021.[lxxiv]

Zeineb bravely represented the signatories of the Open Letter and the independent media. She stood up to defend the right to hold and express diverse political beliefs and opinions. She believed that staying silent in the face of an impending specter of horror and darkness was morally unacceptable. Zeineb was determined to alert the nation to the imminent menace, and she utilized her pen to express her ideas honestly and clearly. During Eritrea's darkest hour in history, she composed the following tribute to the heroes:

The detention of our heroes; I'll call them heroes for we have seen them displaying heroic acts in times of our quest for democracy as they have demonstrated valor and dedication during the war days; won't deter us from taking up further the causes of democracy. Detention of political opponents is not something new in our world. Many repressive regimes have practiced it in view of killing the spirit of democracy.

Mandela has been to prison, Kim, the current President of South Korea was in prison too. The late Corazon Aquino of the Philippines, Lech Walesa of Poland, Vaclav Havel of Hungary, Mahatma Gandhi and many other political leaders have made it after having been subjected to all kinds of coercion. Our heroes will prevail for they have a just cause. They'll for sure reappear in the Eritrean political scene with grace and dignity for they have not committed "crime against the people and the nation." For they have simply followed all the legal and peaceful path toward making their voices heard (Ali Z., 2001).

They have pursued the noblest line of thinking in making the Eritrean people aware of the forthcoming 'debacle' if matters were not set straight immediately. This article is a tribute to you and your noble ideas. Don't give up. Heroes never give up. (Ali Z., 2001).

In remembrance of the independent press, she said,

I'll call them the pioneers of independent thinking. They are not dead. They'll witness their rebirth pretty soon. They too, with grace and majesty. They have already introduced a culture in the Eritrean body politic. A culture of decency, free flow of information, exchange of ideas, public awareness, and courage. A culture daring enough to shake the foundations of the cowardly and lawless regime.

Nor will their closure deter Eritreans' tempered will to fight back. The cyberspace is there as a substitute. It's there to raise their banner high again. Thanks God, we are part of the world community. Thanks God, we can make our voices heard using the technology that human beings like us offered to us (Ali Z., 2001).

Zeineb exposed the machinations and intrigues of the PFDJ to maintain their grip of power. She delved into a wide range of topics, including PFDJ's ideology, the organization's nature, how it thrived in a state of lawlessness and chaos, and its modus operandi.

Zeineb earnestly appealed to the public to prevent the looming crisis by urging them to take action. She also discussed alternative pathways for change and vehemently denounced all acts of cowardice.

Zeineb delved into a diverse array of subjects in her written works, composing a total of sixteen articles. Her explorations spanned topics such as the nature of the regime, the intricacies of secrecy and conspiracy in its politics, the genesis of the organization, the internal power dynamics within the regime, the politics of brinkmanship employed by the governing body, the nature of then ongoing war with Ethiopia, and the impact of this conflict on the bankrupt leadership of PIA, among other facets.

Zeineb diligently kept her readers informed about then swiftly evolving political landscape in the country, ultimately leading to the incarceration of prominent political leaders and media personalities. Through her work, she offered valuable insights into navigating the ongoing struggle for change.

19

ERITREA'S MAIN THREATS
TO ITS STABILITY

A NATION'S STABILITY CAN be imperiled by a complex web of interconnected variables including both internal and external factors. Political stability is jeopardized when authoritarianism prevails, and a lack of inclusivity in the political process fosters disillusionment among a significant portion of society. Economic instability, on the other hand, is fueled by factors such as poverty, high unemployment, inflation, and a scarcity of foreign currency. Furthermore, the presence of poor governance, characterized by a dearth of accountability, fragile institutions, and corruption, poses a significant threat to a nation's stability. This can breed disenchantment among citizens and obstruct the government's capacity to effectively govern.

In addition, limited resources such as water, arable land, and energy can incite discontent among the populace. Importantly, these issues often stem from flawed government policies. In cases where these concerns are not openly addressed, the situation can deteriorate rapidly.

There are several threats to Eritrea's stability and, by extension, its growth trajectory. The first one is Eritrea's domestic policy and how it handles its relationship with its neighbors and the international community. The second set of threats involves outside factors that I will discuss in the following sub-topics.

19.1. ERITREA'S DOMESTIC AND FOREIGN POLICY

Eritrea's stability faces a grave threat from the regime entrenched in Asmara and President Isaias Afewerki in particular.

The nation's economic policies have taken a grievous toll, plunging it into a relentless spiral of decline. Per capita GDP has reached an all-time low, unemployment has soared to record highs, and inflation has surged to alarming levels.

The government's apprehension toward the private sector, or any emerging economically independent segments of society has effectively rendered it impotent. Basic necessities, such as bread and other daily food requirements, are now allocated through rationing. Various efforts to reinvigorate the economy have faltered, with even the president himself acknowledging the government's failures.

Amid this tumult, access to water and electricity has become a luxury as scarcity prevails.

The political situation in Eritrea has driven hundreds of thousands of young people to flee the country in search of better prospects elsewhere. The absence of government accountability is striking with legislative and judicial bodies rendered obsolete for two decades and ministerial cabinet meetings few and far between. Eritrea's stability teeters on a precarious precipice, largely attributed to the regime's grip on power and a series of disastrous economic policies and social policies.

Eritrea's perceived levels of public sector corruption, as measured on a scale where 100 represents very clean and 0 (zero) signifies a high degree of corruption, has been evaluated by Transparency International. The organization's assessment for the year 2021 assigned Eritrea a score of 22 out of 100, placing it at the 161st position among 180 countries, indicating a considerable challenge in terms of corruption control (International T., 2021).

Eritrea has been a consistent source of instability, marked by its persistent conflicts with neighboring countries, such as Ethiopia, Sudan, and Djibouti, along with its interventions in Somalia. Moreover, its support for Saudi Arabia and the United Arab Emirates in their conflict against the Houthis in Yemen further underscores a proclivity for war-mongering in its foreign policy.

Eritrea's antagonistic stance toward regional bodies like IGAD and the AU, as well as international organizations like the UN, has led to its alienation from the global community. Its alignment with nations like North Korea and Belarus in support of Russian aggression in Ukraine reflects the state of mind prevalent within the Eritrean government. This is further illustrated by Eritrea's self-imposed isolation, a phobia of any external influence, and a seemingly paranoid disposition.

The mistreatment of its own citizens and the alarming levels of political persecution have reached astronomical levels. The regime is preoccupied with maintaining power at all costs.

The succession factor has been deliberately glossed over for decades. In the absence of any viable institution – whether it is the political party, the legislative, judiciary, or executive – it is most likely that the nation can find itself in turmoil once change is on the horizon.

These elements collectively form a troubling recipe for instability within the nation. This threatens the nation's fate and for these reasons, Eritrea will always be vulnerable to instability.

19.2 ETHIOPIA

Ethiopia, a country with a population of 120 million, shares a deeply intertwined history with Eritrea. Both nations are situated in the same geographical region, fostering a historical connection that runs deep.

Eritrea, the present-day nation, serves as the cradle of the ancient Axumite civilization. This rich heritage is exemplified by historical sites like Metera, Qohaito, Koloé, and others, which bear witness to the historical significance of this region. Adulis and Zula (located in present-day Eritrea), once vital sea outlets of the Axumite Kingdom, indicate a flourishing maritime history (Munro-Hay, 1991). Notably, the obelisk of Metera, erected in the 3rd century AD during the Axumite Kingdom, features engravings of a crescent with the sun above it, accompanied by Ge'ez writing beneath—a testament to the past (Eritrea, Historical sites worth visiting in the Eritrean Southern region Part I, 2013).

The inscription of King Ezana serves as an invaluable artifact that encapsulates this legacy. However, both present-day Ethiopia and Eritrea have endured tumultuous times since the decline of the Axumite Kingdom. Centuries marked by wars of external aggression from entities like Portugal, Turkey, and Egypt, as well as internal power struggles, which often turned violent, characterized their shared history until the era of Italian colonialism.

It was during Italian colonialism that Eritrea emerged as a distinct entity, while Ethiopia, under the leadership of Menelik II, was still consolidating its own identity. Fifty years of Italian colonial rule in Eritrea, followed by a decade under British Military Administration, contributed to the formation of an emerging entity and a budding sense of nationalism or identity in the region known as "Eritreanism."

The subsequent federal arrangement with Ethiopia did not sit well with Eritrea, leading to a thirty-year war of independence that ultimately resulted in the birth of a new nation, internationally recognized in 1993. The EPRDF in Addis Ababa formally acknowledged Eritrea's sovereignty, marking a pivotal moment in their shared history.

The recognition of Eritrea by the EPRDF regime did not sit well with many Ethiopian elites, particularly the Amhara elite. This influential group consistently voiced their disagreement with this policy, asserting that, from a historical standpoint rooted in the myth of Ethiopia's purported three-thousand-year history, Eritrea has always been an integral part of Ethiopia.

According to their claims, traditional Eritrean leaders have historically acknowledged the authority of the Ethiopian Emperor long before the Italians arrived, which holds some validity. Numerous Ethiopian scholars contended that Emperor Menelik II had made a grave error in signing the Treaty of Wuchale with the Italians[lxxv] (Britannica, n.d.). In their view, Menelik II should have pursued the Italians all the way to the Red Sea during the Battle of Adwa. Some even considered Eritrea to be an inseparable part of the Solomonic Dynasty.

The Amhara elite claims that from a geopolitical perspective, Ethiopia, with its vast population of 120 million people, could not afford to remain landlocked. Being marginalized in regional affairs posed a significant threat to its security. Furthermore, from an economic standpoint, Ethiopia's lack of access to the Red Sea could lead to instability, potentially jeopardizing its economic sustainability. Therefore, Ethiopia was adamant about its claim to a seaport, such as Assab.

In a televised speech delivered to Ethiopian lawmakers on October 13, 2023, Prime Minister Abiy Ahmed gave an official speech concerning the Red Sea issue. He emphasized the critical importance of Ethiopia's access to this port, underscoring that it was a matter of survival for the nation. He urged Ethiopians to initiate discussions regarding the Red Sea, which he asserted would play a critical role in shaping Ethiopia's future. PM Abiy Ahmed explained that the Red Sea and the Nile are intricately linked with Ethiopia, serving as foundational factors that could either drive the country's development or lead to its downfall. He cited geographical, historical, ethnic, and economic reasons, including Ethiopia's rightful claim for sea access, which was established as an agreement within the UN charter[lxxvi] (Addis Standard, 2023).

The prime minister argued that a population as vast as 150 million could not be confined within such geographic constraints. He also issued a caution about the lack of fairness in the utilization of coastal resources among the involved countries, highlighting that an unjust situation could eventually escalate into conflict. Additionally, he outlined possible proposals such as shares in the Grand Ethiopian Renaissance Dam (GERD), Ethiopian Airlines, and Ethio-telecom in exchange for access to the sea. Abiy emphasized the need for leaders in Somalia, Djibouti, Eritrea, and Ethiopia to engage in discussions that extend beyond immediate peace, focusing on sustainable peace. He opposed the idea of postponing conflict to future generations because he thought it was not a viable solution, stating, "We cannot simply defer today's conflict to our children's generation"[lxxvii] (Addis Standard, 2023).

The prime minister emphasized that the port was not an immediate concern for Ethiopia and that a well-informed decision could be made once discussions had commenced. He mentioned Zeila in Somaliland as one option, citing its historical significance during the Ifat kingdom and its proximity. Another possibility lies in Djibouti, which is currently serving Ethiopia's needs. Additionally, Adulis, situated in coastal Eritrea, is another option. He said that Massawa and Assab are also under consideration, with no fixed preference between them; what is essential he said is having a viable access point. The prime minister underscored the importance of pursuing peaceful resolutions, citing Ethiopia's substantial population and military strength. He discouraged actions that might harm other countries and suggested exploring models like Federation or Confederation with Eritrea, despite their differing flags and names, as a means to address historical conflicts[lxxviii] (Addis Standard, 2023).

In light of these circumstances, there exists a perpetual political threat to Eritrea's stability emanating from the south i.e., Ethiopia. Considering the political volatility and instability within Ethiopia, it is not inconceivable to think that a hard-core Amhara elite could ascend to power one day. In such a scenario, it is reasonable to anticipate that it might declare war against Eritrea, ostensibly driven by a desire to restore Ethiopia's historical grandeur and lost glory. PM Abiy's statement about the Red Sea should, thus, be seen within the context of this long-standing claim.

The ongoing Israeli-Gaza political crisis, with its far-reaching implications across the Middle East and the Red Sea region, is shaping a geopolitical landscape reminiscent of the Iraqi crisis in 2003 when the US intervened in Iraq. Whether one approves or not, Eritrea is poised to become one of the players in addressing the Houthi crisis, and it is plausible that Western powers may have already initiated discussions with Eritrea to secure its involvement. One undeniable reality, however, is that regardless of Eritrea's political stance, its relationship with the West is unlikely to undergo a drastic shift, and it will likely continue to be labeled a pariah state.

President Isaias Afwerki may seek to leverage the evolving political dynamics in the Horn of Africa to his advantage, particularly Ethiopia's strategic moves under Prime Minister Abiy (such as the aggressive pursuit of a sea outlet), and the Israeli-Gaza crisis with its ripple effects on the Red Sea. He might aim to rally support among

Eritreans, both within the country and in the diaspora, to bolster his regime. There should be no confusion about these intentions. Regardless, the desire for change in Eritrea will not be hampered by such evolving developments. It will follow its own internal dynamic.

19.3 IS THE WEST IN GENERAL AND THE UNITED STATES IN PARTICULAR A THREAT TO ERITREA'S STABILITY?

The concept of a threat and the interpretation of international politics are fundamentally shaped by one's global perspective. Presently, the global landscape is subject to the dominance of the Western world, primarily under the leadership of the United States, attributable to their economic, political, and military supremacy. It's an undeniable reality, regardless of personal preferences.

Amid this prevailing world order, a powerful and influential player is emerging on the scene—China. China's Belt and Road initiative embodies a shift toward a multipolar world, emphasizing economic globalization, cultural diversity, and extensive utilization of information technology. This initiative seeks to foster connectivity among the continents of Asia, Europe, and Africa, alongside their adjacent seas. It aspires to forge and reinforce partnerships among the nations along the Belt and Road, establishing comprehensive, multi-tiered, and composite connectivity networks. The ultimate goal is to achieve diversified, self-reliant, equitable, and sustainable development across these countries[lxxix] (The State Council, the Peoples Republic of China, 2015). Simultaneously, China has solidified its position as a formidable military force, demanding recognition from the international community.

In reaction to the West's monopoly, various coalitions of nations, such as BRICS, are actively working to challenge this hegemony.

Furthermore, there are emerging regional powers, notably Saudi Arabia and the United Arab Emirates, around the Red Sea region. The unfolding of these geopolitical dynamics and how they will evolve in the forthcoming decades is a story yet to be written. The fate of the global order rests on how these multifaceted players interact and shape the future of international politics.

Eritrea occupies a strategically vital position along the Red Sea, a thoroughfare through which over 10 percent of the world's global trade flows. Spanning from the Bab al-Mandab at the southern entrance to the Egyptian-controlled Suez Canal in the north, the Red Sea holds immense economic importance as a maritime trade route. Its significance is anticipated to endure in the many years to come.

The Western world, particularly the United States, maintains a vested interest in this region. Any disruption to security in this area is a matter of great concern for Western powers and the international community at large. Such a breach can have far-reaching consequences, even extending to the stock market causing significant disruptions.

Eritrea had previously demonstrated a keen interest in engaging with regional politics. Notably, in 2003, during the Iraqi War, Eritrea expressed a desire to join the Coalition of the Willing, a group assembled by the United States, show- casing the country's intent to play a role on the global stage. The Government of Eritrea's statement on the issue reads as follows,

Eritrea
The decision taken by the Bush Administration to complete an unfinished job is very much welcome... The task is indeed one of completing an unfinished job for the sake of the stability and security of the Middle East and the permanent removal of a serious threat without losing another

opportunity. In this vein, Eritrea continues to maintain that the necessary measures must be taken without equivocation.
—Statement by the Government of Eritrea, March 12, 2003[lxxx] (The White House, 2003).

Eritrea was also willing to let the United States build a military base in the Dahlak Islands. In 2002, *The Washington Post* disclosed an ongoing negotiation between the United States and Eritrea, supported by lobbyists. They detailed the content of an issue paper titled "Why Not Eritrea?" that outlined Eritrea's proposal for the United States to use its strategic location in the Horn of Africa as a military staging ground in preparation for a potential conflict with Iraq. According to *The Post*, American officials were considering Eritrea's offer, and General Tommy Franks even visited the country.

Eritrea had retained the services of the law firm Greenberg Traurig, led by Jack Abramoff, who had close connections with Tom DeLay, the then-new House Majority Leader from Texas. As per Greenberg Traurig's contract with Eritrea, which was documented in the firm's registration with the Foreign Agents Registration Act at the Justice Department, Eritrea was paying $50,000 per month to Greenberg Traurig for assistance in advancing its public policy objectives in Washington. This amounted to $600,000 for their year-long engagement, spanning from April 15, 2002, to April 14, 2003 (The Washington Post, 2002).

Padgett Wilson, the director of governmental affairs at Greenberg Traurig, explained that Eritrea's primary goal was to improve its relationship with the United States. Establishing a US military base in Eritrea was seen as a means to attract much-needed capital and encourage American companies to engage in business there ultimately aiding the country in building a middle class and fostering economic stability for US enterprises. The lobbyists acknowledged that some US officials believed Eritrea was not progressing swiftly enough toward democracy, given the government's widespread crackdown on critics and the closure of private newspapers the previous year. However, Wilson maintained that Eritrea was actively addressing these concerns and that a closer relationship with the United States would be beneficial. The issue paper emphasized that, given the current sentiments in the Arab community and the strategic significance of the region, not forming an alliance with Eritrea would be deemed morally unacceptable[lxxxi] (The Washington Post, 2002).

The above two episodes reveal one thing. At least at one point, the regime in Asmara was trying to find its place as a player in the region by making overtures for collaboration with the United States.

The Asmara regime now alleges that the United States is responsible for Eritrea's current predicament. During the commemoration of Eritrea's Independence Day on May 23, 2023, the president expressed his strong disapproval of the "Washington clique," portraying it as the primary threat to Eritrea's stability. In his address, the president highlighted the maneuvers employed by the Washington clique and its allies, aimed at creating a rift between Ethiopia and Eritrea while continuously stoking conflict. He underscored that the defunct NATO Alliance, spearheaded by the "Washington clique," and the discordant financial alliance of the European Union, appear to be futilely attempting to rejuvenate their outdated agendas for global dominance, potentially leading to increased worldwide instability[lxxxii] (Ministry of Information, Eritrea, 2023).

The facts above convey a straightforward reality; the current Eritrean regime is pursuing a flawed and ineffective foreign policy. It is important to clarify that the West's foreign policy does not prioritize Eritrea's national interests over its own, which would be unreasonable. Eritrea, like any other country, prioritizes its national interests. However, in the realm of international politics, the goal is to find mutually beneficial solutions for all parties involved, a win-win solution.

Returning to the question of whether the West and the United States pose a threat to Eritrea's stability, one can only assert that Eritrea must excel in the realm of diplomacy, adeptly navigate tumultuous political landscapes, and demonstrate resilience in situations where complete withdrawal is not an option, but rather integration is the course. Eritrea has the potential to pursue two distinct strategies: the first one entails defying its current political and diplomatic norms. The other involves not only focusing on surviving but also developing the art of thriving in such challenging circumstances. The answer is in the hands of Eritreans, but one should remember that Eritrea is a small and poor nation with a prospect of growth if it manages itself well and the expectations of others.

19.4. ISLAMIC EXTREMISM

For more than three decades, the Horn of Africa has emerged as a significant hub for Islamic extremism, casting a shadow of global terrorism. The year 1989 witnessed the ascent of the National Islamic Front in Sudan, ushering in an era dedicated to constructing an Islamist state that became a magnet for radical Muslim factions worldwide. Throughout the 1990s, Sudan overtly extended its hospitality, providing a secure haven for terrorists to orchestrate operations across the broader Horn of Africa region. (USIP, 2004)

The collapse of the Somali government marked a turning point, giving rise to Al-Shabaab, a Muslim extremist group whose disruptive influence extended beyond Somalia, affecting the overall stability of the Horn of Africa. At the core of Al-Shabaab's agenda is the establishment of an Islamic state, guided by its interpretation of Sharia law (Council on Foreign Relations, 2022). The precarious situation in the Horn of Africa (nations at war, civil wars, etc.) creates an ongoing vulnerability, with the potential for these extremist groups to proliferate into neighboring countries such as Eritrea, Ethiopia, and Djibouti. The constant threat of expansion underscores the need for sustained regional and international efforts to counteract the roots of extremism in this critical geopolitical zone.

19.5. Isaias Afeworki's stance on confederation with Ethiopia: some facts

In his recently published book, "An African Revolution Reclaimed," Mesfin delves into an important meeting that took place prior to the full liberation of the country. According to the book, Isaias called a meeting that consisted of eight members of the clandestine party's Central Committee, along with Mesfin. During the meeting, Isaias emphasized the crucial nature of their collaboration with the TPLF and underscored the importance of their joint efforts leading to an internationally accepted referendum, which would legitimize its outcome. Isaias disclosed that there had been discussions about the formation of a joint government in Ethiopia, incorporating Eritrea. Furthermore, he revealed that an agreement had been reached with the TPLF regarding this initiative (Hagos, 2023).

Mesfin notes in his book that despite the complacency exhibited by other attendees at the meeting, he staunchly opposed the notion of establishing a joint government. He rationalized that such an arrangement contradicted the principles for which the Eritrean people had fought, emphasizing that there should be no compromise when it comes to Eritrea's independence. Mesfin further elaborates, stating,

I concluded by clearly stating that said plan was inappropriate in its approach and unacceptable to me in its substance.

There was no follow-up question not a conversation on the topic. Isaias then said that the issue could then be dropped and dropped it was., not to be brought up in subsequent EPLF Central Committee meeting or any other meeting that I am aware of (Hagos, 2023).

On May 30, 1991, The New York Times ran an article titled "Ethiopia Rebel Faction is to Govern Separately." In this piece, Craig R. Whitney reported that the leader of the rebel group, which had recently gained control of the Ethiopian province of Eritrea, announced plans to establish a distinct provisional government. This interim administration would function independently until a United Nations-supervised referendum on Eritrean independence could be conducted.

Whitney continued to explain that American officials facilitated a conference among victorious rebel groups. The outcome was an agreement, reached on Tuesday, to establish a temporary administration in Addis Ababa under the Ethiopian People's Revolutionary Democratic Front, headquartered in Tigrai Province. Additionally, all-party talks were scheduled to commence on July 1, with the aim of forming a more inclusively structured national provisional government. Despite this, Mr. Isaias, the Eritrean leader, stated that while Eritrea would cooperate with the Addis Ababa administration, it would not become a part of it.[lxxxiii]

The article also highlighted a statement from an American diplomat, noting that the mediator, Assistant Secretary of State Herman J. Cohen, was not surprised by the Eritrean announcement. Cohen, who remained in London, held separate meetings with all the groups involved but offered no further comments on the matter. The report touched upon the accord reached on a national vote.[lxxxiv]

The aforementioned information was disseminated to the public through the media. What added an intriguing layer to this development was the confidential discussions that took place behind closed doors. The mediator, Assistant Secretary Herman Cohen, floated the idea of confederation with three key parties: Isaias Afeworki, Meles Zenawi, and the leader of the Oromo Liberation Front, Mr. Lencho Leta.

Dr. Tesfai Ghirmatsion (former Minister of Agriculture, former Deputy Minister of Foreign Affairs, and Ambassador of Eritrea to the European Union), and I met in Lusaka, Zambia, in 2012 while I was on a mission for a USAID-funded project. We frequently engaged in evening discussions about various topics over dinner. During one such conversation, Dr. Tesfai brought up the surprising revelation that in 1991 Isaias had supported the concept of confederation with Ethiopia. Unaware of this, I expressed my lack of familiarity with the matter. Dr. Tesfai shared, "I took part in some of the discussions mediated by Herman Cohen. During our deliberations, Cohen introduced the topic of confederation between Ethiopia and Eritrea. Isaias expressed his support for Cohen's recommendation. I was taken aback but couldn't voice my thoughts during the meeting as Isaias led the Eritrean delegation. After the session, I approached Isaias and inquired about his endorsement of confederation with Ethiopia. Isaias mentioned he would discuss it later, but that discussion never took place, and Isaias left for Eritrea.

Dr. Tesfai told me that he questioned Isaias's political integrity since.

This incident may be connected to the previously mentioned event as narrated by Mesfin Hagos.

Upon Isaias's arrival in Eritrea, a delegation of high-ranking EPLF officials drove to Tessenei (or possibly Agordat) to extend a welcome. According to a colleague (whose name is withheld for safety reasons), Isaias was in an extremely foul mood and refused to engage with anyone until he reached Asmara.

This possibly indicates that Isaias was still entertaining the notion of forming a confederation with Ethiopia, in stark contrast to Mesfin's position during the February 1991 meeting in Af'abet.

19.6 POINTS TO PONDER

The stability of Eritrea hinges on its capacity to address and mitigate the potential threat to its security. The initial step in addressing this threat involves acknowledging its presence. Equally important is identifying and rectifying Eritrea's flawed domestic policies that have the potential to trigger internal turmoil. It is also crucial to grasp the delicate position Eritrea occupies in the global political landscape, as this could expose it to the risk of an external political and diplomatic offensive that would have severe implications for Eritrea's national security.

To counter this impending assault, Eritrea must utilize several strategies.

First, it should strive to enhance its reputation as a stabilizing and peace-loving nation in the eyes of the international community. A major diplomatic initiative is needed to demonstrate Eritrea's commitment to peace and regional stability and to show it is a reliable security partner in this region while countering the narrative that it has always been part of Ethiopia.

Second, Eritrea should emphasize that Ethiopia's stability is in its own interest and that of the region, and that fostering harmonious relations with neighbors is high on its agenda. Furthermore, it must show goodwill in addressing Ethiopia's security concerns and propose mutually beneficial solution that is in line in line with international norms. The only viable solution is through peaceful negotiation and diplomacy.

Third, Eritrea can also fortify itself by building a strong economy that can weather political crises. This entails implementing sound economic policies, unleashing the potential of the private sector, creating an environment that attracts foreign investment, and bolstering its human resource assets. In addition to economic strength, Eritrea should harness cutting-edge technology to bolster its position among developing economies.

Fourth, building a modern and professional army can serve as a deterrent to potential threats, particularly from neighboring Ethiopia. Exploring military alliances with major global powers is another avenue worth considering, as these alliances can also act as a deterrence to external threats.

Fifth, Eritrea may also need to seriously consider increasing its population size. Demography can sometimes play a role in deterring foreseeable threats from neighbors. According to a report by the National Statistics and Evaluation Office, in the year 2001, Eritrea's Ministry of Local Government estimated the total population of Eritrea to be around 3.2 million.[lxxxv] Assuming a 3 percent growth rate, Eritrea's population can be projected to be approximately 6.1 million in 2023. Given the rapidly growing populations of its neighboring countries, Eritrea should closely examine this demographic aspect.

Sixth, as a rule of thumb, the emergence of extremist tendencies is typically attributed to political, social, and economic crises within a country. Mitigating the threat of Islamic extremism, thus, necessitates a concerted effort by a constitutional government to uphold religious freedom, and basic human and political rights, eliminate arbitrary detention and persecution of believers, foster a robust economy to ensure the well-being of the populace, and collaborate with neighboring countries to collectively tackle this challenge.

Last but not least, Eritrea must make efforts to learn and acquire the art of diplomatic communication. Navigating volatile political situations, especially in the Red Sea region, requires a nuanced approach. In a globalized world where national, regional, and international interests converge, Eritrea cannot exist in isolation. Eritrea should stop playing the "I am the victim" game. Promoting win-win solutions in its diplomatic endeavors should be a core element of its strategy. "Politics is the art of the possible, the attainable — the art of the next best," once said Otto von Bismarck, former Chancellor of the German Reich. There's an invaluable lesson to glean from this axiom.

In conclusion, it is essential to recognize that while certain factors may evolve in the future, there are also elements that will likely remain constant and will have a bearing on Eritrea's stability or instability. These include:

i. The enduring strategic significance of the Red Sea to both the West and East, as well as to the global community.

ii. The persistent recurrence of Ethiopia's claim to access the sea, an issue that will continue to be raised from various corners within Ethiopia.

iii. The ongoing threat posed by Islamic extremism or other extremist tendencies in the region.

iv. The sustained political volatility in the Horn of Africa, stemming from its historical origins and unresolved political challenges, contributing to changes in the alignment of forces.

v. The perpetual potential for proxy wars, driven by the aforementioned factors.

In such circumstances, one does not have a choice but to be resourceful and resilient, mastering not only the art of survival but also the ability to thrive under those circumstances.

20

A UNIQUE TEN-YEAR TIMEFRAME THAT SHAPES ERITREA'S POLITICAL LANDSCAPE: A HYPOTHESIS

I N ERITREA'S POLITICAL narrative, the interval of ten years stands as a distinctive timeframe that profoundly shapes its landscape. My hypothesis suggests that political transformations unfold within a reasonable timeframe, necessitating the expiration of the initial "political honeymoon." This triggers a shift within the internal dynamics of a political movement, resulting in a reconfiguration of the alignment of forces. Such changes transpire gradually as new political issues arise (requiring people to take a stance) within a period allowing for trends to mature—a natural progression akin to a leap from quantitative to qualitative development.

Since the forties, every decade has introduced its own surprise to Eritrea's political scene. For instance, the BMA relinquished its hold to pave the way for Eritrea's Federation with Ethiopia over a ten-year time frame. The tumultuous period gave rise to a new political phenomenon that was explained at length in an earlier chapter.

Similarly, the annexation of Eritrea by Ethiopia, which triggered an armed insurrection, spanned almost a decade.

The emergence of the EPLF occurred a decade after the establishment of the ELF following a very intricate political process.

Following ten years of political tension and civil war between the EPLF and the ELF, it took another decade for the ELF to vacate Eritrea due to its internal political dynamic and the external pressure exerted on it by the EPLF.

It took ten years before Eritrea was liberated following the collapse of the ELF as a political organization.

Further political landmarks include the political movements of the late nineties leading to the birth of G-15 following a decade-long post-independence political honeymoon and euphoria. This movement of high-level politicians shook the foundations of the regime. The regime took harsh measures to silence them. Their only sin was demanding the implementation of a ratified constitution.

Subsequently, an attempt to overthrow the government in 2013 by prominent politicians (also known as the Forto Rebellion) transpired after almost another ten years. The demand was similar to that of the G-15. Regrettably, these two remarkable movements for change did not come to fruition.

A new development surfaced a decade after these major events, marked by a pivotal shift in the relationship between the Isaias regime and Prime Minister Abiy of Ethiopia (following a few years of political honeymoon), signaling the failure of the Isaias regime's policies toward Ethiopia. PM Abiy's statement regarding the Red Sea has raised the specter of war over Eritrea.

The global spread of the Eritrean Blue Wave, represented by the Brigade NHamedu movement, indicates an unprecedented organized effort among the youth, clamoring for regime change and the establishment of a constitutional Eritrea.

It is also worth noting that the regime in Asmara has antagonized the West as never before in its effort to solidify its grip on its power by aligning itself with Russia and China. Previously the West tolerated the regime due to its policy of peaceful containment. Not anymore.

Amid the aftermath of the Eritrean Army's intervention in Ethiopia's domestic affairs, Eritrean parents are yet to be informed about the loss of their loved ones. They are questioning the validity of the policy that the government led them to believe it was aimed at preserving Ethiopia's unity or saving Ethiopia from disintegration. The Eritrean populace is currently leveling accusations against the President for a statement made in Hawasa, Ethiopia. During this instance, he called upon PM Abiy to take the lead and be the representative of the two countries on all aspects of collaboration ("ንስኻ ኢኻ ትመርሓና" "ንስኻ ኢኻ ወኪልና") and tacitly condoned PM Abiy's remarks, which implied that he had President Isaias's authorization to utilize Assab as he saw fit. This development has visibly sparked frustration among the mid-level military and civilian leadership.

Consider how Prime Minister Abiy received a group of high-ranking military officers led by Brigadier General Abraha Kassa at his presidential palace. This meeting took place following weeks-long tour in various parts of Ethiopia, a few months after the signing of the Pretoria Peace Agreement between the Federal Government of Ethiopia and the TPLF. During the meeting, as disclosed by a reliable source, Prime Minister Abiy engaged in conversation with the Eritrean delegation, addressing three key points. First, upon observing that the majority of the delegation members were in their early or mid-seventies, he humorously inquired about their retirement plans. He was particularly staring at Romadan Awlyay whose average age of his peer group is death.[lxxxvi] Secondly, he sought information on when the Federal Government would commence utilizing the port of Assab. Thirdly, he questioned the delegation about their plans for handling the influx of thousands of young Eritreans into Ethiopia. It was evident that Prime Minister Abiy was not anticipating concrete answers from either the head of the delegation or other members, as he was aware that nobody had definitive solutions to these inquiries.

Other visible development is that the Eritrean diaspora is uniting like never before by embracing the Blue Wave. In my view, the resounding call for regime change reverberates louder than ever today.

According to a source whose name I am unable to disclose for safety reasons, the President's inner circle is more isolated than ever before, having dismantled crucial institutions, including the military (as previously discussed).

Recent speeches delivered by the President in various regional forums—such as those in China, Russia, South Africa, Kenya, and Saudi Arabia— strongly suggest signs of his mental instability. It's alarming to witness a leader, unable to provide sustenance for its own citizens, espousing ambitious global strategies.

The above facts and trends foretell an imminent change looming over Eritrea. The choice lies with the people—to align themselves with history or to stand against the tide. It's a challenging choice; indeed.

21

CONCLUSION

21.1. SOME THEORETICAL ASSUMPTIONS AND FACTS

THE PEOPLE OF Eritrea have grown increasingly discontented with the prevailing situation in their country and are yearning for change. Notably, even individuals who currently support the regime are now advocating for the establishment of a constitutional government, the release of political prisoners, etc. They emphasize the importance of a fresh start, putting the past behind us, and are calling for reconciliation, forgiveness, and constructive dialogue or civilized discourse in a YouTube video titled "A Discussion Between Elias Amare and Daniel Teklai"[lxxxvii] (Teklai, 2023).

The main issue lies in the manner through which this transformation will manifest. Within various circles, both in the diaspora and within the country itself, including members of the opposition and even sympathizers of the regime, a multitude of arguments are circulating. Many appear with certainty that change is inevitable. It is simply a matter of time. Conversely, others contend that the Eritrean populace is not yet prepared for change, blaming the regime for instilling fear and conformity into their minds. Some argue that although Eritreans yearn for change, they face challenges in bringing about transformation, primarily because of the oppressive regime that has gripped the nation. Some may argue that they prefer to live under Isaias, at least because they believe he possesses the ability to 'safeguard the nation's security' and deter any threats from the South, particularly Ethiopia. Another perspective upholds that Eritrea stands as an oasis of peace and stability in the tumultuous Horn of Africa, so why bother? A few contend that it is too late for any change to ever take place in Eritrea.

There are also concerns about the future of Eritrea following regime change. Some fear the potential chaos and power struggles that may ensue among the military generals after Isaias departs the political scene given that the question of succession has been deliberately ignored for decades.

No matter when and how there is always a distinct beginning and an end for all aspects of life. This fundamental lesson is imparted to us by both nature and the field of social science. Numerous administrations have arisen and, ultimately, faded into obscurity, yet the people always endure. Political parties, a microcosm of human existence, undergo a cyclical progression—beginning with infancy, traversing youth and maturity, enduring the trials of old age, and ultimately succumbing to the inevitable embrace of decline and dissolution.

In the case of Eritrea's current regime, it has reached the twilight of its existence. Consequently, I believe its days are now numbered. The internal mechanisms that once sustained it are faltering, and its cognitive faculties are no longer functioning at full capacity. In a desperate bid to cling to power, it finds itself in a state of intensive care, fighting an uphill battle against the inexorable march of time.

People cannot remain idle; they should instead work together to hasten the downfall of the regime. To achieve this, one must comprehend the full nature of the regime, including its operational mechanisms, methods of maintaining power, and more.

Dr. Natasha Ezrow, a scholar at Essex University, has conducted extensive research on dictatorships and dictatorial regimes, offering valuable theoretical insights in her scholarly writings and books.

During her TED lecture titled "The Decline of Authoritarian Regimes—How Autocrats Lose Power,"[lxxxviii] Dr. Ezrow provides a definition of dictatorship, characterizing it as any form of government where there is no rotation of executive leadership. She proceeds to categorize five distinct types of dictatorships, which include a single-party system (such as seen in China), military juntas (as exemplified by Argentina), monarchies (like the Saudi monarchy), personalist dictatorships (with leaders like Muammar Ghaddafi and Saddam Hussein who exercise absolute control), and hybrid regimes that incorporate various elements (Ezrow, 2014).

Dr. Ezrow highlights that dictators commonly confront their most significant dangers from elements within their own governments, especially the individuals most likely to stage a coup. She contends that a dictator's ability to stay in power depends on the dynamics of their interactions with the ruling elite (Ezrow, 2014).

The wave of coups d'état in West Africa (Gabon, Mali, Guinea, Chad, Burkina Faso, and Niger) between 2020 -23 attests to the above-mentioned theory.

Dr. Ezrow underscores the importance of an entity that facilitates the rise of dictators to power. This entity may take various forms, such as a military junta, as seen in Argentina, or a single-party system, exemplified by China. She also points out that both the democratic institutions and the organization responsible for propelling the dictator to power tend to be feeble. Consequently, dictators tend to amass power more tightly within their grasp, leading to the development of a personalized dictatorship. Notable instances of this phenomenon include Mobutu in Zaire, Idi Amin in Uganda, Francois Duvalier in Haiti, Saddam Hussein in Iraq, and Ghaddafi in Libya, among others (Ezrow, 2014).

According to her lecture, when a personalized dictator assumes power, their obsession with retaining it, coupled with the absence of established mechanisms for succession, fosters a heightened sense of paranoia. This compels them to take measures aimed at eliminating potential rivals, which involves deliberately weakening the military to prevent coup attempts (a strategy known as "coup-proofing") and undermining their own political party. The military's weakening can be achieved through insufficient training, restricted access to weapons, or the establishment of an alternative military organization designed to counterbalance the traditional military's influence (Ezrow, 2014).

Dr. Ezrow argues that the personalist dictator intentionally weakens his own political party by removing those with significant expertise or the potential to challenge him. Furthermore, she highlights that this type of dictator may also seek to undermine the legislative and judicial branches of government. Additionally, the bureaucracy can be weakened through frequent personnel changes, creating an atmosphere of insecurity and chaos. She suggests that the dictator's aim is to prevent any group from developing expertise or the ability to challenge their rule. She asserts that the personalist dictator actually prefers a state of disorganized chaos, resulting in the complete deinstitutionalization of the regime (Ezrow, 2014).

Regarding the manner in which power transitions occur, she contends that they can turn highly violent. Dr. Ezrow asserts that leaders with a personalistic approach to dictatorship often surround themselves with sycophants who feed them falsehoods and cater to their desires. This dynamic tends to inflate the dictator's ego and subsequently distort their perception of reality and become more delusional. In some instances, these advisors praise them as the best and most exceptional leaders, advocating for their perpetual rule and the elimination of anyone who dares challenge them. These advisors portray their adversaries as feeble. The longer such dictators remain in power, the more they come to identify themselves with the state, essentially personifying it (Frantz, 2011). They become unable to envision a life outside of their association with the state.

Dr. Ezrow argues that due to their inability to distance themselves from the state, authoritarian leaders find it exceedingly challenging to relinquish power. They tend to hold onto power until the very end, as exemplified by figures like Ghaddafi and Saddam Hussein. According to her research, authoritarian leaders have several potential paths they can take, which include proactively initiating reforms and voluntarily stepping down, staying in office until their death, or being forcefully removed from power through means such as a coup, pressure from elites, assassination, or conflicts. Additionally, when violent revolutions occur, international intervention may take place, or nonviolent protests can arise. She asserts that the likelihood of authoritarian leaders being forcibly ousted from power is quite high in dictatorships, standing at 40 percent. Among the remaining scenarios, 20 percent opt for self-initiated reforms, less than 10 percent are influenced by nonviolent protests, and 20 percent remain in office until their demise[lxxxix] (Ezrow, 2014).

21.2. HOW DOES THE ABOVE THEORY APPLY TO ERITREA?

The Eritrean regime perfectly fits the profile of a personalist dictatorship as explained above. The regime strategically utilized the PFDJ as its launching pad/organization, fully aware of the weak state of most institutions. From the outset, the regime recognized that the primary threat would arise internally, especially from individuals who had played prominent roles during the war of independence.

To maintain its grip on power, and in the absence of established mechanisms for succession, the regime has systematically eliminated and continues to eliminate potential rivals. Notable examples include the Reformist movement spearheaded by G-15, and members of the Forto Rebellion. General Sebhat Efrem's situation serves as another poignant illustration—he narrowly survived a life-threatening attack at his home but remains paralyzed. Former ministers like Berhane Abrehe were consigned to prison, left to languish in obscurity. Ambassadors Mohammed Ali Umaru and Abdu Heji, Senai Kifleyesus, Al'azar Mesfin, Tesfai Ghebreab, Kiros Habtemichael, Idris Ab'are, Miriam Hagos, Senait Debessai, Aster Yohannes, Siraj Ibrahim, etc.,[xc] also find themselves incarcerated, their freedom also denied.

Isaias weakened the army from the very beginning. He vehemently opposed the establishment of a professional army. Even after a significant number of former freedom fighters were demobilized, there was never any intention to rejuvenate the military forces. The crisis of 1997, involving neighboring Ethiopia, exposed the vulnerabilities of the regime. The regime was caught unprepared. The deliberate attempt to weaken the military had its adverse ramifications. Afterall, the Ethio-Eritrea crisis could have been resolved peacefully on a negotiation table.

As mentioned earlier, there existed a golden opportunity to establish a military academy aimed at producing an elite corp. However, the dictator instead implemented the "National Service" program as a means to counterbalance the influence of the traditional military and thus, deinstitutionalized the army. No other person could explain better how the military was rendered the private domain of the dictator but Mesfin Hago. Mesfin—who served as both chief of staff and Minster of Defense in Isaias's government—in his most recently released book entitled *An African Revolution Reclaimed—A Memoir of Eritrea Freedom Fighter Mesfin Hagos*. He has the following to say about how Isaias weakened the army and turned it into his own fiefdom,

> He treated the military like his worn private domain. Instead of allocating a budget and affording the minister or the chief of staff some freedom of action, he kept doing things himself, or he would come and tell us what to do without consultation. Such failure—sluggish institutionalization and professionalization, and excessive presidential intrusion—combined to weaken the military as an institution and hurt the country (Hagos M., 2023).

Mesfin's frustration was captured again in the following statement from the same book. He continues,

> Consequently, my position as minister and the ministry as an institution were hallowed out. The ministry's essential branches were gutted, one branch at a time, causing friction between us and irreparably damaging our relationship—on both a personal and a professional level. The ordeal was reflected in five institutions, the air force, the navy, the national service, the ground force, and the office or role of the minister (Hagos M., 2023).

Furthermore, the regime intentionally and systematically eroded its own political party's foundations by eliminating party congresses and Central Committee meetings. It has almost been thirty years since the last congress (the Third EPLF Congress) was convened.

This erosion also extended to the legislative and judicial branches of government, with twenty- two years having passed since the last session of the legislative body (the National Assembly). Chief Justice Teame Beyene was dismissed from his position following his protest against the President's continuous interference in the Ministry of Justice's internal affairs. In addition, a Special Court was established in parallel with the High Court, further undermining the judicial system's independence.

Ministries often find themselves marginalized, as they are frequently bypassed by the ruling party. There is a significant consolidation of power within the President's office, leading to the complete deinstitutionalization of the government. Also, the question of succession is difficult to fathom at this juncture.

Loyalty holds significant importance within this regime. The dictator closely associates himself exclusively with individuals who are blindly loyal to him. He only welcomes perspectives that align with his own values and desires. As per my sources, any attempt by members of his inner circle to raise concerns is met with disdain. A case in point is Mr. Yemane Ghebreab. According to reliable sources, Yemane finds himself in an awkward situation with Isaias. Rumor has it that his position is shaky. One cannot fail to notice his absence in several diplomatic missions the President is undertaking these days.

A colleague recounts an incident that took place in Massawa during a rare cabinet meeting. During this meeting, a member of the cabinet raised concerns brought forth by the general populace. In response, the President immediately inquired about the source and the person responsible for assembling this information. This left the cabinet ministers perplexed, and the President's ensuing anger was so intense that he abruptly departed the meeting and returned to Asmara. By the way, the average age of the so-called cabinet of ministers is 76–77.

I also recall an episode that occurred at the "Ghibbi" or Government Palace around 1994. The President convened a meeting to discuss the relocation of ministries from the capital city to other administrative zones. The proposed idea was for some of them to be dispersed across the various zonal centers (capitals). The rationale behind this proposal was to generate employment opportunities for the residents of the administrative zones and promote an equitable distribution of resources. The meeting was attended by government officials, including Director Generals and Ministers, as well as party representatives.

The initial response was voiced by Dr. Ner'ayo Teklemichael, who emphasized the gravity of the matter and stressed the need for meticulous consideration and thorough research before any decision could be made. Following Dr. Ner'ayo's comments, I took the floor and argued that the public sector's role in generating employment is limited, with most opportunities arising from the private sector or through other development programs. Additionally, I raised concerns about the logistical challenges and lack of coordination that might arise if ministries were dispersed throughout the country.

In an alternative approach, I proposed designating specific cities for distinct roles. Asmara, I suggested, could be the political capital, Massawa, a financial center, Dekemhare, a cultural hub, and perhaps Keren, a tourist destination, given its favorable climate.

The third speaker, Eden Fasil, weighed in on the matter, expressing a lack of support for scattering ministries throughout the country with the exception of the Ministry of Marine Resources. Eden's reasoning added an element of humor to the discussion. He quipped, "At least the ministry would be well-positioned to catch fish that dare to peek above the sea" (ብዉሑዱ ኣብኡ ኮይኖም ርእሱ ዘዘቐልቀለ ዓሳ ክሕዙ ይኽእሉ).

The meeting was scheduled to resume in the afternoon, but the President did not show up.

Criticizing the government is often equated with criticizing the dictator, and vice versa, blurring the distinction between the two. In Eritrea, this extends to the point of labeling anyone who criticizes either the government or the dictator as a traitor, and often paying a hefty price.

Isaias shows no inclination to willingly surrender power; only a violent challenge seems capable of compelling such a change. In Eritrea, Isaias appears uninterested in reform or voluntary resignation, as these concepts do not seem to align with his agenda. It is probable that he will strive to maintain his grip on power until his passing. Consequently, the most plausible avenue for change in Eritrea lies in the forceful removal of the president, an outcome that appears increasingly likely.

The aforementioned argument is not without merit. There have been instances where the President faced challenges not only from external forces (opposition outside PFDJ) but also from insiders. The reform movement of G-15, for example, posed a significant threat to his survival. Such a substantial threat had not been seen prior to that incident. Another noteworthy instance of opposition emerged in 2013, known as The Forto Rebellion, led by a coalition of high-level party, military, and government officials, including ministers and governors.

The way in which the dictator manages his relationships with the elite fails to endure beyond the initial honeymoon period. The alignment of power dynamics has consistently relied on the positions individuals have taken at different junctures in the history of the front, first within EPLF, and later on PFDJ. Collaboration among them only occurs when the political interests of these individuals converge. However, political developments are fluid and can morph or undergo rapid transformations. In such situations, it is not a must for individuals to hold identical stances on various issues. In the context of a personalized dictatorship, like the one in Eritrea, there exists no mechanism for amicably resolving differences. Violence can emerge as the sole, albeit undesirable, means of resolution.

Eritrea is not unique in the sense that the current regime will remain in power indefinitely, as some of the supporters argue. However, I do not foresee a change driven by outside forces or through external intervention. Among the scenarios outlined above, probably, discontented factions within both the military and the civil service currently operating under the regime will eventually take action to alter the prevailing situation, despite Isaias' regime's efforts to prevent it. Information from my sources suggests that such movements exist within Eritrea. The specifics of their organization and how they will bring about change are subjects for future historical accounts. However, one thing is certain: change is on the horizon.

21.3. THE ROLE OF THE OPPOSITION IN THE DIASPORA

The role of the opposition in the diaspora is pivotal, but it hinges on the imperative need for consensus regarding its mission, values, and approach. To effectively support the movement for change within Eritrea, the diaspora must rally around several key principles and actions.

First and foremost, unity is key. The diaspora is confronted with significant challenges arising from the current state of the country, making it imperative for Eritreans abroad to unite in solidarity. Internal divisions and conflicts do not bode well for the pursuit of change.

Unity should not be perceived as an effort to bring all like-minded individuals under a single organization because as the historical context indicates, it is rather difficult to achieve. What is essential, however, is a convergence of ideas and shared beliefs. It is critical to establish a common political platform that can serve as a catalyst for instigating positive change. The opposition must articulate these shared beliefs and ideas.

There seems to be a broad consensus on the necessity for change among the people,. Additionally, there is widespread support for the establishment of a constitutional government immediately following the change—a government characterized by checks and balances. The concept of forming a transitional government has also been discussed within various segments of the opposition for some time. It is imperative for the opposition to communicate its stance clearly on this matter.

Second, internal divisions within the diaspora must be set aside in pursuit of the overarching goal: regime change and the establishment of a constitutional government. The focus should remain on these common objectives. As discussed earlier in the book, the diaspora is highly fragmented and unwieldy. It would not be an exaggeration to say that the opposition often spends more time vilifying each other than targeting the regime in Asmara. Attacks and counterattacks are the norm within the diaspora, and at times, they become highly personalized. Moreover, the opposition is frequently seen dedicating too much time to peripheral issues rather than addressing fundamental matters.

Third, the diaspora must come together to address these nuisances and help the younger generation develop a culture of civility, tolerance for differences, and a commitment to the mission and political issues, rather than personalities. It is heartening to see that the Global Yi'akel Movement, Felsi, Bright Future, and other political platforms have taken significant steps toward promoting constructive dialogue within the Eritrean community across the world. This is an encouraging development.

Fourth, civilized discourse should be the cornerstone of the diaspora engagement, providing a platform to constructively address differences. Opposing opinions should not only be tolerated but celebrated. Effective communication across party lines is crucial to promoting collaboration and unity. It is unrealistic to expect all opposition parties to unite under a single umbrella, given the diverse perspectives, approaches, and geographical dispersion of the diaspora. What truly matters is the quality of political discourse that is based on civility and tact (ናዕውነትን ውሕልነትን). Individuals can still align with specific groups or ideologies, but the key is to identify some common ground to use as a launching pad for collective efforts. While it's a challenging endeavor, it is achievable, and there are many supporters of the Eritrean people case who may be willing to extend a helping hand in the effort.

Fifth, media outlets representing the diaspora, especially YouTube channels, should exercise caution and responsibility when disseminating information. It is imperative to avoid spreading false or unsubstantiated news and refrain from using harsh language. Their credibility will be at stake should they prefer to do so. The presentation of diaspora media outlets often leaves much to be desired; however, it's important to note that not all of them fall into this category.

There are individuals within the diaspora who repeatedly release unsubstantiated news. Additionally, some social media outlets within the diaspora exhibit divisiveness, sow seeds of political hate, and prioritize attacking personalities over addressing critical issues. Perhaps the most concerning aspect is the time and effort that the diaspora community invests in vilifying one another.

I have heard from reliable sources about how the people of Asmara and the country in general perceive this situation. They often view the diaspora as ineffective, lacking credibility, and, to put it mildly, unhelpful to the cause of bringing about positive change. It is crucial that this unhealthy trend comes to an end.

Sixth, it is important that former freedom fighters not be unfairly labeled as bandits (ሽፍታ). The sacrifice and firm commitment displayed by those who fought for Eritrea's independence should be revered and celebrated. Many individuals, including me, find it disheartening and frustrating to witness how certain media outlets depict former members of the EPLF.

The tens of thousands of comrades who were unable to witness the realization of Eritrea's independence were not, and are not, bandits. They are no different from you and me, having devoted their careers, youth, and even their lives to a noble cause. They did what was expected of them. Were they let down? The answer is a resounding "yes." It is crucial that we differentiate between those who wholeheartedly dedicated themselves to the cause and those who betrayed it, ultimately becoming the root cause of our trials.

By misrepresenting the sacrifices of our martyrs and veterans, we inadvertently undermine the pursuit of change and the establishment of a constitutional Eritrea.

Seventh, a call for unity should be extended, urging the diaspora to mobilize millions of Eritreans under a common banner, advocating for regime change and the establishment of a constitutional government. Wholehearted support should be provided to the movement for change within Eritrea, strengthening the collective effort for change.

Eight, financial support to the dictatorial regime in Eritrea, whether through the 2 percent tax or other revenue sources, must be actively opposed by the diaspora. As detailed in earlier chapters of this book, one of the primary sources of income for the Asmara regime is the long-standing 2 percent tax imposed by PFDJ decades ago. This practice is commonly referred to as "milking the diaspora."

The opposition should wholeheartedly support any initiatives aimed at denying the regime this cash flow.

The young Eritrean diaspora movement should strengthen its strategies for countering the regime's influence abroad, effectively organizing and rallying around actions such as refusing to pay the 2 percent tax, boycotting regime-organized festivals, and persuading others to join the cause. However, their actions shouldn't solely rely on taking countermeasures. It's imperative for them to explore various strategies to outmaneuver the regime's political tactics.

Ninth, diplomatically isolating the regime in Asmara, wherever it may be, and the exposure of its atrocities against its own people are crucial actions to be taken by the diaspora. It can play a significant role in making the plight of our people heard by the international community. It can effectively convey their grievances and concerns to foreign governments, international organizations, and the media. Additionally, through this effort, it can pressure the regime to stop harassing its citizens, establish the rule of law, protect human rights, release prisoners of conscience, and, in the best-case scenario, prompt a change in its behavior.

Diplomacy can also facilitate mediation efforts between a government and the opposition, although this is highly unlikely to occur in the Eritrean context. The advocacy efforts led by the diaspora in various forums can be instrumental in raising awareness of human rights abuses, advocating for investigations, and supporting initiatives to hold perpetrators accountable. Furthermore, diplomacy can foster international solidarity with the Eritrean people, potentially leading to partnerships among interested groups working together to address the challenges faced by the Eritrean population.

The diaspora's diplomatic initiatives can provide critical support for Eritrean refugees scattered across the globe and help reinforce international legal frameworks that protect their rights. Through diplomatic statements, speeches, and media coverage, these efforts can effectively raise public awareness about the predicament the Eritrean people are undergoing. Increased awareness can subsequently generate public pressure to take meaningful action.

It is imperative that these efforts are meticulously planned and executed to maximize their effectiveness.

Tenth, diaspora communities often face unique challenges related to identity, integration, status, cultural preservation, etc. Eritrean community groups can play a crucial role in supporting the diaspora in addressing these issues. They can offer language classes to ensure that the diaspora community's local language is passed down to future generations. They can create resources like books, websites, and apps to facilitate language learning. They have the capacity to organize cultural events, festivals, and workshops to help diaspora members maintain their cultural traditions and pass them on to younger generations and establish cultural centers to showcase history, art, and traditions. They can provide support services for newcomers, including help with finding housing, employment, and navigating legal and immigration processes. They can organize programs or workshops to help diaspora members integrate into their new society. They can offer counseling or support groups for diaspora members who may be experiencing stress, isolation, or discrimination, and foster a sense of belonging and community through social gatherings and events. They can advocate for the rights and interests of the diaspora community, both within the host country, and encourage members of the diaspora to participate in local politics and engage with government agencies to address their needs.

Eritrean Community Centers can create networking and business support to help Eritreans get access to resources for starting or growing businesses. They can even provide financial literacy programs to support economic empowerment and encourage diaspora members to engage in community service and volunteer activities to give back to their host communities. They can initiate diaspora-focused media outlets, such as newspapers, radio stations, or online platforms, to share news, stories, and information relevant to the community and use social media and other digital tools to connect diaspora members across the globe. They can offer legal aid and information regarding immigration, citizenship, and other legal matters, advocate for fair immigration policies and support those facing legal challenges. Community groups that support the diaspora could and should collaborate, seek funding opportunities, and continuously assess the evolving needs of their community to provide effective and sustainable support. Building bridges between the diaspora community, the host country, and the country of origin can lead to positive outcomes for all parties involved.

Eleventh, exploring the establishment of a government in exile, as attempted by various opposition groups (including the Eritrea Govt In Exile Group) should also be considered in order to give voice to the voiceless Eritrean peoplexci (Eritrea-Gov in exile, n.d.). Eritrea- GiE envisions quantifiable and measurable progress toward successfully establishing a democratic government in Eritrea. It advocates for the restoration of democratic institutions, peace, and security for all, with personal safety and property protection in every corner of Eritrea. It intends to give impetus to the current struggle and aspiration of all peace-loving Eritreans. It sets out to achieve its goal through the Office of Secretariat, General Assembly, and Executive Board[xcii] (Eritrea-Gov in exile, n.d.).

In summary, the role played by the diaspora is pivotal, and it requires unity of ideas, a clear focus on shared goals, constructive discourse, responsible media representation, and the desire for a principled democratic government in Eritrea. This being the case, the diaspora needs to take into account one simple fact. No matter how much the diaspora contributes or how tirelessly it works toward the cause of change, it is my conviction that change will ultimately originate from within, driven by insiders (ኣብ ውሽጢ፡ ብደቂ ውሽጢ). Let the diaspora consistently recognize that justice-aspiring Eritreans inside Eritrea (both within the military and outside its framework) could make formidable allies to the cause of change. The diaspora's strategy should thus focus on how to build the bridge between them and forces of change within Eritrea thereby collectively constituting a powerful force for an inevitable positive change. ብዕራይ ኣብ ዘበለ እንተበለ ዕርፊ ኣጽንዕ as the saying goes, which translates into "never let your vision blur no matter how circumstances shift."

21.4. THE ROLE OF MOVEMENT FOR CHANGE INSIDE ERITREA

Within Eritrea, I believe a passionate movement (although little is known of the way it is organized) for change seems to be in the making. This is led by like-minded Eritreans (comprising elements from the military, the security apparatus, civil servants, religious institutions, and other sections of the society) who are deeply troubled by the current situation in their country. These individuals are willing to make necessary sacrifices to rescue Eritrea from the brink of disintegration, and their sole agenda is the salvation of their nation.

There is a need for this movement to set forth a comprehensive vision for the future of Eritrea, outlining a series of crucial objectives.

In a country mired in crisis—enduring perpetual warfare, economic decline, a mass exodus of its youth, a culture heavily militarized, unceasing national service requirements, and severe scarcity of essential resources like water and electricity—the foremost imperative must be the restoration of normalcy (ንቡር ወይ ንቡርነት). This entails the reestablishment of a tranquil and functional society, where the rule of law is upheld, fundamental services are delivered, and citizens can lead their daily lives without the specter of political persecution looming over them. The restoration of normalcy necessitates the revival of economic stability and enabling citizens to access basic necessities.

It envisions a scenario where children can savor their childhood without being inundated by political rhetoric and a place where the youth can aspire to a promising future, complete their education, find employment, establish families, own homes, and raise children in security. It means that farmers can tend to their land without disruption, workers can earn a sustainable livelihood to support their families, and parents and grandparents can relish peaceful retirements. It also involves showing respect for churches and allowing them to provide spiritual services to their communities unhindered. It means the respect of local traditions. This transformation embodies the aspiration for a society where peace, stability, and prosperity are not merely ideals, but are the lived reality of every citizen.

Drawing a political transition roadmap is thus the first step toward the restoration of normalcy followed by growth and stability. This requires crafting a political roadmap that lays out a clear path toward a constitutional Eritrea, built upon fundamental democratic principles. The plan articulates the vision and objective of the transition. It delineates the scope of the political transition, identifies potential risks, and highlights areas that require attention. The roadmap also talks about the time frame, roles and responsibilities of the different bodies, and other pertinent matters. It also plays a critical role in managing change effectively, minimizing disruptions, and ensuring that the desired outcomes are achieved during a transition process.

Setting a timeframe is essential to ensuring progress and to demonstrating the movement is committed to transitioning Eritrea to a democratic system by specifying key milestones and deadlines. This ensures that the transition stays on track and is completed within a reasonable timeframe.

The movement should define the composition of a transitional government and establish its limitations, ensuring that it operates in the best interest of the people. The transitional government is expected to facilitate the transition from the day the change has been affected until a constitutional government is set up.

Calling a national conference will facilitate open, transparent, and inclusive consultation. This should call upon Eritreans from all walks of life, including political entities, civic organizations, religious and traditional institutions, prominent individuals, and the diaspora, to participate in the ratification of the draft political transition road-map through a national conference. Equal female representation in the entire process is not choice but a priority.

Drafting a constitution in an inclusive way is another major task of the transitional government. The movement should aim to look into the existing constitution and draft a new one through an inclusive and participatory process, reflecting the diverse perspectives and aspirations of the Eritrean population.

It is also important to demonstrate a commitment to creating an environment conducive to civil discourse and ensuring an inclusive and transparent transition process toward a constitutional government. The movement should actively promote a culture of resolving differences through dialogue, championing unity and understanding.

Throughout the transition, the movement should prioritize the rule of law to maintain order and justice. The stability and security of the general populace should be a top priority to protect Eritreans as they pursue change.

The transitional government should initiate a process of peace and reconciliation to heal divisions within the nation. This requires specific strategies and a deep understanding of the situation in question. The success of these efforts often depends on the commitment and goodwill of all stakeholders as well as the support of the broader international community.

The transitional government should seek to ensure good relations with neighboring countries and the international community as a whole in accordance with international norms and standards.

As part of their commitment to human rights, it should aim to facilitate the release of all prisoners of conscience.

Lastly, the transitional government should be dedicated to providing essential social services to meet the needs of the Eritrean population.

In their pursuit of change, the movement inside Eritrea should envision a brighter, more democratic future for their beloved nation, where the principles of justice, equity, freedom, and prosperity prevail. This should be made to the Eritrean people.

21.5. A VISION FOR A NEW ERITREA—THE DEVELOPMENT PERSPECTIVE

In the vision for Eritrea, there lies a nation that commands respect from its neighbors and the international community. This reverence does not solely stem from its hard-fought war of independence, but rather from a multifaceted approach. It encompasses qualities such as exemplary governance, a robust and modern economy, a highly educated human resource base, astute diplomacy in its foreign policies, and a genuine concern for the well-being of its population.

Central to this vision is a commitment to the rule of law, the cornerstone upon which a just and orderly society is built. It is a commitment to uphold economic development based on the principles of equity and social justice and anchored in local communities and a governance structure that fosters consensus building and representation. Traditional laws that once dictated village norms should evolve, shedding backward traditions that have historically discriminated against women and marginalized groups. The path to change may be gradual, but it is steady, favoring a slow and continuous transformation over abrupt disruptions. Change is perceived as positive when it is sustainable, aligning with the idea that an individual's life can be cut short, but the life of a society should endure.

The preservation and celebration of Eritrea's values, traditions, history, and beliefs are vital components of this vision. Even in the face of adversity, pride in one's identity is paramount, acknowledging that history is a complex tapestry that offers valuable lessons, even from its darker chapters. Reclaiming Eritrea's rich history, including the Axumite civilization and its various historical sites, is of utmost importance. Similarly, a reclamation of the nation's mythology, such as Belew Kelew, adds depth to the cultural narrative. This vision promotes respect for history and traditions while providing incentives for those who contribute to the nation's prosperity.

We aspire to witness Eritrea living in peace with its neighbors, treating them with respect, fostering regional collaboration toward shared objectives, and advancing peaceful conflict resolution mechanisms.

Religious freedom is another pillar, recognizing the role of faith in societies and its potential to contribute to stability. Respect for the elderly, consensus-building, and a belief in the organic course of change are integral. Change should be seen as a natural progression, occasionally requiring direction or catalysis but never as destruction. Lessons are drawn from past institutions, whether colonial or otherwise, to inform contemporary practices. The aim is to create a society where "normalcy" prevails, where people can earn a living, practice their beliefs without fear, express themselves freely, and enjoy their rights as citizens/human beings.

In this vision, parents raise their children in harmony with their values and aspirations, fostering love, affection, and a carefree childhood. The justice system operates transparently, ensuring that the rule of law applies to all. Predictability reigns in a nation guided by laws, policies, and norms. Tolerance toward diverse views and opinions is embraced, and social justice is upheld through the fair distribution of the nation's wealth and investment in vital services like education and healthcare.

Eritrea's development primarily depends on the mobilization and utilization of local resources, the institutionalization of community-based programs, and the promotion of grassroots initiatives. Inclusivity and attentive listening to the needs of the people are paramount. Establishing centers of excellence, including educational institutions and research centers, is prioritized to promote innovation and creativity.

This vision paints a portrait of a future Eritrea where prosperity, stability, and cultural richness coalesce, ensuring a nation that commands respect, not only for its history but for its promising future.

The vision promotes a fair and equitable distribution of national wealth among its population and does not intend to create a wide gap between the rich and the poor.

APPENDIX 1

MY MOTHER'S LAST LETTER - BEFORE SHE PASSED AWAY IN 1989

Mio caro semere solomun.

Come stia, noi tutti stiamo bene oltre che il vostro gran desiderio,

Oricevuto la vostra cara letera sono molto contenta, Non vedo l'ora di rivedervi, perche quando arrivato, Schianbel, Michele, ero gia arrivata, mi a raccontato tutto sono molto contenta, e spero, Anche a noi vi vedro, con la auito del Signore!

Caro figlio mio, questa guerra la finisce solo, Dio, viviamo con la speranza, non so fina quand finisce?

Spero che sara al piu presto, perche voi siete, I miei fratelli e sorelle e miei hadarei come solomun semere mio basta che state bene, e la Madonna vi dia, Sra salute e vita lunga, non vi preccupate di noi, Stiamo stiamo tutti bene, anche gloria sta bene con i Suoi figli, e tutti i nostri fratelli e sorelle. Figlio mio adesso se trovo visa vado Italia a vedere, afache e cognere, anche giermen a trovare singsolmu, sono contenta di trovare olganese osefasc cafueb, mbb tutti stiamo bene, mi sento un sogno la, Mio caro figlio non so cosa raccontare dall contentezza demu seicar semere maar eta baro patrio to gigna begadulotat vi benidica vi dia forza e prace, semere mio perdu non ti sposi? mi dispiace tanto, perche non fate i figli per finissce ti racomando, deamommo, anche chidane non era figlio.

Baci e abracie Saluti,

Buon Natale.

e Buon Anno Anno di Pace.

Tua cara, Mamina Sorel Si addaterio,

MIO CARO Semere Solomon,
Come stai? Noi tutti stiamo bene oltre che il vostro gran desiderio.

Ho ricevuto la vostra cara lettera. Sono molto contenta. Non vedo l'ora di vedervi. Perche quando arrivato Shambel Michale era gia arrivato. Mi ha racontato tutto. Sono molto contenta. E spero anche a voi vi vedro con l'auito del Signore.

Caro flglio mio, questa guerra la finisce solo.

Dio, viviamo con la speranza, non so fina quando finisce.

Spero che sara piu presto, perche voi siete i miei frattelli, sorelle, e mie Hadarei come Solomon.

Semere moi, basta che state bene. La Madonna vi dia la salute e vita lunga. No si preocupate di noi. Stiamo Stiamo tutti bene. Anche Elena sta bene con I suoi figli e tuuti I nostrum Fratelli e sorelle.

Figlio mio, adesso si trovo via vada all'Italia a veder Abatie ed Agnese anche germania a trovare Angilina.

Son contenta to trovare Alganesc, Assefasc e Caleb e Melete. Tutti stanno bene. Mi sento un sogno.

Mio caro figlio, non so cosa raccontare del contesteza.

Semere Scicor, Semere Me'ar, bravo patriot Gigna Tegadlotat. Vi bendica, vi dia forza e pace.

Semere mio, perche non ti sposi ? Mi dispiace tanto. Perche non fate I figli per piacere. Ti racomando.

Amore mio, anche Chidane non ha figlio.

Baccii ed abracci e salute

Buon Natale
Bou Anno
Anno di pace
Tua cara, Madalena Yosief

ENGLISH TRANSLATION OF THE LETTER

My Dearest Semere Solomon,

I trust this letter finds you in good health. While we are all well here, our hearts ache with the void left by your absence.

Receiving your heartfelt letter brought immense joy to my heart. The anticipation of seeing you again is overwhelming, especially after meeting Shambel Michael, who shared so much about you. I am filled with happiness and pray that, with the Lord's help, we will soon be reunited.

My dear son, this seemingly endless war continues to weigh heavily on our hearts. We cling to hope, uncertain of its conclusion. I fervently pray for a swift resolution, as you are not just my son but also my brothers, sisters, and the other half of my being, Solomon.

Semere mine, it warms my heart to hear that you are doing well. May Our Lady bless you with continued health and a long life. Please, do not worry about us; we are all in good health. Elena and her children, along with our brothers and sisters, are also thriving.

If I obtain a visa, I plan to visit Italy to see Abatie and Agnese, and perhaps even Germany to visit Angiolina.

The thought of reuniting with Alganesc, Assefasc, Caleb, and Melete feels like a dream come true.

Words fail to express the overwhelming happiness I feel, sweetie. You are a brave patriot and a valiant freedom fighter. May God bless you with strength and peace.

Sweetie, concerning your personal life, have you considered marriage? I regret to hear that you have no children. Please, consider my recommendation to start a family. On a related note, Chidane also remains without children.

Sending you kisses, hugs, and wishes for good health.

Merry Christmas and a Happy New Year!

Year of Peace!

Your dear Madalena Yosief

ENDNOTES

Chapter 2

i. https://www.unhcr.org/publications/unhcr-global- appeal-1999-eritrea Accessed on September 19, 2013

ii. Tedros Tesfai's, Where did things go wrong for the party of the people? Awate.com January 21, 2001

iii. The Complicated Nature of Red Sea Geopolitics Oct 27, 2021 Charles W. Dunne, https://arabcenterdc.org/ resource/ the-complicated-nature-of-red-sea-geopolitics/ Accessed on September 19, 2023

iv. The Danger of African Liberation Movements https:// issafrica.org/iss-today/the-danger-of-african-libera- tion-movements Accessed on September 19, 2023

v. The Danger of African Liberation Movements https:// issafrica.org/iss-today/the-danger-of-african-libera- tion-movements access on September 19, 2023

Chapter 3

vi. The Fund for Peace is an independent, nonpartisan, non-profit research and educational organization that works to prevent violent conflict and promote sustain- able security. It promotes sustainable security through research, training and education, engagement of civil society, building bridges across diverse sectors, and developing innovative technologies and tools for policymakers. A leader in the conflict assessment and early warning field, The Fund for Peace focuses on the problems of weak and failing states. Its objective is to create practical tools and approaches for conflict mitigation that are useful to decision-makers. The Fragile States Index (FSI) is an annual ranking of 178 countries based on the different pressures they face that impact their levels of fragility. The Index is based on The Fund for Peace's proprietary Conflict Assessment System Tool (CAST) analytical approach. Based on comprehensive social science methodology, three primary streams of data — quantitative, qualitative, and expert validation — are triangulated and subjected to critical review to obtain final scores for the FSI. Millions of documents are analyzed every year, and by applying highly specialized search parameters, scores are apportioned for every country based on twelve key political, social, and economic indicators and over 100 sub-indicators that are the result of years of expert social science research. Source: Fragile States Index | The Fund for Peace Accessed on September 12, 2023

vii. The Security Apparatus indicator considers the security threats to a state, such as bombings, attacks and battle-related deaths, rebel movements, mutinies, coups, or terrorism. The Security Apparatus also takes into account serious criminal factors, such as organized crime and homicides, and perceived trust of citizens in domestic security. In some instances, the security apparatus may extend beyond traditional military or police forces to include state-sponsored or state-supported private militias that terrorize political opponents, suspected "enemies," or civilians seen to be sympathetic to the opposition. In other instances, the security apparatus of a state can include a "deep state", that may consist of secret intelligence units, or other irregular security forces, that serve the interests of a political leader or clique. As a counterexample, the indicator will also take into account armed resistance to a governing authority, particularly the manifestation of violent uprisings and insurgencies, proliferation of independent militias, vigilantes, or mercenary groups that challenge the state's monopoly of the use of force. Source: Fragile States Index | The Fund for Peace Accessed on September 12, 2023

viii. The Group Grievance Indicator focuses on divisions and schisms between different groups in society—particularly divisions based on social or political characteristics—and their role in access to services or resources, and inclusion in the political process. Group Grievance may also have a historical component, where aggrieved communal groups cite injustices of the past, sometimes going back centuries, that influence and shape that group's role in society and relationships with other groups. This history may in turn be shaped by patterns of real or perceived atrocities or "crimes" committed with apparent impunity against communal groups. Groups may also feel aggrieved because they are denied autonomy, self-determination, or political independence to which they believe they are entitled. The Indicator also considers where specific groups are singled out by state authorities, or by dominant groups, for persecution or repression, or where there is public scapegoating of groups believed to have acquired wealth, status, or power "illegitimately," which may manifest itself in the emergence of fiery rhetoric, such as through "hate" radio, pamphleteering, and stereo- typical or nationalistic political speech.

ix. The Economic Decline Indicator considers factors related to economic decline within a country. For example, the Indicator looks at patterns of progressive economic decline of the society as a whole as measured by per capita income, Gross National Product, unemployment rates, inflation, productivity, debt, poverty levels, or business failures. It also takes into account sudden drops in commodity prices, trade revenue, or foreign investment, and any collapse or devaluation of the national currency. The Economic Decline Indicator further considers the responses to economic conditions and their consequences, such as extreme social hardship imposed by economic austerity programs, or perceived increasing group inequalities. The Economic Decline Indicator is focused on the formal economy—as well as illicit trade, including the drug and human trafficking, and capital flight, or levels of corruption and illicit transactions such as money laundering or embezzlement. Source: Fragile States Index | The Fund for Peace Accessed on September 12, 20 x. The Human Rights and Rule of Law Indicator considers the relationship between the state and its population insofar as fundamental human rights are protected and freedoms are observed and respected. The Indicator looks at whether there is widespread abuse of legal, political, and social rights, including those of individuals, groups, and institutions (e.g., harassment of the press, politicization of the judiciary, internal use of military for political ends, repression of political opponents). The Indicator also considers outbreaks of politically inspired (as opposed to criminal) violence perpetrated against civilians. It also looks at factors such as denial of due process consistent with international norms and practices for political prisoners or dissidents, and whether there is current or emerging authoritarian, dictatorial or military rule in which constitutional and democratic institutions and processes are suspended or manipulated. Source: Fragile States Index | The Fund for Peace Accessed on September 12, 202323.

x. The Human Rights and Rule of Law Indicator considers the relationship between the state and its population insofar as fundamental human rights are protected and freedoms are observed and respected. The Indicator looks at whether there is widespread abuse of legal, political, and social rights, including those of individuals, groups, and institutions (e.g., harassment of the press, politicization of the judiciary, internal use of military for political ends, repression of political opponents). The Indicator also considers outbreaks of politically inspired (as opposed to criminal) violence perpetrated against civilians. It also looks at factors such as denial of due process consistent with international norms and practices for political prisoners or dissidents, and whether there is current or emerging authoritarian, dictatorial or military rule in which constitutional and democratic institutions and processes are suspended or manipulated. Source: Fragile States Index | The Fund for Peace Accessed on September 12, 2023

xi. The State Legitimacy Indicator considers the representativeness and openness of government and its relationship with its citizenry. The Indicator looks at the population's level of confidence in state institutions and processes, and assesses the effects where that confidence is absent, manifested through mass public demonstrations, sustained civil disobedience, or the rise of armed insurgencies. Though the State Legitimacy indicator does not necessarily make a judgment on democratic governance, it does consider the integrity of elections where they take place (such as flawed or boycotted elections), the nature of political transitions, and where there is an absence of democratic elections, the degree to which the government is representative of the population of which it governs. The Indicator takes into account openness of government, specifically the openness of ruling elites to transparency, accountability and political representation, or conversely the levels of corruption, profiteering, and marginalizing, persecuting, or otherwise excluding opposition groups. The Indicator also considers the ability of a state to exercise basic functions that infer a population's confidence in its government and institutions, such as through the ability to collect taxes. Source: Fragile States Index | The Fund for Peace Accessed on September 12, 2023

xii. The Human Rights and Rule of Law Indicator considers the relationship between the state and its population insofar as fundamental human rights are protected and freedoms are observed and respected. The Indicator looks at whether there is widespread abuse of legal, political, and social rights, including those of individuals, groups, and institutions (e.g., harassment of the press, politicization of the judiciary, internal use of military for political ends, repression of political opponents). The Indicator also considers outbreaks of politically inspired (as opposed to criminal) violence perpetrated against civilians. It also looks at factors such as denial of due process consistent with international norms and practices for political prisoners or dissidents, and whether there is current or emerging authoritarian, dictatorial or military rule in which constitutional and democratic institutions and processes are suspended or manipulated. Source: Fragile States Index | The Fund for Peace Accessed on September 12, 2023

xiii. World Report 2023 EVENTS OF 2022, Human Rights Watch, https://www.hrw.org/sites/default/ f i les/med ia _ 2023/01/ World _ Repor t _ 2023 _ WEBSPREADS_0.pdf Accessed on September 19, 2023

xiv. Human Rights Watch, World Report 2023, https:// www.hrw. org/world-report/2023/country-chapters/ eritrea Accessed on October 15, 2023

xv. Amnesty International Report 2022/23—The State of the World's Human Rights Amnesty International Report 2022/23:

The state of the world's human rights - Amnesty International Accessed on September 20, 2023

xvi. Coup Attempt by Rebel Soldiers Is Said to Fail in Eritrea, Jeffrey Gettleman, January 21, 2013 https:// www.nytimes. com/2013/01/22/world/africa/coup- attempt-fails-in-eritrea. html Access on September 20, 2023

xvii. Amnesty International Report 2022/23—The State of the World's Human Rights Amnesty International Report 2022/23: The state of the world's human rights Amnesty International Accessed on September 20, 2023

xviii. Situation of human rights in Eritrea - Report of the Special Rapporteur on the situation of human rights in Eritrea, Mohamed Abdelsalam Babiker (9 May 2023) Situation of human rights in Eritrea : (un.org) Accessed on October 11, 20, 2023

xix. The Heritage Foundation's Index of Economic Freedom has served as an essential policy guide that analyzes and highlights the state of economic freedom in countries around the globe. Over time, the Index has recorded profound advances as the cause of freedom has swept the globe, empowering everyday families and workers to thrive and hold their political authorities accountable. 2023_IndexOfEconomicFreedom_ FINAL. pdf (heritage.org) Accessed on September 12, 2023

xx. Eritrea Economy: Population, GDP, Inflation, Business, Trade, FDI, Corruption (heritage.org) Accessed on September 12, 2023

xxi. Human Capital (worldbank.org) accessed 12 September 2023

xxii. Eritrea: Development news, research, data | World Bank accessed 12 September 2023

xxiii. VOA News (2021) UAE Dismantles Eritrea Base as it Pulls Back After Yemen War. https://www.voanews. com/a/

africa_uae-dismantles-eritrea-base-itpulls-   back-after-yemen-war/6202212.html. Accessed 3 April 2023War. https://www.voanews.com/a/africa_uae-   dismantles-eritrea-base-itpulls-back-after-yemen- war/6202212.html Accessed 12 September 2023

xxiv. Final Report and Recommendations of the Senior Study Group on Peace and Security in the Red Sea Arena, senior_study_group_on_peace_and_security_   in_the_red_sea_arena-report.pdf (usip.org) Accessed on September 19, 2023

xxv. Elena DeLozier, "UAE Drawdown May Isolate Saudi Arabia in Yemen," Washington Institute for Near East Policy, July 2, 2019; Melvin, "Foreign Military Presence"; and David Wainer and Samer al-Atrush, "UAE Ran Covert Arms Flights to Aid Libya's Haftar, UN Finds," Bloomberg, May 15, 2020

xxvi. 2023-forum-report.pdf (ibrahim.foundation) Accessed on September 12, 2023

xxvii. World Economic Outlook, Rocky Recovery, IMF World Economic Outlook, April 2023: A Rocky Recovery (imf.org) accessed 12 September 2023

Chapter 4

xxviii. Louise Fox - editor, Robert Liebenthal—editor, Attacking Africa's Poverty: Experience from the Ground. Contributors: (Washington: World Bank, 2006) 26, https://openknowledge.worldbank.org/   server/api/core/bitstreams/23392c87-efd7-5ba0- b055-474e33c9da68/content Accessed on October 11, 2023

xxix. Webster's II New Riverside University Dictionary, (Boston: The Riverside Publishing Company, 1984)

xxx. http://info.worldbank.org/governance/wgi/index.asp Accessed on October 11, 2023

xxxi. P Rogers, Kazi F Jalal, and John A Boyd, An Introduction to Sustainable Development (London: Earthscan, 2009), 62

xxxii. Peter P Rogers, Kazi F Jalal, and John A Boyd, An Introduction to Sustainable Development (London: Earthscan, 2009), 62

xxxiii. Robert Calderisi, The Trouble with Africa, Why Foreign Aid is not Working (New York: Palgrave Macmillan, 2006), 160

xxxiv. Paul Collier and Jan Willem Gunning, "Explaining African Economic Performance." Journal of Economic Literature 37, no. 1 (1999): 64-111.

xxxv. Paul Collier, New Rules for Rebuilding a Broken Nation, TED Global, 2009, http://www.ted.com/ talks/paul_collier_s_ new_rules_for_rebuilding_a_ broken_nation.html

xxxvi. United Nations Economic and Social Commission for Asia and the Pacific, https://www.unescap.org/ttdw/ ppp/ppp_primer/51_functions_of_a_regulator.html Accessed on September 25, 2023

xxxvii. James M. Cypher, and James L. Dietz, The Process of Economic Development (New York: Routledge, 2004) 362, Questia, Web, November 6, 2011

xxxviii. Rosalyn McKeown, Education for Sustainable Development Toolkit, July 2022, Accessed on October 11, 2023

xxxix. OECD, A Policy Framework for Investment: Human Resource Development Policy, 25-27 October 2005, Rio de Janeiro, Brazil https://www.oecd.org/invest- ment/investmentfordevelopment/35518811.pdf Accessed on October 11, 2023

xl. James M. Cypher, and James L. Dietz, The Process of Economic Development (New York: Routledge, 2004) 19, Questia, Web, November 6, 2011 xli. James M. Cypher, and James L. Dietz, The Process of Economic Development (New York: Routledge, 2004) 19, Questia, Web, November 6, 2011

xlii. Eritrea Options and Strategies for Growth, The WBG, November 10, 1994 https://documents1.worldbank. org/ curated/es/401511468752060584/pdf/multi0page. pdf Accessed on September 21, 2023

xliii. The Eritrean diaspora and its impact on regime stabil- ity: Responses to UN sanctions, Nicolle Hirt, African Affairs, Volume 114, Issue 454, January 2015, Pages 115–135, https:// doi.org/10.1093/afraf/adu061 https:// academic.oup.com/ afraf/article/114/454/115/2195155 Accessed on September 21, 2023

xliv. The Eritrean diaspora and its impact on regime stability: Responses to UN sanctions, Nicolle Hirt, African Affairs, Volume 114, Issue 454, January 2015, Pages 115–135, https:// doi.org/10.1093/afraf/adu061 https:// academic.oup.com/afraf/ article/114/454/115/2195155 Accessed on September 21, 2023

xlv. Nation-building, Alberto Alesina and Bryony Reich, Harvard University, February 2015, https://scholar.harvard.edu/files/ alesina/files/nation_building_ feb_2015_0.pdf Accessed on September 21, 2023

xlvi. https://datahub.itu.int/dashboards/umc/?e=USA &c=ERI Accessed on October 11, 2023

Chapter 6

xlvii. Alemseghed Tesfai, ፌደረሽን ኤርትራ ምስ ኢትዮጵያ ካብ ማቲየንሶ ክሳብ ተድላ 1951—1955 (The Federation of Eritrea with Ethiopia—From Matienzo to Tedla 1951 -1955), Hidri Publishers, June 2005

Chapter 7

xlviii.   "ንኣርብዓ ዓመታት ዝተቐብረ ጉዳይ" (A case that has been buried
          for forty Years—1972—2013, Tesfay Temnewo, 2013, Leck,
          Germany
xlix.   Dehay Eritrea ኣብ መጽሓፍ ተጋዳላይ መስፍን ሓነስ ዝተሞርኮሰ
          ሰፈሕ ዝርርብ! ደሃይ ኤርትራ, August 11, 2023 https://www.you-
          tube.com/watch?v=vHu2FNfIphY Accessed on October 11,
          2023

Chapter 8

l.   A movement within the ELF that opposed the ELF Leadership's
          approach to unity which later joined the EPLF.

Chapter 9

li.   www.ehrea.org Accessed on October 11, 2023
lii.   According to Ahmed Al Qaisi, he was detained on the direct
          orders of the Secretary-General of the Front following a heated
          confrontation on the eve of his detention, during which Qaisi
          referred to the Secretary-General as Pinochet. His alleged
          offense was his suspected association with an Eritrean Islamist
          Group in Sudan. In an effort to establish his guilt, the Front's
          Foreign Intelligence Unit (referred to as 72) apprehended a
          member of the said Islamist Group in Sudan. Tragically, this
          individual died from suffocation while being transported to
          Eritrea in the vehicle.
liii.   Zatanna, Coup within ELF led by Abdalla Idris and the
          Death of Melàke Tekle, https://zantana.net/coup_within_
          elf_and_the_death_of_melake_tekle/#:~:text=They%20

ambushed%20the%20participants%20of,with%20EPLF%20 undermining%20the%20front. Accessed on January 29, 2024

Chapter 10

liv.   Interview with Pres. Isaias Afwerki on regional issues & domestic development programs - ERi-TV, January 8, 2022 https:// www.youtube.com/ watch?v=0qaGpf0HsoQ

lv.   France's Hollande: Eritrea 'Becoming Empty' as Residents Leave, VOA, November 11, 2015 https://www.voanews. com/a/eu-offers-african-nations- 1-8-billion-but-some-question-response/3052919.html Accessed on October 11, 2023

lvi.   Futile Acts of Subversion, Eritrea Profile, Ministry of Information, Eritrea, September 5, 2023 https:// shabait. com/2023/09/05/futile-acts-of-subversion/ Accessed on October 2, 2023

Chapter 11

lvii.   Stephen Kotkin is the John P. Birkelund Professor of History and International Affairs in what used to be called the Woodrow Wilson School and in the History Department of Princeton University, as well as a Senior Fellow (adjunct) at the Hoover Institution at Stanford University. He directs the Princeton Institute for International and Regional Studies and co-directs its program in History and the Practice of Diplomacy, which he founded. He also founded Princeton's Global History Initiative. His scholarship encompasses geo- politics and authoritarian regimes in history and in the present. Kotkin has published two volumes of a three- volume history of the world as seen from Stalin's desk: Paradoxes of Power, 1878–1928 (Penguin,

November 2014) and Waiting for Hitler, 1929–1941 (Penguin, October 2017). The final installment, Totalitarian Superpower, 1941–1990s, is underway. He writes reviews and essays for Foreign Affairs, the Times Literary Supplement, and The Wall Street Journal, and served as the business book reviewer for The New York Times Sunday Business Section. He is an occasional consultant for governments and some private companies. PhD UC Berkeley (1988).

lviii. Modern Authoritarianism and Geopolitics: Thoughts on a Policy Framework, Stephen Kotkin, Apr 11, 2022 https://www.youtube.com/watch?v=E7ZtsajvV98 Accessed on October 11, 2023

lix. United Nations Institute of Training and Research (UNITAR), Location of Places of Detention Centers in Eritrea Identified by the Commission of Inquiry of Human Rights in Eritrea, Analysis with WorldView-3 Data Acquired September 24, 2015 and January 23, 2016 and Landsat-8 Data Acquired May 29, 2016, June 6, 2016 https://www.ohchr.org/sites/default/files/Documents/HRBodies/HRCouncil/CoIEritrea/UNOSAT_COIE_070616.pdf

lx. Escaping Eritrea (full documentary) | FRONTLINE, FRONTLINE PBS | Official, May 4, 2021, https:// www.youtube.com/watch?v=jquCbpLYw7Q Accessed on October 2, 2023

lxi. PBS, Frontline, 500,000 Refugees, 'Slavery-like' Compulsory Service, No National Elections, Border Conflicts & Secret Prisons: 5 Human Rights Crises in Eritrea, May 4, 2021 https://www.pbs.org/wgbh/ frontline/article/5-human-rights-crises-in-eritrea/

lxii. Dan Connell, He Didn't Do It For Them, Middle East Report 238 (Spring 2006) https://merip.org/2006/03/he-didnt-do-it-for-them/ Accessed on October 16, 2023

Chapter 12

lxiii.   Modern Authoritarianism and Geopolitics: Thoughts on a Policy Framework, Stephen Kotkin, Apr 11, 2022 https://www. youtube.com/watch?v=E7ZtsajvV98 Accessed on October 2, 2023

Chapter 14

lxiv.   Ministry of Education, Eritrea, National Education Policy, Asmara, 2003 http://www.eritreaem- bassy-japan.org/data/ National%20Education%20   Policy%20Feb%202003.pdf Accessed on October 13, 2023

lxv.   LWF will continue humanitarian aid in Eritrea for further 12 months: Only NGO program in operation there News and Press Release Posted 14 Jul 1998 https://reliefweb.int/report/ eritrea/lwf-will-continue-humanitarian-aid-eritrea-further-12-months-only-ngo-program Accessed on January 23, 2024

lxvi.   Peace through education: An interview with Dr Teame Mebrahtu, August 8, 2017, Centre for Comparative and International Research in Education https://cire- bristol. com/2017/08/08/peace-through-education-   an-interview-with-dr-teame-mebrahtu/ Accessed on October 4, 2023

lxvii. Peace Corps Suspends Program in Eritrea; All Volunteers are Safe and Sound, Peace Corps, Friday, June 5, 1998, https://www. peacecorps.gov/news/ library/peace-corps-suspends-program-in-eritrea-all- volunteers-are-safe-and-sound/ Accessed on October 5, 2023

lxviii. The gross enrollment rate is defined as the number of children enrolled at a specific level of education, regardless of age, expressed as a percentage of the official school-age population in a given year for a given level of age-specific education.

Chapter 15

lxix.   Modern Authoritarianism and Geopolitics: Thoughts on a Policy Framework, Stephen Kotkin, Apr 11, 2022 https://www.youtube.com/watch?v=E7ZtsajvV98 Accessed on October 11, 2023

Chapter 16

lxx.   USAID, USAID Policy Framework 2011-2015. 3, https://2012-2017.usaid.gov/sites/default/files/documents/1870/USAID%20Policy%20Framework%202011-2015.PDF (Accessed on January 24, 2024)

lxxi.   UNDP, Human Development Report 2011, Sustainability and Equity: A better Future for All http://hdr.undp.org/en/media/HDR_2010_EN_Complete_reprint.pdf (accessed on January 24, 2024)

lxxii.   Ibid

Chapter 18

lxxiii.   Eritrea Hub, The Open Letter signed by the G15— now Eritrean political prisoners, Asmara, September 15, 2021, https://eritreahub.org/the-open-letter- signed-by-the-g15-now-eritrean-political-prisoners Accessed on October 16, 2023

lxxiv.   Committee to Protect Journalists (CPJ), '15 Journalists imprisoned in Eritrea, September 16, 2005, https:// cpj.

org/2005/09/15-journalists-imprisoned-in-eritrea/   Accessed
on October 16, 2023

Chapter 19

lxxv.   Treaty of Wichale, Wichale also spelled Ucciali, (May 2, 1889),
           pact signed at Wichale, Ethiopia, by the Italians and Menilek II
           of Ethiopia, whereby Italy was granted the northern Ethiopian
           territories of Bogos, Hamasen, and Akale-Guzai (modern
           Eritrea and northern Tigray) in exchange for a sum of money
           and the provision of 30,000 muskets and 28 cannons https://
           www. britannica.com/event/Treaty-of-Wichale Accessed on
           October 11, 2023
lxxvi.   A population of 150 million can't live in a geographic prison"—
           PM 321Ahmed, Addis Standard, October 14, 2023 https://
           addisstandard.com/feature-a-popula-   tion-of-150-million-
           cant-live-in-a-geographic-prison- pm-abiy-ahmed Accessed on
           October 14, 2023
lxxvii.   Ibid
lxxviii.   Ibid
lxxix.   The State Council, The Peoples Republic of China, Full text:
           Action plan on the Belt and Road Initiative, English version,
           March 30, 2015 english. gov.cn https://english.www.gov.cn/
           archive/publica- tions/2015/03/30/content_281475080249035.
           htm
lxxx.   The White House, Press Release by the White House, March 26,
           2003, Washington, DC, The White House https://georgewbush-
           whitehouse.archives.gov/info-   cus/iraq/news/20030326-7.
           html Accessed on October 13, 2023
lxxxi.   Judy, Sarasohn, Eritrea Pushes to Get U.S. Base, By Judy
           Sarasohn, Washington, DC, November 21, 2002 https://

www.washingtonpost.com/archive/politics/2002/11/21/ eritrea-pushes-to-get-us-base/   f730d0da-a727-43c1-ae16-15c8b06ae7a3/ Accessed on October 13, 2023

lxxxii. Ministry of Information, Eritrea, Keynote Address By President Isaias Afwerki on 32nd Independence Anniversary, Asmara, May 24, 2023 https://shabait. com/2023/05/24/key-note-address-by-president-isaias- afwerki-32nd-independence-anniversary/

lxxxiii. https://www.nytimes.com/1991/05/30/world/ethiopian-rebel-faction-is-to-govern-separately.html Accessed on January 25, 2024

lxxxiv. Ibid

lxxxv. Eritrea, Demographic and Health Survey, 2002 National Statistics and Evaluation Office Asmara, Eritrea ORC Macro Calverton, Maryland, US - May 2003 https://dhsprogram.com/ pubs/pdf/FR137/FR137.pdf Accessed on October 22, 2023

Chapter 20

lxxxvi. Robert De Niro teasing his friend Don Rickles about his age while celebrating his 90th birthday.

Chapter 21

lxxxvii. ዘተ - ኣብ እዋናዊ ኩነታት ምስ ዳኒኤል ተኽላይ - ኤልያስ ኣማረ - (Discussion on current events with Daniel Teklai and Elias Amare) Dehai Eritrea Streamed on September 24, 2023 https://www.youtube.com/live/ MAhvByBxXFc?si=JVCOXWdmsFy04nVx Accessed on October 7, 2023

lxxxviii.Dr. Natasha Ezrow is a Senior Lecturer in Government at the University of Essex. She has recently completed a new book

Failed States and Institutional Decay, and she published two books in 2011 on dictatorships. Dictators and Dictatorships is an introductory textbook and The Politics of Dictatorship is a research monograph on the duration of authoritarian regime types.

lxxxix. Authoritarian breakdown -- how dictators fall | Dr. Natasha Ezrow | TEDxUniversityofEssex, https:// www.youtube.com/watch?v=6ECTcaSXe1I Accessed on October 7, 2023

xc.   Eri-platform.org

xci.   https://eritreagovexile.org/our-mission-and-strategic-aims/

xcii.   https://eritreagovexile.org/

REFERENCES

Addis Standard, A population of 150 million can't live in a geographic prison"—PM Abiy Ahmed, Adhanom, Addis Abeba, October 14, 2023

Alesina, Alberto and Bryony Reich, Nation-building, Harvard University, February 2015

Ali, Zeineb, A decade since 1991: Life under PFDJ, Asmarino. com, January 30, 2002

Ali, Zeineb, A call from a sister, Asmarino.com, September 22, 2001

Amnesty International, Amnesty International Report 2022/23— The State of the World's Human Rights

Babiker, Mohamed Abdelsalam, UNHRC, Situation of human rights in Eritrea - Report of the Special Rapporteur on the situation of human rights in Eritrea, United Nations, May 9, 2023

Bairu, Herui Tedla, Eritrea and Ethiopia—A front row look at the issues of conflict and the potential for a peaceful resolution, Trenton, The Red Sea Press, 2016

Brixiova, Zuzana, Ales Bulir and Joshua Comenetz, The Gender Gap in Education in Eritrea in 1991-98: A Missed Opportunity?, IMF, 2001

Britannica, Treaty of Wichale, Wichale

Calderisi, Robert, The Trouble with Africa, Why Foreign Aid is not Working, New York, Palgrave Macmillan, 2006

Centre for Comparative and International Research in Education, Peace through education: An interview with Dr Teame Mebrahtu, August 8, 2017

Collier, Paul and Jan Willem Gunning, "Explaining African Economic Performance, Journal of Economic Literature 37, no. 1, 1999

Collier, Paul Collier, New Rules for Rebuilding a Broken Nation, TED Global, 2009,

Committee to Protect Journalists (CPJ), 15 Journalists imprisoned in Eritrea, New York, September 16, 2005

Connell, Dan, Conversation with Eritrean Political Prisoners, Trento, The Read Sea Press Inc., 2005

Connell, Dan, He Didn't Do It For Them, Middle East Report 238 (Spring 2006)

Council on Foreign Relations, Al Shabaab, December 6, 2022

Cypher, James M. and James L. Dietz, The Process of Economic Development, New York, Routledge, 2004

Delozier, Elena DeLozier, UAE Drawdown May Isolate Saudi Arabia in Yemen," Washington Institute for Near East Policy, July 2, 2019;

Due, Charles W., The Complicated Nature of Red Sea Geopolitics, Arab Center Washington, DC., October 27, 2021

Dunne, Charles W., The Complicated Nature of Red Sea Geopolitics, Arab Center Washington, DC, Oct 27, 2021

EHREA

Eri-ptaform.org

Eritrea Hub, The Open Letter signed by the G15—now Eritrean political prisoners, Asmara, September 15, 2021,

Eritrea-Gov in Exile Group,

Ezrow, Natasha M., and Erica Frantz, Dictators and Dictatorships— Understanding Authoritarian Regimes and their Leaders, Bloomsbury, London, 2011

Ezrow, Natasha, Authoritarian breakdown -- how dictators fall, TEDxUniversityofEssex, November 5, 2014

Fox, Louise and Robert Liebenthal, Attacking Africa's Poverty: Experience from the Ground. Contributors: The World Bank, 2006

Fund for Peace. Fragile States Index

Georgis, Andebrhan Welde, Eritrea at a Crossroads: A Narrative of Triumph, Betrayal and Hope, Houston, Strategic Book Publishing Rights Co., 2014

Gettleman, Jeffrey, Coup Attempt by Rebel Soldiers Is Said to Fail in Eritrea, New Yor Times, January 21, 2013

Hagos, Mesfin, An African Revolution Reclaimed - A Memoir of Eritrea Freedom Fighter, Trenton, The Red Sea Press, 2023

Hagos, Mefin, Interview with Mesfin Hagos on his book (ካብ መጽሓፍ ተጋዳላይ መስፍን ሓጎስ ዝተምርኮሰ ሰፊሕ ዝርርብ, Dehay Eritrea, August 11, 2023

Heritage Foundation, Population, GDP, Inflation, Business, Trade, FDI, Corruption,

Heritage Foundation, Eritrea Economy

Hirt, Nicole, The Eritrean diaspora and its impact on regime stability: Responses to UN sanctions, African Affairs, Volume 114, Issue 454, January 2015

Human Rights Watch, World Report 2023 Events of 2022, 2023

Human Rights Watch, Escalating Crackdown in Eritrea, Reformists, Journalists, Students At Risk, September 2001

IMF, World Economic Outlook, Rocky Recovery, April 2023

International Telecommunications Union, Datahub

Kim, Anthony B., 2023 Index of Economic Freedom, The Heritage Foundation, February 2023

Kotkin, Stephen, Modern Authoritarianism and Geopolitics: Thoughts on a Policy Framework, Stanford CDDRL, April 11, 2022

McKeown, Rosalyn, Education for Sustainable Development Toolkit, July 2022,

Mesfin, Berouk, The Danger of African Liberation Movements, Institute for Security Studies, July 22, 2008

Ministry of Education, Eritrea, National Education Policy, Asmara, 2003

Ministry of Information, Eritrea, Futile Acts of Subversion, Eritrea Profile, September 5, 2023

Ministry of Information, EriTv, Interview with President Isaias Afewerki, January 8, 2022

Ministry of Information, Eritrea, Keynote Address By President Isaias Afwerki on 32nd Independence Anniversary, Asmara, May 24, 2023

Mo Ibrahim Foundation, Global Africa: Africa in the World and the World in Africa, Forum Report, July 2023

Movic, Peter, Eritrea, Option, and Strategies, The World Bank, Washington, DC, 1994

National Statistics and Evaluation Office, Asmara, Eritrea ORC Macro Calverton, Maryland, US - Eritrea, Demographic and Health Survey, 2002, May 2003

The New York Times, Ethiopian rebel-faction is to govern separately, May 30, 1991

OECD, A Policy Framework for Investment: Human Resource Development Policy, 25-27 October 2005, Rio de Janeiro, Brazil

PBS Frontline, Lila Hassan, Escaping Eritrea (full documentary) | FRONTLINE, FRONTLINE PBS | Official, May 4, 2021

PBS, Frontline, 500,000 Refugees, 'Slavery-like' Compulsory Service, No National Elections, Border Conflicts & Secret Prisons: 5 Human Rights Crises in Eritrea, May 4, 2021

Peace Corps Suspends Program in Eritrea; All Volunteers are Safe and Sound, Peace Corps, Friday, June 5, 1998,

Reliefweb, LWF will continue humanitarian aid in Eritrea for further 12 months: Only NGO program in operation there News and Press Release Originally published 14 Jul 1998

Rogers, Peter P, Kazi F Jalal, and John A Boyd, An Introduction to Sustainable Development, London, Earthscan, 2009

Runde, Daniel, The American Imperative, Reclaiming Global Leadership through Soft Power, New York · Nashville, Post Hill Press, 2023

Sarasohn, Judy, Eritrea Pushes to Get U.S. Base, The Washington Post, Washington, DC, November 21, 2002

Singh, Somia, Stockholm Syndrome: A Psychiatric Diagnosis or Just a Myth?, International Journal of Trend in Scientific Research and Development (IJTSRD), Volume 6 Issue 2, January-February, 2022

Solomon, Semere, Being Responsive to Locally Led Development: Beyond, Channeling Funds to Local Organizations, Creative Associates International, September 26, 2023

Solomon, Semere, U.S.-Africa leaders summit: How can the US contribute to Africa's development?, Creative Associates International, December 5, 2022

State Council, The Peoples Republic of China, Full text: Action plan on the Belt and Road Initiative, Beijing, English version, Mar 30, 2015

Teklai, Daniel, Interview with Daniel Teklai, ዘተ - ኣብ እዋናዊ ኩነታት ምስ ዳኒኤል ተኽላይ - ኤልያስ ኣማረ - (Discussion on current events), September 24, 2023

Temnewo, Tesfai, "ንኣርብዓ ዓመታት ዝተቐብረ ጉዳይ - 1972 - 2013", (A case that has been buried for forty Years—1972—2013), Leck, 2013

Tesfai, Alemseghed, ፌደረሽን ኤርትራ ምስ ኢትዮጵያ ካብ ማቲየንሶ ክሳብ ተድላ 1951—1955 (The Federation of Eritrea with Ethiopia— From Matienzo to Tedla 1951 -1955), Asmara, Hidri Publishers, June 2005

Tesfai, Alemseghed, ኣይንፈላለ 1941 -1950, Asmara, Hidri Publishers, 2001

Tesfai Alemseghed, ኤርትራ ካብ ፈደረሽን ናብ ጎበጣን ሰዉራን 1956- 1962, Asmara, Hidri Publishers, 2016

Tesfai Tedros, Where did things go wrong for the "party of the people?" Asmarino.com, January 21, 2001

UNDP, Human Development Report 2011, Sustainability and Equity: A better Future for All

United Nations Economic and Social Commission for Asia and the Pacific, A Primer to Public-Private Partnerships in Infrastructure Development

United Nations Institute of Training and Research (UNITAR), Location of Places of Detention Centers in Eritrea Identified by the Commission of Inquiry of Human Rights in Eritrea, Analysis with WorldView-3 Data Acquired 24 September 2015 and 23 January 2016 and Landsat-8 Data Acquired 29 May 2016, June 6, 2016

UNHCR, UNHCR Global Appeal 1999—Eritrea, December 1, 1998

USAID, USAID Policy Framework 2011-2015

USIP, Terrorism in the Horn of Africa, 1994

USIP, Final Report and Recommendations of the Senior Study Group on Peace and Security in the Red Sea Arena, 2020

VOA, UAE Dismantles Eritrea Base as it Pulls Back After Yemen War, VOA, February 18, 2021

VOA, France's Hollande: Eritrea 'Becoming Empty' as Residents Leave, VOA, November 11, 2015

Webster's II New Riverside University Dictionary, Boston, The Riverside Publishing Company, 1984

White House, Press Release by the White House, Statement of Eritrea, March 26, 2003, Washington, DC,

World Bank, 2020 HCI: Country Briefs and Data,

World Bank, Worldwide Governance Indicators, A global compilation of data capturing household, business, and citizen perceptions of the quality of governance in more than 200 countries and territories.

World Bank, Eritrea Options and Strategies for Growth, The WBG, November 10, 1994

World Bank, Eritrea, Development, news, research, data

INDEX

ABOUT THE AUTHOR

The author brings forth a wealth of over three decades of progressively advancing senior-level experience in the domain of national and international development.  This expertise has been honed through the orchestration of multifaceted initiatives on behalf of respected entities such as the United States Agency for International Development (USAID), the United Nations (UN), and during an esteemed tenure as a senior civil servant within the Government of Eritrea.

Semere Solomon's journey toward a career in international development and humanitarian assistance was more of an intricate path than a linear trajectory. As a young man, he took up arms to fight in Eritrea's war of independence, later assuming a significant role in the Education Ministry within the nascent government. Departing from his homeland, he pursued further advanced degrees and embarked on a career in global development, amassing over twenty-five years of rich experience. His professional footprint extends across diverse regions, encompassing Africa, the Middle East, South East Asia, and Central Asia.